AF371384

THE SUM OF ALL DOUBTS

THE SUM OF ALL DOUBTS

March towards
'The True Face of Tribalism'

JOE MINTSA

JANUS PUBLISHING COMPANY
London, England

First Published in Great Britain 2004 by
Janus Publishing Company Ltd,
105-107 Gloucester Place,
London W1U 6BY

www.januspublishing.co.uk

Copyright © 2004 by Joe Mintsa
The author has asserted his moral rights

British Library Cataloguing-in-Publication Data
A catalogue record for this book
is available from the British Library

ISBN 1 85756 509 6

Cover Design Nathan Cording

Printed and bound in Great Britain

To

Elaine

TABLE OF CONTENTS

ACKNOWLEDGEMENTS

I would like to acknowledge the devotion of those very Christ-like people around me who put their investments into the realisation of this book.The whole congregation of CCK (Church of Christ the King) in the city of Brighton & Hove, England, and especially my cell group, are the ones I want to thank first. And I am particularly indebted to the Revd Stephen Whittington and his wife Joanna for the miraculous friendship that they created between their family and me, as well as the special support that they gave me.

I very much appreciate the nearness and sympathy of such people as David Nolent of the University of Sussex; Fiona Lawrence and Liza Kordalski of the Brighton Friends Centre; Sue Erlam and Zina Bratovic of the Brighton Community Base; Kate Wiggett of Brighton & Hove City Council; Chris and Helen Evans of CCK; and Audrey Federa, my advisor.

I shall not overshadow my friends of my home university lobby, 'le Cercle de Vision Parfaite' ('the Brain Circle'), in Libreville, who shared my visions and made valuable contributions to the shaping of my insights at their earliest stages. Joseph Désiré Ebang, Alfred Placide Mbongo, Rodrigue Minso, Christian Bouyomba and Alex Ndoutoume are the ones of whom I think.

May God be with them all.

CHAPTER 1

OF LOGIC AND MISCONCEPTIONS

Pope's Avenue was a popular venue because of its famous pubs; the most attractive pubs in the town. From the junction with Gabosep Street, near Mekie-Me-Kwule Catholic High School, down to its embouchure on the Boulevard of Triumph, the street was the most exciting place to go with friends for an endless, and even aimless, gossip around a glass of beer. Pope's Avenue would make everybody's life beautiful from 5 p.m. to seven the following morning – especially the two nights between Friday evening and Sunday morning, every week.

The pavement would be reduced by three-quarters, busy with plastic tables and chairs to host the multitude overnight; and motor traffic would be almost impossible due to the massive crowd. People of all ages would flow down to the avenue and remain there drinking, chatting, eating hot tropical dishes served in the open air, laughing, and courting the most attractive angels of the night. Pope's Avenue was the right remedy for stress, depression, solitude, and even celibacy. You wouldn't come back empty-handed from the magic place.

Now, four friends – Ngule, 21, Bifun, 20, Ebongué, 25, and Amanoofwom, 22 – gathered around a table for a drink in one of the most popular pubs of the avenue. Amanoofwom was back from a long trip, and the cocktail was a welcome invitation from his three friends, who had not seen him for nine years. This was about five weeks after his arrival. It was delightful to have Amanoofwom around again after such a long period of absence. It was on a Friday afternoon. The four friends were there tasting the beauties of the magical venue in a fading equatorial sun, breathing the hot wind that was blowing off the seafront, and sipping from their cool glasses.

Amanoofwom, was in the spotlight among his friends after his trip

"So, what is the news in Messanza?" Amanoofwom started.

"Oh, the news! Well, ask Ebongué, the minister," teased Ngule.

"Cool down, man. I am not a minister." Ebongué reacted swiftly to extricate himself from the provoking allegation.

"Bloody hell! Look at that!" Bifun exclaimed unexpectedly.

"What!" The other three briskly turned round to scrutinise an elegant silhouette that was passing by.

"Cool down, man! She is not even a bit beautiful. Just look at the way she walks." Ngule discouraged the group with the disdainful assessment.

"Will you forget about girls and tell me a bit about Messanza?" Amanoofwom insisted.

"What do you want to learn about Messanza that will be more important than catching a nice and colourful bird for the night?" derided Ngule.

"I couldn't guess you were going to grow so wicked! You were not like this when I left. What is going on?"

"Nothing, man…I just wanted to make sure she was crispy and crunchy," assured Bifun concupiscently.

"Ha ha ha…" The three sketched a vicious laugh while Amanoofwom observed them in a disgruntled mood.

"Is this, then, the only thing I have to learn about Messanza?"

"My goodness! What do you want to know about Messanza? All we've got here is shit. Do you want to learn about our shit?"

"What is that shit, then?"

"Well, Messanza's gone belly up. We now have to count on strangers who are trying to volunteer to get us up. That is what Messanza has become, a beggar. Are you satisfied?"

"Who are those strangers who are trying to help you up?"

"The Americans."

"What! Do you want to talk about Revd Sullivan's Foundation?" Ebongué queried.

"Yes," Bifun replied confidently.

"No, man. They are not strangers here. These are our brothers who went to America 300 years ago, and they are just coming back to their original land to help their brothers."

"Oh! This sounds interesting. What is this Sullivan's Foundation and what is it trying to do for us – you said?"

"Well, Sullivan is one of the greatest African American figures who visited our country about…I think…two months ago. And, according to what was stated in the press, he has just initiated a new impetus to drive black Americans back to Africa – I mean, not really come back, but get them create businesses with Africans…" Bifun started a praiseworthy account of the event.

"It was really exciting to see him discussing the future of Africa with young people," Ngule confirmed.

"That man is really a great man!" Ebongué declared. "Even the president looked at him like a god."

"Of course, if you are the master of the beasts, you will still feel inferior to the slave of man," Amanoofwom replied unexpectedly.

"No, man! Such a reasoning is too comparative. Yet, as you know, 'comparaison n'est pas raison'," launched Bifun.

"This is one of the silliest sayings the French language has ever produced. For there is no way to reasoning where comparing is banned. Tell me: how can you reason without comparing?"

Ngule, who was a former student in the department of ancient philology, had been listening to them carefully, and, as Amanoofwom asked that question, he started a very intellectual reply.

"I really think that it is possible to reason without comparing."

"How?" Amanoofwom asked searchingly. To which Ngule began to expound. "I remember one of my classmates asking the same question to our tutor of Latin about five years ago, and the tutor said that we could, of course, give non-comparative assertions just by using absolute superlatives. He explained that absolute superlatives are used to express the highest degree of attributes when the objects described are viewed as being unique and are not compared to anything else. He illustrated this with the sentence: 'Hic hortus pulcherrimus est.' Is this not relevant?" Ngule posed a question to conclude.

"This is very surprising of you, man!" Amanoofwom exclaimed. "For whoever looks into this sentence will notice that you would never know that a garden is 'very beautiful' if, in your experience, you have never seen what a less beautiful garden looks like. If you have no idea of something filthy, how will you know that something else is clean or even very clean?

"If, in our world, we had only clean things, we would never know that they are clean. And, likewise, if all things in the world were strictly equal, adjectives would not exist in our languages, for you would never regard something as small while there exists nothing bigger. And that is the principle of reasoning, I mean *comparison*."

"Er, yes, this seems to work with physical descriptions. But what about purely abstract concepts?" Ngule posed another question.

"Even in the universe of abstractions or theoretical contentions, a *non-comparative* reasoning is revealed as falling short as well. Imagine a man trying to demonstrate the truthfulness of an assertion to you, and you come up to conclude that he is right. At the first onset, it seems that your conclusion does not hold from a comparative analysis, since there was nobody else trying to demonstrate the opposite or anything different. But you forget that, while acting the judge, you were yourself at the same time that apparently missing challenger who was trying to demonstrate the opposite to play the comparing part. What I mean is that, if you admit that he is right, this is simply to reckon that you are wrong yourself. Because, how could you find that he was right if, in your mind, you did not try to make up some arguments and find them unable to stand against his demonstrations? Otherwise, you would have said to him, 'I don't think so,' and you would then prove him wrong. But how would you know that you 'don't think so' if you did not compare his contentions to the ones you would then brandish against him to prove him wrong?

"In fact, the listening process of the human mind is so analytical that every single line of reasoning that is perceived always triggers – consciously or unconsciously – an automatic counter-reasoning to play the comparing part. But the mechanism is so quick that we never take notice that we really made use of comparison before approving of or rejecting something. And yet, in reality, we will never know what is right or wrong if we do not compare. For all that is right is right because something else is wrong, and vice versa. Now, tell me if you can really reason without comparing."

"I understand, but the fact is that we do not really perceive comparison when we reason. Why say that there is comparison if we do not perceive it?" said Ngule.

"Of course, the fact that you do not perceive something does not mean that the thing does not exist. You might just be blind."

"Probably."

"No. It is not a supposition. The truth is that 'Il n'y a point de raison sans comparaison'. I mean, there is no reasoning without comparing."

"I think that you are a bit right," Ngule partially approved.

"What?"

"I said, you are right, but maybe not totally."

"You are really surprising. How can a man be 'maybe not totally' right? Tell me that I am right if you find so, or that I am wrong it if this is what you find, for rightfulness and wrongfulness can never be partial. What is right is right, and what is wrong is wrong."

"You are too absolutist, Aman! Imagine yourself in a situation in which you pull the trigger of a gun unconsciously and end up killing somebody. The judges will prove you innocent because you did it unintentionally and your case will be ranged in the category of involuntary crimes. However, because you will have shed blood, you will be sentenced for a short period of time."

"What does this mean?"

"It means that you are innocent but partially condemned because you killed anyway. You can see, through this example, how the truth about your innocence becomes altered because of the bloodshed."

"Bifun, do you take time to listen to yourself when you speak? How to justify the sentence of an innocent person? Either you are proved guilty or innocent. But you cannot be both at a time."

"The problem is blood, Aman!"

"No, Bifun! Blood is not a big deal. The main concern is to seek to respect logic in everything that we do. That is the only option that makes things work soundly and truthfully."

"I understand that logic, soundness and truthfulness are important. But you have to try and understand that nothing is absolutely true. Everything is relatively wrong, and every rule admits exceptions."

"That is what we do in order to find a compromise so that nobody is absolutely left in oblivion. For example, we want to relieve the relatives of the deceased by imprisoning the killer, and at the same time satisfy the killer by telling him that his act is worth five years' imprisonment but that he would be imprisoned for one year for killing involuntarily. But this is complaisant and has nothing to do with truth. Truth is absolute. A man who kills involuntarily is truly innocent since what we judge is not the act of killing but the intention of doing harm. Condemning an involuntary killer is like condemning a man who gets killed in an accident while driving his own car. Such a sentence is sheer nonsense."

"I know, Aman, but there can be some exceptions. For example, if it is found that the killer had an argument with the deceased a few months earlier. That argument may not even be linked to the circumstances of his death in any way, but it can play a part in the killer's sentence, albeit he should be released for being proved innocent."

"That is an exception, and I know that exceptions exist, but do not make some up where there are none. Not every single involuntary killer will have had an argument with the victim beforehand. Unless it is the case, the rule of innocence in involuntary killing will remain absolutely true as long as no facts have proved it wrong. And it should not be declared wrong or partly true just for the sake of some sort of general relativity that doesn't affect it yet matter-of-factly. Therefore, if a particular fact happens to prove the killer guilty in any way, this will simply be an exception."

"Of course, 'l'exception confirme la règle'," launched Ebongué.

"What are you talking about, Ebongué?" Amanoofwom asked. "Tell me: if the exception proves the rule, what will disprove it then? Is it the rule itself that will disprove itself? It may be technically observable that, by means of comparison, you will make the rightfulness of an argument 'A' definite by resolving that another argument 'B' is wrong. In this case, B's flaws look very much like something that is proving A's strengths. And, of course, they prove them. But the trouble is that things don't work like that between rules and their exceptions. The role that exceptions play, rather, is to try and prove that the rule is not almighty and that it does not work in every single case. In this sense, exceptions are diseases for the rule; that is, they reduce its range and expanse. They fight it. They limit it. They act like a demon that wants to overcome a few among the chosen to prove how limited God's power is. Is this a new way of proving things? An exception is an exception, and all it does is to try and kill the rule. You know, I observed a phenomenon somewhere in the world. Some people have created a blind obsession for feminine emancipation and political correctness in their nation. And this phenomenon has trapped them into some kind of non-sexist grammar that has destroyed the beauty of their language. What they have tried to do is to raise woman as an exception to man within the mankind rule. It is very funny. If you go there, you will hear them mercilessly entangled into that wordy and redundant 'he or she', 'him or her', and 'his or her'. Others, for example, give orders to their secretaries: 'If somebody wants to meet me, they must show you their ID before you let them in.'

"I tell you, he will be very famous who will demonstrate grammatical coherence in such a sentence. For, at school, you were told that the indefinite pronoun 'somebody' is singular, so no wonder if the verb that accompanies it is put into the singular form; hence the phrase 'if somebody wants to meet me'. But look, these people are putting it together with the plural personal pronouns 'they' and 'them', and the plural possessive adjective 'their', to dodge the use of 'he', 'him' and 'his' – which stand for mankind – because they want to avoid skimping on women. Is this grammar?

"If the time has come for women to take over our 'mankind' label, why do we not just give them the seat and call our species 'womankind'? We will then say: 'If somebody wants to meet me, she must show you her ID before you let her in.' With such a gender overthrow, grammar will not be smashed.

"I tell you, whenever exceptions tend to gain too much credit, the rule will tend to fall and give way to the destruction of its beauty.

"Is it because the world population is said to have a female majority that we have to kill 'mankind' and neutralise ourselves?

"Can you now see the disasters that can be caused to a rule if an exception becomes too much powerful? And you say that 'the exception proves the rule'! Are you normal? I tell you, if somebody says to you 'the exception proves the rule', tell him that 'it rather proves itself to rise as a counter-rule'."

"In this case, the exception is true and the rule is true as well, and they both coexist!" said Ebongué.

"No. They both exist, but one is true, and it is absolutely true; and the other is wrong, and absolutely wrong; because two truths cannot be opposed if they reside within the same universe."

"Do you then mean that the 'woman principle' is wrong and that the 'man principle' is the only one that is true?"

"Yes. That is my point. But do not get me wrong. What I am saying is that, if we call our species 'mankind', then it will be foolish for us to be afraid of skimping on women in purely grammatical terms. Besides, even in a very practical point of view, a woman still loses her identity, her name, once she gets bound to a man in the marriage contract; which means that 'man' + 'woman' = 'man'. Here, 'woman' is neutralised or simply engulfed into 'man'. Is this not enough to understand that our species is still acting 'mankind' and that nonsexism is a mistake?

"Thus, if trying to raise women to the same level as men while we still call our species by the name of 'mankind' is responsible for the rise of such grammatical fallacies in our language, it goes without saying that there is something wrong somewhere. Consequently, everything cannot be true at a the same time. This is why, as I told you, if you find two truths opposed within a subject, you have to make sure that the subject really exists. And, likewise, if you find the same truth valid in two subjects that are opposed, just forget about that truth."

"What if we really want to give equal credit to women and men?"

"I have just said it. There are only two possibilities: either 'mankind' is invalid or nonsexist rules are incorrect. But the two cannot be true at a the same time, unless they are considered in two different universes that are themselves opposed to one another."

"In this case, what is the outlet?"

"The outlet to what?"

"I mean, what we can do to phase out the fallacy."

"Well, there are two possible solutions, I believe: either we create a hermaphrodite term to design our species and match it with singular pronouns (subject and object) and a singular possessive adjective of similar nature; or we maintain 'mankind' and fall back into onto the original 'if somebody wants to meet me, he must show you his ID before you let him in'. Only one of these rules can help avoid gender fallacies in grammar. But if we maintain both at a the same time, we cannot expect our grammar to be logical in terms of gender. I know that some theorists stand against language creation through such creeds as: 'Let us follow language the way it moves forward instead of dragging it to the way we want it to come.' But this is losing control of language and killing it just the way it is being killed with this gender problem."

"But, look carefully, if you create a hermaphrodite term between men and women, you will simply have raised women to the same level as men. What does it change?"

"What it changes is that they will both be raised to the same level, but instead of being distinguished as two opposed terms – 'him' and 'her' – they will, rather, be melted and expressed with one single absolute term making one single absolute truth."

"But, how can you stand so obsessively against something already so common as partiality in human reasoning?"

"Because, as I already made it clear, truth is not something partial. What is true is true and what is wrong is wrong; and if you do not know where truth is, this does not mean that truth does not exist, or even that it is partial. We regard things as partly true for three main reasons: ignorance, fear and shame. Firstly, you will never be absolutely convinced of something that you do not understand. That is ignorance. Secondly, if you are reluctant to explore your truth to the full for fear of facing some unexpected consequences, you will start absconding behind a partial conviction. But you are not partly convinced; you are simply affected by cowardice. That is, the fear of going further. And, thirdly, Dr Anthony Campolo, for example, said: 'We met the enemy, and we found that they are partly right.' But, I tell you in truth, you will acknowledge that your challenger is *partly right* if you are ashamed to reckon that you are *completely wrong*. That is, the shame of declaring oneself wrong."

"I understand you, Aman. But imagine yourself being absolutely convinced of something, and you meet somebody else who says he strongly believes in the contrary. What will you do?"

"He will simply be wrong, unless I am wrong, because diversity of opinions does not hold from diversity of truths. There is always one single truth in every single subject. Therefore if there arises a controversy over a subject and the contenders seem to find truth everywhere at a the same time, or nowhere at all, then the subject is not framed. Hence, the subject needs to be redefined so that truth can be found in all its glory and be strictly distinguished from anything wrong. However, you can find, in a subject, one main truth and several contributory truths. But they will never be opposed in principle to each other. And anything opposed to them will simply be null and void within the subject or the universe considered; because, if you deal with different universes at a the same time, it will be very difficult for you to find one sovereign truth unless these universes are not themselves opposed to each other. That is why those who created a non-Euclidean geometry to proved Euclid wrong in regard to the two meridians that meet at the pole while they are both perpendicular to the equator are wrong. Because, they seem not to be aware of the astounding fact that every single meridian is itself twice perpendicular to the same equator. In fact, it is an infinity of times perpendicular to it as long as it keeps revolving across it, which makes the nature of such a line very wanting. Moreover, an asymptotic parallel is not parallel to its supporting axis from P_A to P_B over a sensible distance. Therefore, instead of believing that Euclid had failed to consider the spherical case, the truth is rather that the Euclidean plan is the only one in which we find straight lines. Thus, if you do not take notice that you are dealing with two universes that are opposed to one another, you will tend to think that truth is everywhere at the same time, or even that it is partial. But you have to be very careful. Partiality does not exist in matters of truth. Partiality is a disease. It mutilates truth. It kills it. That is why compromising is the art of the liars and the unsuccessful."

"This is very dangerous, Aman. I mean, what you say is not wrong in itself. But the point is that er…I don't know…em…well, what I want to say is that you are taking the risk of becoming a dictator should you do politics. I mean, I am really scared."

"No. I will never be a dictator. Dictatorship is political delinquency, whereas absolutism is the expression of seriousness and determination about a leader's political ambitions. The only problem with political absolutism is that, if your ambitions are wrong, you will be absolutely wrong and therefore an obnoxious leader. But if your ambitions are genuine, you will then be absolutely truthful.

Here, the real problem hinges at the question as to whether your ambitions are absolutely harmful or absolutely beneficial. And what I am trying to show you is that the absolutely wrong and the absolutely true can never work together."

"In this case, what is the place of democratic parliaments?"

"What do you mean?"

"I mean the systems in which opposition and power work together."

"This does not exist."

"You must be going mad, Aman! You are not going to deny the existence of observable phenomena for the sake of pure logical thinking."

"No. I will never do that, my dear Ngule."

"Aman, never say 'never'!"

"But what if I die just after saying 'never'?"

"You will always find a way out. That is your knack."

"No. My knack is not to always find a way out. The thing is that there is always a way out that you cannot see because you do not have time to get closer to things and look at them carefully. Your political coexistence that you are trying to classify among observable phenomena is not observable at all."

"You are just killing me, Aman. I know that you have not been here for years. But do you not know Menganga, Oyon and many others who have been ministers in the president's government while they oppose the president?"

"This is one of the most stupid things that I have ever seen in my life. Anyway, you know that this will never work. Just see for yourself how they have been resigning all the time because all activities that they wanted to carry out were rejected for tending to oppose the government's views. That is what I am saying to you. You just lack refined perception. Two opposed ideologies can never work together. All those who want to try it are doomed to failure, for you cannot work with somebody who is opposing you. Political opposition has one single function. It plays a 'bug off' role that consists in censuring the government by bringing out its fouls. The main objective of this job is to create a negative image of the government before the people so that the constituencies would change their mind at future elections. However, the positive side of such a job is to allow the government to correct its mistakes if truly in error. That is all that the opposition can do in a real democratic system – but never work with the party in power."

"What about the French? Have you tried to consider that case at all?"

"What is the case of the French?"

"They sometimes have an opposition majority in their parliament; which means that the government is often held by the opponents, and this does not impede the president at all."

"Your French system is simply a legislative disorder, for it implies that the president will have to keep from carrying out his own political projects and rather work on opposition bills that will be imposed onto him. This is simply nonsense; for, as a president, you cannot be held to overlook your own political projects and rather consider those of your opponents. You will have to resign!"

"Aman, you are really terrible."

"I am not terrible, Bifun. You just don't have time to look into things and unveil their real face. You glibly pass over phenomena and start contending nonsense. Do not forget that 'an aerial view of an agglomerate city centre always gives you the impression that even ants have a valuable destiny in life. But you will not understand that men are not like ants until you land in them and start approaching them.' And, likewise, if you try and get closer and closer to the ants, you may end up finding that they are not very different from men. You have to get closer and closer to things to understand them and find where truth lies. And yet, you know that 'O se ki ádegue mbek á meyinbe, ve á mekohga'. Ideas are not something that you can joke about. You cannot negotiate your ideology with your opponents."

"But, Aman, do not forget that ideas evolve."

"Of course, I know this. But an idea that evolves simply improves in quality. It will never change into the opposite. If an idea changes into its opposite form, this will imply that its former stance was wrong. In this case, the idea does not evolve, but it corrects itself."

"No, no, no. I can't just get it. Can you give me an illustration of your ideas that evolve in quality or change in form?"

"Em, I don't know…em…"

"Look! If you cannot describe your point through practical cases, then you are wrong."

"No! I am not wrong! Sometimes, examples are very hard to find straightaway. You need to browse your active memory to find one; and this can take seconds, minutes, hours, and even days, months and years. That is why, if you fail to find an illustration today, this does not mean that the illustration does not exist. It might simply be sleeping somewhere in a disabled area of your memory, or it is somewhere in life but you have never come across it."

"Aman, you are really funny! Are you trying to defend your failure to illustrate your point?"

"No. I tell you, my point is true, but I am just short of practical cases that match with it; and this does not mean that the cases do not exist anywhere at all."

"And you want me to trust your point just like that, and believe, just like that?"

"No. Never believe until you are absolutely convinced."

"Is this to encourage me not to believe you?"

"Yes. Don't believe me until you understand my point and find it relevant and practical."

"Listen, you are saying that finding an illustration can take minutes, hours, days, weeks, months, and even years. Now, if you happen to die before you find and an example for your point, what will I do?"

"You will have to browse through life by yourself to find a good illustrative case for yourself. And, until you find one, do not believe me."

"Anyway, I do not feel like questioning your convictions any more. My only concern is that, if you keep so strongly clung to an idea because you find it true, this can become seriously harmful in a negotiation process. Have you ever thought of this?"

"My dear Bifun, I do not care about dianoetics. The only way I can negotiate about ideas is to get people to understand that truth is with me, and that they need to move with me; or get them to convince me that truth is with them, and that I need to move with them. This is all that I can do. I have already hinted that democracy is not about diversity of truths. Democracy is about the search for one single truth supported by the majority of people and then adopted by the political apparatus that is in charge of the nation."

"But how do you explain the fact that the majority of people keep on changing their choices between parties that are opposed by principle?"

"What do you mean?"

"I mean, at one election, they can find truth in conservatism, and then at the next election they rather turn to the liberals, socialists or whoever else."

"You know, Bifun, there is nothing that I have found so improbable as parliamentary representation. You choose a man for what you want. But the man acts for what he wants. Thank God if both of you coincidentally want the same thing. Some elected politicians often veer round and betray the ideas upon which they were chosen. How do you then want the constituencies to keep on trusting them? You see, even the rabble knows when its ideas are not met. Can you now understand why you should not negotiate about the ideas and principles that you find true? Truth is something that you have to keep, and live with, or die with."

"In this case, your truth is really going to kill you."

"Let me die, then."

Bekale Be'Nguema, a young journalist working for a national television channel, was coincidentally in the same pub that afternoon, having a drink with his girlfriend and one of his cousins. They were sitting around a table next to the four friends. Bekale Be'Nguema had been following the conversation of the four friends with critical attention, and had been very touched by Amanoofwom's relevance, and especially his repeated references to God in his interventions.

Bekale Be'Nguema was a daily broadcaster and the presenter of a programme called *Questions about God* that was telecast on Sundays. Bekale Be'Nguema found Amanoofwom interesting enough to be a guest on the programme the following Sunday. He quickly approached the four friends while they were pushing their chairs back as a sign of leaving.

"Excuse me, brothers! My name is Total Bekale…"

"Who doesn't know you here?" Ngule interrupted him and He went on, "A journalist is like the president. There is nobody who has never seen him, unless he is blind."

"By the way," intervened Bifun, "how is your programme? I have not seen you on TV for about two Sundays. What is going on?"

"Rightly, I am here in front of you for that very reason. I have been working on a special subject that is going to be telecast next Sunday. The debate is on the beginning, I mean, creation; and, following your conversation and especially your interventions," he pointed at Amanoofwom, "I found that you could be a guest next Sunday, if you do not mind, or if you have time."

"No, no, no. I can't go on TV." Amanoofwom hesitated.

"No, man! What do you lose? Just go there for a good chat! That will be great for us to see you on TV!" Ebongué cheered his friend up, and that was also Ngule and Bifun's reaction.

"But I do not have a suit."

"No, man, you don't need a suit. Anyway, I buy you the latest Smalto that exists on the market tomorrow morning. I pour all my bank account into it 'cause I wanna see you on TV, man."

"Yes, I will contribute," assured Ngule.

"Me too," concluded Bifun.

"OK, I go."

"I thank you, brothers, for convincing him," Bekale Be'Nguema said happily, opening his pouch. He then withdrew a couple of sheets, stapled up together, instructing: "Well, here you have a rough view of the main points of the debate, you can keep the copy. And, as you know, the telecast starts at two in the afternoon. But it would be great if you were there at half past one, just for the setting preparations."

"We will be there," confirmed Ebongué. "I will give him a lift and then go back home in a rush to view the event."

"OK, thank you so much."

"Thank you."

"À dimanche prochain."

The four friends left the pub and Ebongué's 4X4 hummed for an all-out destination throughout Messanza that Friday evening.

CHAPTER 2

OF THE BEGINNING

It was two o'clock in the afternoon on that Sunday when the screens turned on, the soft esoteric music sounding in the background, and the lights flashing from the ceiling of the studio. A young man appeared as usual, holding a sophisticated microphone with his right hand while his left hand was holding an unfolded A4 sheet. He barely looked at the paper when he started:

"Good afternoon, ladies and gentlemen, welcome to *Questions about God.* This afternoon, we are going to have a debate on 'The Beginning'; I mean 'Creation', or even beyond. So, ladies and gentlemen, 'In the beginning God created the heavens and the earth. Now the earth was formless and empty, darkness was over the surface of the deep, and the Spirit of God was hovering over the waters.' All this happened just before God said, 'Let there be light.' And then, suddenly, there was light. And everything was created from these commands, according to the sacred Scriptures. And we believe. However, as human beings, our brains have also commanded: 'Let you seek and find more about what you believe.' We are here this afternoon not only to disclose what we have found in our extra search, but also to go further with the search. To have some elements of response to the question as to what did happen in the beginning, we have invited intellectual personalities of different areas and experiences to share the question with us. And, to start with, here we have Mr Ondo Mebiam. He has a doctorate in structural linguistics and is a teacher of generative grammar in Nkorebot University. He is also known as a devoted believer of the sacred word. Hence we invited him today.

As the faces kept on blipping one by one through the screen, Bekale Be'Nguema went on introducing the guests:

"Sima Minko is a cosmologist and teacher of physics at Bikôndôm College.

"Ngwa Beyem is a historian of renown. He teaches archaeology at Melen High School. He is the founder of Minzeng & Co. and is chairman of Save the Children's board of trustees.

"Father Aba'a Memin is an ordained minister in the Roman Catholic system and has been serving at the Regina Immaculata Congregation for 25 years."

"Kapla Bikuk-Ebuh is a neurologist and presently works as a general practitioner at Wessa Medical Centre. He is the author of *God, Herbs and Pills.*"

"Dr Eyang Alouga is a man of letters who teaches the Nguess language at President's University. He has just published *Historical Analogy between North America and Sub-Mboga: A Review on Dark Skin Condition.*

"We also have Mr Yans Milo Mi'Mbot. Mr Mbot is an anthropologist and he lectures in community behaviourism at President's University."

As Bekale Be'Nguema turned to the last face, he said: "And, eventually, we have Mr Amanoofwom...But he just got stuck there. Yielding Amanoofwom's details the way he had for the other guests proved to be a big problem. He had none of these data. He had forgotten to ask for Amanoofwom's personal details prior to the meeting. After a three-second pause of clever reflection, however, the journalist instantly continued with a skilfully fallacious fill-in.

"Mr Amanoofwom is a young man who has been studying modern anthropology abroad, and he has just come back home, and we warmly welcome him back.

"Ladies and gentlemen, here is the question: what really happened in the beginning? What does the Milky Way tell us today about the beginning?

"Well, we know that God created the world," Ondo Mebiam started straightaway. "This is undeniable. Suffice it that you look around to notice that there is an intelligent being that had devoted its knowledge to produce such a beautifully structured universe. The holy word already says that in the beginning God created heaven and the earth. This is not something we even need to think about. It is written, and it is true."

"Who is this God, then?" Bekale Be'Nguema posed the question to the pious man.

"Well, as you may be aware of it, it is written, in addition, that in the beginning was the Word, and the Word was with God, the Word was God, in fact."

"Is this, then, to say that God is simply a magical word that had uttered or had been uttered by itself to create our world?" he asked again.

"It is not a magical word. It is a holy word," replied Ondo Mebiam, annoyed by the pretty cynical question of the young journalist.

"So, if God is simply an intelligent and holy word, then He cannot be physically described," deduced Bekale Be'Nguema.

"Of course, no," assured Ondo Mebiam.

"In this case, in which sense is man made in His image and likeness?" Bekale Be'Nguema opened the debate another way round with a question of empirical logic.

"This is not physical. It is moral and spiritual." Ondo Mebiam made explicit his view with a symbolistic stance.

"OK. But how can we describe Him anyway in this moral and spiritual imaging?"

Father Aba'a Memin intervened to stop what he termed a 'pernicious discussion', stating that the most important thing to learn in the chapter on the beginning was how great God is and how much we should consequently pay tribute to such a greatness by worshipping Him. And he added that man's intelligence is so limited that he cannot understand spiritual realities, and especially the mystery of God. Man just needs to enjoy the grace and be thankful to the Father.

But Kapla Bikuk-Ebuh opposed that.

"I really believe that, in the beginning, man did not know anything about his body. People used to die of some diseases that have become a piece of cake to medicine today. Thus, if we had remained seated to be amazed by the complexity of our body, we would not cure these diseases today. And, likewise, we need to pursue spiritual realities as well, and especially God. Maybe this will help us find an easier remedy for several mental and spiritual defects that a lot of people suffer today."

This was an idea that Sima Minko approved and welcomed. He thought that looking further into the universe was indispensable, for man not only to understand his own life but also to grasp the essence of the visible as well as the invisible universe around him. For this, he began to reveal some of the important findings that he had come upon as a cosmologist.

"The question of the beginning is quite hard to deal with. What we have now is just very impressive approximations of the way the universe started and then expanded. Many of us are still stuck to the opinion that the universe has no edge in space, nor a beginning in time. And this uncertainty has made us stray to the study of stars: their composition and evolution. However, we recognise that a very brilliant Englishman called Hawking produced an impressive pattern of the beginning a few decades ago. This, if examined, seems to propound that our universe started with a zero volume state and then expanded. In some descriptions, this is known as a singularity in theoretical physics; that is, a reversed relation between volume and mass in which volume nears zero while mass nears positive infinity. This simply suggests that, if the universe was created by God, God himself must be outside the universe and that he must have created it out of nothingness. Because, the fact that mass nears zero or gets to zero implies that there was nothing. Consequently, if God resided within the universe, then He might Himself have begun to exist in that singularity, which would suggest that God Himself might have been created out of nothingness and, therefore, that He should be the same age as our universe. In this case, if the explosion of the singularity started 15 million years ago, it follows that God would be Himself fifteen 15 million years old, the same age as our universe. In a sense, to answer the question of our journalist, I would say that in the beginning was nothing. And then nothingness suddenly exploded once upon a time into a little atom the volume of which was nearly equal to zero; and just a few seconds after the atom began to rapidly expand. And that is where we can substantially start our study of God. And that is what we, cosmologists, are doing."

Ngwa Beyem, the historian, was very impressed by Sima Minko's relevant account, but said that he preferred the first possibility to the second one. He could not believe that God could be the same age as our universe.

"No. Do not let us be so silly as to think that God is the same age as our universe, or that He expanded from nothingness. God must be something older than our universe, for we say that He created it. He must therefore reside outside the universe, and must be bigger, greater and older."

"Moreover," carried on Kapla Bikuk-Ebuh, "we all have studied some principles of physics, and we can see that, if the beginning had been a singularity, then the beginning cannot be represented, for singularity implies the impossibility to reach the beginning, since we can never reach a state of singularity with matter, whatever the nature of it."

"Why?" Sima Minko asked impulsively.

"If you reduce the volume of matter," Kapla Bikuk-Ebuh started to expound, "and keep its mass intact or increase it, density will inevitably increase. But matter shall come to a state from which you will be able to compress it not for a jot more, and therefore volume will never approach zero. However, if we imagine that we can decrease the volume of matter to infinity or to zero, then there will come a time when volume, mass and density shall all start decreasing proportionally down to zero until there is nothing left. Because there is no realistic way in which the volume of a piece of rock can be compressed down to zero while its mass gets to positive infinity. Mass and volume shall disappear and nothing will be left. This state of 'nothing left' – not even mass – should make it clear that it is impossible to have a state of singularity. Therefore, the universe can never have experienced a state of singularity. Unless singularity is a one-way system; I mean, we can go from singularity to matter, but never the opposite." But even in this case, mass cannot start from positive infinity while volume starts from zero."

"Besides," approved Eyang Alouga, "I know that I am not a scientist in the mathematical sense, but we popularly say that, in science, 'Rien ne se crée, rien ne se perd, mais tout se transforme'. Consequently, the universe must not have come out of nothingness just like that, if 'nothingness' really means 'nothing'. There should have been something else from which the universe had come. It might not have necessarily been material. But there should have been something, turned into what we can see today."

"Right, anyway, we all seem to agree that in the beginning was 'something'. But what was it, in fact?" Bekele Be'Nguema asked.

"The evolutionists say that in the beginning was an atom." Kapla Bikuk-Ebuh started trying to borrow a picture that was certainly not his own to find a way out with. "And they have tried to give a very elegant explanation of the way in which the atom created the universe. Perhaps God is an atom. Professor Dawkins, the successor to Hume and Darwin, has tried hard to explain the very improbable, and many of us tend to admire his explanations even though their degree of intricacy makes them quite difficult to grasp. But the atomic organisation of the universe up to the formation of every single living being is not very awkward. However, what I do not quite well understand in the evolutionist mindset is their courageous renunciation of purpose in creation. I can understand that, if atoms are at the origin of creation, it would go without saying that creation has no purpose since atoms are not said to be able to think and design any kind of purpose. But what makes me feel very bad about this is that the universe, and especially the human beings that came out of the atom, seem to have the ability to think and, in consequence, a purposeful life. I have never been able to explain the interruption between the unthinking atoms and the resulting thinking men; I mean, that special thing that intervened in the middle of the atomic build-up process to turn atomic combinations into thinking beings while the atoms themselves do not think. The question that I am posing here is that of an intelligent God that had created intelligent beings like men, but that, if that God may be like an unthinking atom, how then could that atom build thinking beings – or should we simply forget about atoms in all creation debates?"

Father Aba'a Memin's face betrayed a lurking smile, expressing his satisfaction at the evolutionists' deadlock, as delineated by his fellow Kapla. It is well known that clergy people are antipathetic to the evolutionists and sympathetic to creationists. A bad stumbling point in the evolutionist camp would always be a good springboard on the creationist side. What more would one need to show that evolutionism is a disgraceful mistake? This was an unmissable opportunity for Father Aba'a Memin to turn on his hatred for evolutionism.

"That is exactly what the evolutionists do not understand," he started energetically. "Our creator, our living Father, the omnipotent, the omnisapient, created this universe intelligently and purposefully to make it intelligent and purposeful in its turn. He did not intervene in the middle of the atomic combination to invent intelligence into it. He is the starting point of everything. I do not need to explain myself any further to make it any clearer. The striking reality is that we are intelligent because our creator is intelligent, period!"

"Be careful, Father!" Eyang-Alouga came up with an audacious warning. "Suppose the atomic combination out of which the universe was made was blind, and man, a mere atomic combination, had no intelligence in the beginning, and your omnisapient being was simply the one that came as a serpent to reveal intelligence to Adam and Eve. What I mean is that God, as an omnisapient principle, might have just interfered in the middle of the atomic blind build-up to put intelligence into it. Is this not what the Scriptures want to tell us?"

"No, Eyang." Sima Minko interposed instantly.

"Why not?"

"Because such an alternative poses a big problem."

"What is it?"

"The problem is that, if the serpent was built up through the same atomic blind combination, how could it possess intelligence on its own and try to hand it over to man? Where did it, then, get that intelligence from?"

"You did not follow me very carefully, brother Sima. What you have to put in mind is that the serpent is not the result of your atomic blind build-up. The serpent is an intelligent outside creature travelling around the cosmos. It simply stops for a few seconds at a station at which it finds a strange atomic combination process with no intelligence. The serpent is simply a benefactor. It does not want to go back to its abode and leave that poor atomic creation in total ignorance. It then takes a few seconds to instruct the poor ignorant before flickering back to its original world."

"In this case, where did the serpent come from? Where is its original world that you are talking about?"

"This is not my business, brother Sima. The only thing that I need to set clear is that my universe started with an atomic blind combination and that a strange serpent came from an unknown world to instruct us and then went back."

"Your vision is very straightforward, but it poses two more problems from which we cannot get away like that. First of all, it is not very comfortable to leave that serpent alone without trying to discover where it came from and where it lives now, and what the real purpose was for it to instruct beings that had no friendship with it. And then, when we look at the Scriptures, we will see that the serpent did not instruct beings that had been built up through a simply blind atomic combination. What the serpent said to the ones that it instructed was that they would be like their Creator should they agree to receive the intelligence that was being offered to them. This implies that there was already a creator and that this creator was intelligent. But, perhaps, the creator was not willing enough to instruct its creation. Here, the creator was certainly acting like a jealous father who does not want his children to be as powerful as himself. But the serpent, the father's neighbour, finds this inhumane. He then has to do his job as an external benefactor. From here, it is no longer possible to ignore the existence of an intelligent creator over the atomic combination. The serpent is simply an outside benefactor. This is where it becomes quite difficult to come to an agreement with the evolutionists, who deny the existence of an intelligent being in the very beginning, even though the creationists themselves have yet big trouble giving a proper description and definition of their intelligent creator."

Something started to become a bit embarrassing at the rostrum. Bekele Be'Nguema was the most who was feeling the worst about it. The man that he had so avidly admired in a pub at Pope's Avenue had not said a word since the debate had begun, but, judging by his facial expression, he did not seem very distant either. He seemed to be interested while saying nothing. What was wrong with him? In this situation, Bekele Be'Nguema had a double problem. He was afraid of being sacked for starting to pick unknown freaks that ended up saying nothing in such an important debate. Somebody else could have taken that freakish guest's place and could have said something instructive. Then the journalist was eager to prove to himself that he was not absolutely wrong in picking Amanoofwom. What to do? The journalist resolved to boldly force the freak into the debate, whatever the resulting catastrophe.

"Brother Amanoofwom, brother Sima Minko has just tried to shed light on the real problems that make the argument troublesome for both the evolutionists and the creationists around the question as to what happened in the beginning for creation to be so well organised and, perhaps, purposeful. Is there anything that you can say about it?"

"Yes, ummm…I first have to saying a big 'thank you' to the evolutionists who discovered that the creation of our universe started at the atomic level. This is true indeed. The primeval thought that created the universe started its material job at the atomic level. However, the problem of the evolutionist is in thinking that these atoms were propelled to their duplication as well as their intricate interconnection into complex bodies up to forming beings of all kinds in a non-purposeful way, as well as the subsequent idea that the creator and organiser of these atoms into beings was blind.

"Everything that the brothers have said this far is brilliant and very enlightening. I even was tempted to say that we do not really have much more to dig into about the disagreement between the evolutionists and the creationists. The point at which each one of them has stumbled has been made quite clear by brother Sima Minko. However, I would like to look into some prominent arguments propounded by the two camps and see if they are absolutely wrong or not. I will start attacking the evolutionists, and then turn to the creationists. I will have to speak about all this quite glibly because I do not think that we have much time. But I will try to be as clear as possible, though very concise.

"I have already said that I do not find any guilt in the evolutionists saying that creation started at the atomic level. However, deeming creation blind is simply irrelevant. First of all, if we suppose that man designs engines like motor cars for well-determined purposes, how can we explain that the one who created man created him without any purpose in mind? How can man's mind be purpose-directed while the mind of man's creator had no purpose in creating him?

"Let us look into things a bit more carefully. If the evolutionists recognise that a package like Solitaire that is installable on a computer is meant to work on its own using complicated tricks to defeat the players without the assistance of its builder, it will not be very difficult to understand that the builder of living beings built them for a purpose that they can now achieve without the assistance of their builder. We shall certainly define the purpose for living beings to be built by the creator, but let us first settle the case about the existence or the non-existence of purpose at all.

"Suppose that you give birth to a child. You might not be a very conscious parent to define with precision the reasons why you came to have a child, but the work of nature will help you understand why this happened to you. First of all, the birth of a child is a mere biological consequence of sexual intercourse. At first sight, it looks very naïve to try and connect sexual desire to impregnation in terms of purpose. It is not self-explanatory. But why do living beings, and especially man, have sex or commit to any form of mating? Are there no reasons? Let us first forget about plants' pollen, not to exclude it but to avoid complicated explanations for nothing. Let us also avoid talking about animals, fish, birds and insects that are yet nearer to man for the same reasons.

"Man has sex for survival. The way you battle to satisfy your hunger is the same way you battle to satisfy your sexual needs to survive. If you repress them for a while, you will not repress them for life. However, there is a sequential or periodical difference between man's capability to resist hunger and his capability to resist sexual desires. You might not be able to resist hunger for 24 hours, but you might resist sex for years. And, if you go on resisting sex for years and years, you might not die, but you will be disturbed. This is psycho-biologico-somatic. Trying to cut down such disturbances in order to have an equilibrated existence is man's reason to seek sex, and impregnation is a consequence of man's trying to survive impending or expressive disturbances due to the lack of a sexual life. But that consequence is not external to the idea of survival. It is not like saying that, if you think about your mother while making love with your wife, it is not to say that you have been making love with your mother. Survival is sought both in orgasm and reproduction.

"If you are really clung to the idea of survival – I don't see a man trying to neglect it – you might not want to survive just for a few days, months, years, decades, or even centuries. You might try to be eternal. But *knowing* that your body is meant to disintegrate, the only solution for your genes, blood or spirit – whatever – to go on living eternally as you wish is to give birth. You might not see this when you go to bed with your partner, but the idea is there in you.

"A short-sighted observer or a narrow-minded thinker would not see purpose in creation, just the way many people today do not see why they should have kids if they can enjoy life with no burden. They do not hold onto such a position because they do not see any greater opportunity to enjoy life with, but because their telescope is not far-reaching enough to see it. What I mean is that you cannot refuse to give life if life was given to you. Only those who have never been born can have a good reason for this. And, likewise, man's mind cannot be design-directed while the mind that created it is blind. How can a computer programme be purposeful if its designer's mind is not? If a computer programme fails to explain to itself the reasons why man created it, this would not mean that man did not assign it to a determined purpose. Now If we turn to the above layer of the hierarchy of creations we would henceforth find that, if man fails to find out the reasons why the Creator created him, this would by no means imply that the Creator did not have any purpose in creating him. And, conversely, if the Creator – or whatever the machine or natural impulse that made human beings – is purpose-less, it will go without saying that human life has no purpose itself. I think that we can perceive the implications of such a logical conclusion.

"Purpose is generated by thought. Only the absence of thought can result in the absence of purpose. If we break the faulty contrast that the evolutionists had tried to create in order to overshadow the inherent contradiction of their vision, we can understand that the evolutionist arguments simply tend to make thought a human illusion. Here, one might wish René Descartes had never been born. The 'cogito ergo sum' principle, for which Descartes developed such a long discourse to demonstrate that thought is the basis of man's awareness of his existence, is hereby illusive. In fact, man is aware of nothing. His mind – if he has a mind at all – is but an intricate web of electronic conductors that make it possible for the wavy blind messages to travel through his spinal system for the execution of obscured attitudes. Here, man's body structure, in every part of every single organ, is but a jumble of blind mechanisms interconnected and organised in such an amazingly ordered and relevant way that we think – without really thinking – that there is purpose somewhere. What I mean is that we think that we think, but we don't. Our achievements are – I would not dare say intuitive, for intuition refers to *spiritual* insight – but sheerly mechanical, with no foresight. Humanity has no future. Here, our human civilisations may be seen as a clutter of termite hills. Presumably, if men do not think, how much more would the termites fail to have the ability to think? Is this the kind of story that the evolutionists want to tell us?

"Creation is amazingly complex. Living beings sometimes look very much like sophisticated machines. But complexity and sophistication are not the opposite of purpose. Richard Dawkins, the genius who studies machinery of evolution, himself recognises purpose in complexity. But I have very often been so surprisingly impressed – not to say disappointed – by the hasty and incongruous conclusions drawn by Dawkins, in which he has always sought to create an abrupt contrast between complex machines and complex beings. Once, browsing through *The Blind Watchmaker*, I was so shocked by the conclusion of the genius after his brilliant exposition on the flabbergasting similarity between the pulse radar mechanism and the echolocation technique of bats. Dawkins says: 'A bat is a machine, whose internal electronics are so wired up that its wing muscles cause it to home in on insects as an unconscious guided missile homes in on an aeroplane.' But this is – I have to say it again – so surprising, because after exposing such a perfect similarity between an artificial machine and a natural machine, Dawkins breaks into an unexpected contrast by saying: 'Our experience of technology prepares us to see the mind of a conscious and purposeful designer in the genesis of sophisticated machinery. It is this second intuition that is wrong in the case of living machinery. In the case of living machinery, the "designer" is unconscious natural selection.' Such a reasoning is what I may call 'an argument from personal stubbornness'. Dawkins seems to run away from logic by engaging personally with the admission that, if you have two perfectly comparable machines, you should arbitrarily regard one as having been built by a *conscious* manufacturer and the other as having been built by an unconscious manufacturer. But the question is: how can you justify consciousness in one and unconsciousness in the other if they can both produce similar works? How can you explain that the creator of a dog was unconscious while that of an airliner is conscious? Dawkins won't answer this question correctly until he admits that the designer of the Anglo-French Concorde was dumb.

"Dawkins comes up again with an analogous contrast: his eleven-month-old monkey-like randomising typist or the random-typing computer babytalk program. The random typist goes 'WDLDMNLT DTJBKWIRZREZLMQCO P', but the target phrase to reach out of this gibbering series of characters is Shakespeare's sentence 'Methinks it is like a weasel'. Let us cut it short. The sentence is finally reached in generation 43 after several anagrams, one after another, by selection. But, surprisingly – again – Dawkins concludes that while: 'In each generation of selective breeding the mutant progeny phrases were judged according to the criterion of resemblance to a *distant ideal target*, the phrase 'Methinks it is like a weasel', life (on the other hand) isn't like that. Evolution has no long-term goal. There is no long distance target.' Once again, we have an abrupt negation that seeks to arbitrarily set difference in things that are similar. We could take several more examples of that ilk, and we will still meet the same contradiction. But how can we justify the fact that the most appropriate illustrations that the evolutionists use have a conscious target but that they just come up to abruptly deny that this is also what happened in the case of creation? If there were not a distant target to be reached in the so-called 'apeline', why did the chimps suddenly stop turning into men – if they had even ever turned into men at all?

"My feeling is that evolutionism still has a long way to go to get rid of that stunning contradiction created by Darwin himself when he wrote that: 'The process of cumulative selection constituted anything but chance, but the simple forms from which this process started came about by chance.' Here, Darwin seems to have to accuse simplicity to raise a chance argument, not because simple things do not need a designer, but because it would be too wrong to try and contend that complex things have no designer.

"To try and defend Darwin, Dawkins uses the argument of a step by step atomic build-up into beings by taking the picture of a 'regressive eye' from the present form of the normal eye that he calls X to X', the least different predecessor of the normal eye, then X", the least different predecessor of X', then X''', the least different predecessor of X", and so on back probably to X'''''''''''''''''' (- 1,000,000,000,000), or the eye in its smallest and simplest form – say, its atomic form. This, to say that, because of the simplicity of the primeval forms of beings, they could not be purpose-directed. However, he comes to recognise that, as it is impossible for the heterogeneous parts of a complex being to be thrown at random to assemble a well-working being like a whale, a swallow, a man or an airliner, it goes without saying that living beings started to be purposeful in their evolutionary process as they grew complex. What Dawkins says here is that the atoms, for being so simple in the beginning, were dumb, but that they gained a sudden self-awareness and understanding of their own build-up into living beings by the very fact of growing complex in their fight for survival. Again, complexity seems to be the right convict for purpose.

"Let us take an airliner. The present airliner is so different from the earliest von Zeppelin version of a flying machine, but does this mean that von Zeppelin had no purpose in inventing the simplest airliner, or that the Anglo-French Concorde is the only purposeful flying machine for being so sophisticated? Is this to say that, because of the recent achievement of the automatic piloting system and the intricacy with which its coordinated electronic network works, there was no purpose in the very initial conception of the ailerons of the airliner? Moreover, in the making of an airliner, the manufacturers do not produce the whole machine in a single wham. An airliner is made step by step, part by part. But does the fact that the builders of the airliner started to conceive the shape and behaviour of the ailerons before installing an electronically complicated cockpit over years or decades, or even centuries, imply that they had no purpose in mind when they started to conceive the ailerons? Even the first tiniest spare that, yet, might have been preceded by the first tiniest element – say, the first screw – did not come into existence purposelessly out of the hands of the manufacturers for being first, tiny, and simple.

"No matter the time it took for man to imagine a device capable of taking over from the horse or the camel to help him travel more efficiently, the purpose was always there, while the abilities for man to create and improve the airliner had to travel all the way from its lowest primary perception in man's mind up to its complete improvement and final materialisation. And, likewise, no matter the time it took for the Creator to produce every single atom and cell up to putting them to work together in the form of complex beings such as a dog, a seagull or a man, the purpose was already there from the very inception of every first atom, from which the building of every single being started. And that purpose could not be dissipated because years, decades, centuries, millennia or tens of thousands of millennia had stridden past and generations vanished.

"In fact, the evolutionists have two problems related to their radical subjectivism. They have faith neither in logic nor in the spiritual subtleties of our universe. It is not surprising if the Scottish empiricist Hume is one of their ancestors. The only thing in which the evolutionists believe is what I may call 'the Universe of Possible Mechanics'. But not every single imaginable mechanism is achievable in the mainstream of physical and spiritual laws that govern our existence. For example, it is right that nobody would like to see somebody whom he loves dying. God himself would not like to see human beings dying. But because it has proved to be inevitable for any organic body to deteriorate and vanish, God has not been able to fight against such a law. The account, in the Scriptures, that says that, because man had sinned, God found Himself under the obligation to snatch life from him so as to punish him is misleadingly metaphorical. God simply could not do otherwise. I already said to a brother of mine one day that God does not fight against bacteriological laws. For example, very few people living in equatorial Africa don't suffer from malaria, and almost a quarter of them die. However, this doesn't mean that God doesn't love equatorial African people. The reality is simply that they live in an infested environment; and there is nothing God can do about it. If your body is damaged, it is damaged; and, if you have to die, you have to die. God has no power to fight such a law. Miracles occur for those who believe that they occur; but if they really do occur they concern but a tiny minority of cases. And yet, as we may be aware of it, rules are not built upon the minority of cases, but rather upon the majority, the minority constituting but exceptions.

"'The Universe of Possible Mechanics' in which the evolutionists live has resulted in it being impossible for them to cope with nonsensual truths. When Darwin writes that the atoms did not need to think in order to interconnect to each other in the building of living machines, and that they did so only for the sake of a fortuitous fight for survival, he could not stop and ask himself whether it was possible for a being that has no idea of what survival means to start fighting for it. But because it was not possible for him to observe the existence of thought in the atoms, as he could observe it in himself by sensual perception, he just rejected it subjectively.

"Denying consciousness and the existence of the unknown is, in fact, man's enterprise to excuse his ignorance about or indifference towards things whose substance he cannot grasp. For example, we have been brought up to consider that it is sheerly instinctive for a mother lion to protect its baby lion, but that protection of progeny is conscious and purposeful in the human world. But where is the difference? Because we know nothing about the mother lion's consciousness, we just deny it arbitrarily. But if we are unable to have access to something, does this automatically imply that the thing does not exist at all?

"I know some linguists and entomologists who have given us such a thorough description of the organisational skills of some insectile societies that they would give you the impression that they are talking about human beings. Why should this be regarded as instinctive? Do we need to study the brain and the spinal system of the bees to understand that they are fully aware that they need to build a hive to have babies? Did we need such a study in the first place to conclude that human beings are conscious? But because we have no knowledge of the bee's consciousness, we just negate it whimsically. And this is exactly what the evolutionists have done with the denial of consciousness in creation. They just cannot understand it.

"The biggest problem with philosophy – I find – is that its visions have often come into existence as a result of opposition, the younger visions tending to negate the older ones. In such a merciless challenge, little effort has often been allotted to the search for truth, but most of the work has, rather, turned to the rage of trying to prove somebody wrong. Evolutionism has been turned into the negation of a conscious creator from an attack on creationism to such an extent that its arguments have often failed to observe methodological reasoning. Here, the problem of the evolutionists in trying to invent a blind watchmaker in creation lies in the fact that they had rather focused their argument on their divergence with the creationists who saw the creator in the form of a craftsperson-designer, a kind of man who, according to their vision, made a machine later dubbed the universe. The trouble for the evolutionists, at this point, has been taking for granted a non-phenomenological man of whom the creationists themselves have failed to give a proper description and definition.

"If it is true that there was an atomic sequence in the creation of the universe, but not everything started at the atomic level. The evolutionists simply started their investigations halfway, and ignored any possible hindsight. But, those, the creationists, on the other hand, who tried to break the atomic glass to find what was behind were simply unfortunate. Their picture of a living man that starts giving verbal commands to nothingness to miraculously get a well-organised universe in six days is amazingly untenable. Because, if there were a man, where did that man come from? The place where he might have been born is certainly not very important in this question. The main problem is about having a man who has no begetter. The creationists did not tell us anything about the parents of the creator, or whatever the machine that might have made him, and then the manufacturer of that machine, and so on. They simply said, 'In the beginning, somebody named God created the universe.' Who is courageous enough to believe in this?

"If you are a believer and believe in an intelligent being that created the universe, you are probably not wrong. It might be true that there was someone there. But who is he? How is he? Where did he come from?

"Indeed, it may be true that the chain of creation goes further back before the atomic sequence where some kind of purposeful mind over creation may be found. But those who tried to go back there simply could not justify the presence of such a man in the void. (I unconsciously called this 'a man' because of my background education, but I do not really know if it can be a man.)

"The Scriptures say that when God came down as a man his mother did not need to have sex to give birth to the child-God. Perhaps her counterpart mother of the creator in his primeval form also did not need to mate in any way to give life to the creator. But who is that woman? How is she? Where did she come from? I do not even know if we can already call this 'a woman' at all. Anyway, the creationists have never held any talk like this. It even seems to me that the question of the possible mother of the creator is too far-fetched. We want to know the Creator himself in the first place. Either he had parents – or, at least, a parent – or he had come about by himself; our problem is in understanding the nature of an individual that starts uttering commands to nobody to end up getting our beautiful universe made. That is what the evolutionists could not understand. And, as a result of failing to understand it, they had to negate it flatly. In fact, they really had no choice but to push as far as possible the obvious negation of such a strange magician-artisan that nobody knows. And, as a consequence, they have had to invent something mechanical that could unconditionally replace the inexplicable.

"The theological reality today is that the creationists cannot explain the presence of their 'man' in the void. I have myself several times put to many of them, some of whom even lead important congregations, the questions as to how that man is and where he came from. But, surprisingly, none of them could give me a clear answer to the question. Some have had to conceal their failure to give an intelligible answer to that question behind the idea that the Creator is spiritual – spirits cannot be described. Others have preferred to fling the question into the blasphemy box.

"I will first drop a lid on the blasphemy box because, anyway, it is already closed. Let us then try to follow the fibres of the 'indescribable spirit' and see where they can take us. At first, all creationists, and especially believers, call the Creator by the name of 'Father'. The Scriptures also tell us that the Creator said: 'Let us make man in our image.' But it seems that our commentators of the Scriptures have never taken this sentence seriously. Who was the Creator with when *they* made man together? Was it a professional sculptor-helper or a sexual partner? However, there is no mention anywhere in the Scriptures that there had existed another somebody in the same image as the Creator in His vicinity. Moreover, the Creator is not believed to have ever mated with His female counterpart – if there had been a female all. All the goddesses that we know are said to be mythological and have been banned from theological and religious mainstreams. Here, the Creator has no sculptor-helper in his own image, and is not believed to have had a wife, nor even to have mated in fornication. However, he is believed to be the father of man. This is far beyond anything probable. I do not know if we need to follow these wires either. However, let us pose a few questions before we definitely decide whether or not it is worth continuing the debate.

"A very important side vision of the creationists is that the creator made man in the way of a craftsperson-sculptor by means of dust, while that creator is, at the same time, regarded as the father of man. But the man who created the airliner by means of steel is not the airliner's father. He is simply its creator. The ambiguity or the non-applicability of the creator's fatherhood towards his creation is the first criterion upon which it turns out to be quite difficult to clearly make up our position whether the Creator is a creator or a father. The question can be left open for free choice. But such a democracy is not very consistent. Those who will toss their slip into the ballot box for fatherhood will not be able to explain their choice, since it will be very hard for them to talk about a single father with no sexual experience.

"Let us suppose that *in vitro* semen build-up might have already existed in the very beginning, but *in vitro* semen build-up is not uni-sexual or homosexual, or even autosexual. Who, then, was the distant female? Moreover, if creationists and believers condemn cloning and biotechnological manipulation of human cells, it is far more probable that the Creator in the name of whom these condemnations are expressed might have hated such practices. This gate is also locked. The Creator has no wife, no girlfriend, and might never have practised any kindred artificial reproduction. However, he is believed to be the father of man. How? I even think that such a question is no longer useful; and the adoption window – the only one left – cannot be opened either in an argument in which no other individuals are believed to have existed at the same time as our Creator. So we cannot be adopted children of the very Creator who created us.

"Let us even suppose that the existence of the Creator's friends –

certainly those who begot us before we were adopted by the Creator (but why call him Creator in this case?) – had certainly been overshadowed in the Scriptures for some reasons, but this would not prevent us from knowing our Father. An adoptive child knows his adoptive father. The question that I am trying to open here is that of our knowledge of our father, however possibly adoptive. The creationists, and especially the believers, still say that they cannot describe their father. But how can we justify the claim that a being is the begetter of some form of beings while it remains impossible to describe it? The begetter of a sheep is but a sheep. You do not need to look any further to draw such a conclusion. But if the begetter of man or the universe is not a man or a universe, how can we justify such an engendering?

"This question came too soon. I should have started saying that the creationists do not really regard our Creator as a true man or a real universe, while they believe that He is the father of man and the universe. How is it, then, that the begetter of man and the universe is not a man or a universe like the sheep is the begetter of sheep? I shall have already locked the biological side of this question as well, because it will never work. The Creator is not believed to have had sex. Here, I feel that the creationists will need to transcend the Scriptures and tell us in truth who the Creator was with when *they* made man in *their* image. Or, shall we consider that this sentence might have been poetically misconstrued by the translators of the Scriptures, who put it into the plural? Shall we, then, correct the Scriptures?

"The question of the Creator's fatherhood towards creation can even go some way further still. We are still in the description problem but no longer in terms of biological engendering. The preoccupation here is to look into the foundation of man's inability to describe the Creator that, yet, he calls 'Father'. How is it that a son cannot yield a proper description of his father? Because, in order for this to happen, there can be only two possibilities: either the father died without leaving any picture of himself when the child was still but a baby – but did the mother and any other person who might have known the father die at the same time? – or the child was born blind. I have already excluded the probability of a mother and the father's friends as decided a bit earlier. Here, the question is: did the Creator die at the time when humanity was still but a baby, or was humanity born blind?

"Suppose that the Creator died when humanity was still at the stage of mental babyhood; but how can we justify the claim of the creationists that their father is alive? Or else, let us consider that the Creator is not dead, shall we then regard humanity as a blind creature? If the only alternative left then is that humanity is blind, how can we justify the claim of some believers who shout so loudly that their eyes have been made open thanks to the mysterious revelations of a special messenger born in the Middle East? Did that special messenger open their eyes to everything but to their father? We can go on and on asking such questions layer by layer down to infinity; we will not find a proper description of the Creator by His offspring. Either by the premature death of the Creator or by the blindness of His Creation, the questions will not find a downright answer. I thereby suspect that we regard God as our father the way we regard Herodotus as the father of history, or Auguste Comte as the father of sociology, or Henry Ford as the father of the modern car engine. Man is a piece of art, a machine, a sophisticated device designed by a very intelligent being. But a designer that cannot be described remains a big problem to solve.

"My own feeling on the matter is that the evolutionists' discovery that our organic universe had experienced an atomic stage proceeding from the combination of simpler units into more complex ones is absolutely true; but their failure to understand that there is no creation without a purpose is simply incongruous. And this is not just a spiritual matter; it is even methodological. Because, if you have a proper understanding of logic, you can't support the idea that man is a thinking being if you believe that his creator is dumb. Or else, suppose that there was no creator at all. But you can't see the atoms and genes as thoughtless units if they can make some well-structured combinations resulting in the building of thinking beings – unless you don't believe that men think. But, in this case, you should start admitting your own dumbness and give up your beliefs, for beliefs are about thoughts. You can't believe in something and hold a debate on it if you can't think about it in some primary ways.

"On the other side, the creationists too are not wrong in sustaining the possible existence of purpose in creation with a purposeful mind behind it, but their inability to give a proper description of their creator is just regrettable. You don't need to think twice to understand that you can't talk about something you can't describe. I understand that, unlike some of the creationists who choose to run away from the description question, there are some others who tend, rather, to maintain that the Creator is a man; no wonder if they call him 'father'. But a man that can't be seen the way I can see you – men – remains very wanting.

"We need to have a clear picture of what really happened to understand and believe in who the Creator really is and how he created life. For example, it may seem obvious that a son is the son of his father. But a sensible son will still wonder how it is that he is the son of his father. Is it something conventional? Did his father find him somewhere and then pick him up to make him his son? Do babies fall out of the sky with a note hooked around their neck or somewhere else on their body, saying that their father should be Mr X? What I mean here is that a sensible son will not understand what really happened for him to be the son of his father until a reproduction lesson is thoroughly delivered to him. And, likewise, if we are sensible creatures of our Creator, we will not be at ease – whatever, believers, atheists or researchers – until we have a clear picture of what really happened for us to be the creatures of our Creator.

"I understand that the majority of us prefer to make ourselves dumb about the matter to avoid what we may regard as aimless worries. But if you are a normal human being, you won't be satisfied with sitting back there and believing that you were created by something you can't describe and that created you in a way that you haven't got a clue about.

"The truth is, as I see it, that material existence sprang from the atomic combination sequence (just as the evolutionists discovered it), and, equally, that the universe that came about thereof has a well-designed purpose planned by some kind of intelligent designer (exactly as the creationists perceive it). However, the question remains as to who that designer really is. How is he? Where does he come from? I will leave that question open to Father Aba'a Memin, who, I suppose, represents the creationists in this talk."

Bekale Be'Nguema was more than relieved, and everybody was petrified, not because Amanoofwom had said anything more impressive than the other guests had said beforehand, but simply because nobody expected him to be able to speak like that. Bekale Be'Nguema knew that Amanoofwom could do it, but he could not prove it before he had spoken. The young Fanghish journalist got such a motivation to continue the debate that he did not waste a second in cheering Father Aba'a Memin up for him to face Amanoofwom's question. But Father Aba'a Memin rather reacted in a very surprising way.

"Young man, you who are asking me such an indecent question, how do you think the Creator is and where do you think He had come from?"

"No, Father. This question is not mine. The question is yours, as a creationist. Tell us how your father is and where he comes from."

"This is what is terrible with young people when they are given freedom of speech. They do not know how to frame the approaches and follow the rules. This debate is not meant to be a one-to-one confrontation. We are all seeking truth. I understand that, so far, we creationists have not been able to give a technical explanation and justification of everything in which we believe. But this is what faith is all about. However, we are at work trying to improve the visions that underlie our faith. If somebody discovers a trustworthy pattern, we will not fight it for the sake of being creationists. We have never fought the atomic vision of the evolutionists. It is true that nature works through atomic combination and genetic replication. Nobody can deny this. But our position is that there is a designer behind all of it, which the evolutionists do not want to concede. Your own conclusion after your brilliant analysis was perfect, and that is our position too. If you have something better to offer, then go on."

"I am sorry, Father, for having harassed you so badly. I have to recognise that your position is quite clear, and it seems that it is my position too. However, you have just said something else that shocked me a bit. You just said that faith is about the inability to explain and justify the object of faith. Where do you get such a definition of faith from?"

"Read the Scriptures, my son, and you will understand it."

"Where is this written?"

"Young man, I have already said that this talk is not a one-to-one confrontation."

"I am sorry, Father. I did not mean to harass you again. But I simply want you to tell me where this is written."

"Read, for example, the letter of the Apostle Paul to the Hebrews and you will understand what faith stands for."

"What does that letter say?"

"My God! Well, Paul says to the Hebrews, with the revelation of the Spirit, that, 'Faith is the substance of things hoped for, the evidence of things not seen.' Are you satisfied?"

"Be careful, Father. What Paul says here is totally the opposite. Paul is giving us a double definition of the notion of faith, which is no way near the rejection of justification and demonstration. Listen very carefully to Paul. At first, Paul says that faith is the substance of things that we hope for. Imagine that you are sick and have faith that you will be healed. Your hope for healing is the *substance* of your faith. But you will not be able to *substantiate* such a faith until you feel well. Here, your liberation from sickness is the justification of your faith. Now, imagine that you fall sick and hope to be healed and live for years until you die. How would you be able to substantiate such a faith? What Paul intelligently means, maybe without saying it, is that our faith will be *substantiated* once the things that we hope for come true. And that will be the bedrock of our faith. That is what the phrase 'the substance of things we hope for' means.

"Then, later, Paul says that faith is the evidence of the things that we cannot see. Follow Paul very carefully again. For example, you can write a physical equation to express the existence and functioning of electrons while the electrons themselves are not observable by eyesight. Here, not only is the equation a theoretical *evidence* of the existence and functioning of the electrons, the electricity that is but the direct effect of their existence is also fully observable to us. So we have a full evidence of the electrons albeit we cannot see them. This is what the phrase 'the evidence of things we cannot see' means. This is what Paul says.

"The true revelations of the Spirit have never fought against their own substantiation and justification. Man is the one who fights against the evidence of everything that he cannot prove. And this is not the business of the Spirit. I fully understand that we can suppose that the existence of the universe is the evidence of its Creator. But the trouble is that we still fail to make a sensible connection between the two the way we can express the connection between the electrons and the electricity in physics or that of the primitive and the derivative in algebra. How can we methodologically express creation by the Creator? I cannot help leaving this question, once again, to the creationists."

It was obvious, according to what people sensed, that the talk had finally come to a dead end. Where else could anyone pave a way out? The pressure on the participants was like a spherical involution. It was all-in. The evolutionists could not definitively categorise as blind the mind of a bacterium that builds a purposeful universe; and the creationists could not explain the mysterious appearance as well as the functioning of an individual who utters foolish commands to nothingness to get a beautiful universe created. Where else could we delve into and expect to find an outlet? Bekale Be'Nguema had certainly gone too far with his programme in trying to find the proof of God in a limited human mind. If physics could prove that electricity was generated by electrons, who, among our evolutionist and creationist guests, could prove that the universe had been generated by God and, more importantly, that there was purpose in such a generation and, above all, that the generator himself had a purpose-directed mind? Amanoofwom was certainly not the one to tell such a story.

CHAPTER 3

OF THE PRIMEVAL THOUGHT

The silence on the rostrum was getting more and more embarrassing. The guests seemed very exhausted, not in energy, but in ideas. The journalist too was kind of short of questions, not because he could not ask any questions at all, but because there was only one question, and it would be recursively unintelligent, I mean redundant, to go over the same question again and again. What to do? Well, let us try something.

"Dear guests," Bekale Be'Nguema started after about 30 seconds of muteness on the podium. "We still have 47 minutes to go. Can we take up our challenge and duty to break the wall of enigma about what really happened in the beginning?" he asked desperately.

"Yes, brother Bekale," Amanoofwom responded quite confidently. "Before we try and break the enigma, I just want to remark that I am quite shocked by the fact that we have given too much value to our evolutionist and creationist vests that real and fresh revelations are being mistakenly overshadowed. Why depend upon such unfulfilled visions of God if we know that the Primeval Thought is the alpha and the omega of the beginning?"

"What?" Bekale Be'Nguema was startled.

"Don't be surprised, brother Bekale. The truth is that there has always been existence in the beginning. But in the beginning – which is not a beginning but eternity before creation – existence was obscure and mute, and it was with the Primeval Thought."

"What is it?" Eyang-Alouga frowned at the strange declaration. And everybody rhythmically turned his head to Fridio Wúlyem Amanoofwom like the puppets on a TV show.

"What was it in the beginning?" asked Sima Minko, astonished and lost.

"I said that in the beginning was the Primeval Thought."

"What is it?" asked Ngwa Beyem insistently.

"The Primeval Thought was the first intelligent principle that existed before our universe was created."

"Where does it come from?" enquired Eyang-Alouga derisively.

"The Primeval Thought has no place of birth from which He might have come. It is the spiritual principle from which our universe had come."

"How is it in reality?" Bekale Be'Nguema asked, to make things understandable, and certainly to put to Amanoofwom the question of description that he himself had put to Father Aba'a Memin a bit earlier.

"The Primeval Thought is extremely beautiful if you see it. But it is a mystery. It has no age and is physically formless. It is a concentration of energy with no supporting substance. That energy can take any form, but only when it comes to material realisation. And, to be a bit more precise, that energy can be described as an amalgam of ideas and images representing something like a project; a business project, for instance.

"Let us imagine that a student has just finished his degree in business, and that, instead of looking for a job, he rather wants to start his own business, and he has, for that, designed a beautiful business project. The project is technically designed on papers, but he has the whole design in his mind. I mean, when you have the mastery of your project, you do not need the paperwork to have a clear picture of it. The picture is constantly in your mind; and you can even contemplate the whole thing because it is in your mind. And, if you are very effective, you can even give a presentation on your project with no documents in hand because you know everything by heart.

"Now, if that school leaver dies – say, at midnight – the ideas and images that he had in his mind to achieve his project will not die with him. For ideas and thoughts do not die. They are a form of spirit. What becomes obvious here is that all that exists or is about to exist, even artificial things, has a spirit. Its spirit is the mental picture that represents its reality just as one can see it in one's mind. This picture never dies. If you happen to forget about something that you have experienced or conceived this does not mean that this picture does not exist any more. It will simply have lapsed into your inactive memory, and it can pop up again at any time.

"So, as spirits do not die, the ideas and images that the school leaver had in his mind will continue to live, condensed in one single compound and floating in the dark at one o'clock in the morning, just an hour after his death. And they will remain tied up in the form of a beautiful business project. That business project will never cease to exist in the air. It is an eternal living energy formed together by an actively thinking mind that was conscious of its existence. But, as the project has got detached from that active mind, it has ceased to be conscious of itself, but it is still a thought, even though it is no longer supported by an active mind. It is therefore an unthinking thought floating in the air.

"However, as a project, it bears some form of energy, thanks to which it could become a real company just as its designer had planned its achievement. That energy, I mean that inactive and finite business project, may then, thanks to the law of affinities, be attracted by the mind of somebody who has just won a lottery, and who is silently wondering what to do with the lot. And it will be like: 'Wow! What a good idea! I will try it!'

"Once the business is set out, its daily work will depend on the organisational skills of the management, while its whole picture will be dependent on and sustained by the energy from which it came into existence. In the beginning the business may be run on the basis of some general marketing rules being studied at business schools. But as it grows and gets attuned to the realities of the local market, the manager may then cease to cling to mere theories learned at school, and will adapt his productive scheme to the local demand. It will then become a very practical management. Moreover, the school leaver might have had a number of business projects in his mind. All of them will survive as several compounds created by a common mind. They will then be a set of projects. Each of these business projects will tend to burst out into a different company as they may be attracted by different individuals over time.

"The Primeval Thought works the same way. It is a compound of energy pictured as a set of projects that bang off at times into universes, each of them having the ability of begetting an intelligibly growing mechanism intended to achieve the project just the way it was delineated. Let me then start by saying that the real image of what we call God is just like the school leaver's business project, and it works just the way I explained. What I mean is that in the very beginning there was an amalgam of ideas and images tied up in a good compound. That compound was in the image of our universe. It was that project that banged off into something visible just the way we can observe it today.

"However, the difference between the school leaver's project and the Primeval Thought hinges at two levels. First of all, the Primeval Thought was not created by the mind of an individual who had lived previously and then died. It was formed out of itself. And that formation did not take place at a certain time. It is an eternal process that has been eternal before creation. Secondly, the projects that stem from the Primeval Thought do not integrate the mind of living individuals. Instead, they create their own individuals.

"Another important thing is that if the school leaver's project or projects live very long, they may accumulate very much of their energy and get somehow improved by creating several little aspects related to their design but which might rather develop themselves as additional projects. And this may tend to increase the number of similar projects in the air. The number of projects created by the Primeval Thought is unlimited. We cannot count them and they will keep on being created and banging off into an infinite number of universes. For example, if we consider our time and suppose that the Primeval Thought has already created 12 projects, five of which have already been banged off into universes this far, then there might be three projects more to be banged off into three other universes out of our knowledge in seven billion years. This will make it eight existent universes and four still in project in seven billion years. Perhaps at that time there will be two more projects at a very rudimentary stage, but not at the same level. The Primeval Thought is a self-created thought in the form of a set of an infinite number of well-structured projects."

"But how can we justify the presence of such a thought in the void? Where does it come from?" Father Aba'a Memin posed the question, perhaps to take his revenge on the question that Amanoofwom himself had put to him previously.

"It is not very difficult to understand. Some people might have looked at man and concluded that man *thinks* because he is endowed with a spinal system through which the information perceived from the external world travels. It is the internal reactions of the nervous system as it is hit by that information that turns into something like a mind even though this mind is no longer as observable as the nervous apparatus itself. The mind of man – or that of any living being that possesses the ability to *think* – is thus created by a kind of electronic analysis of external perceptions by the nervous machine. This means that the *thinking* faculty of living beings is but the result of that electrical activity. *Thought* is therefore but the product of external perceptions as they are analysed by the nervous package. This might perfectly match the sudden awareness of atoms – now in the form of living beings – once they began to have the ability to observe the world around them. Hence consciousness suddenly came about. But, if space was bleak and obscure in the beginning, how could some kind of thought take shape then? From which observations could such a thought be formed if there was nothing observable?

"There are two types of thought: active thought and reactive thought. Reactive thought is the one that I have just hereon expounded. It is the kind of thought that helps babies to improve their understanding of the world as they grow. The more they perceive the more they assimilate. But the problem here is that a baby is not a mindless being in the first place. It simply has to accommodate itself to its new world. The fact that a 30-year-old Englishman looks very like a stupid child once he lands in China does not mean that he is mindless. He simply does not yet understand the Chinese language and habits. He will, therefore, need his reactive abilities very much to start understanding his new Chinese world.

"Active thought, on the other hand, exists not as a result of internal electrical reactions to external perceptions, but rather by the intrinsic ability of mind to imagine possible creations by itself. This is the kind of thought that conceives and creates new realities. It is that kind of thought that existed in the beginning and had imagined the universe in its entirety without any need for perceiving some preexisting realities. However, the question remains. Where does it come from? How can its presence be justified in the void?

"The presence of such a thought in the void is justified by the void itself. The void is space, and space is presence. Wherever you have some space, there is some form of presence that you might not see but it is there, and it is in the form of a thought, and that thought fills the entire space that exists. If you close an empty bottle, there will be some space in the bottle, and that space represents a presence in the form of a thought or a picture that you will not be able to perceive by sight. That thought or that picture is everywhere in the bottle. It is a thought. That particular thought that is in the bottle may be achieved if it accumulates sufficient creative energy. But this can take millions of years. That thought can also be achieved if it is intercepted by the mind of somebody who is trying to fix a drawer with no glue in hand, and he might instantly find another way to do it efficiently. What I am trying to say here is that we do not invent ideas. Ideas exist in huge amounts in space, because space itself is huge. But our minds simply attract ideas from space according to our needs and aspirations.

"Some people will tell you that 'suffering breeds great art'. But it is not enough for a man to suffer to become very clever. Some people are very pleased to suffer because they believe that they cannot do any better due to certain circumstances, or somebody might have convinced them that suffering is necessary or that they deserve to suffer. Whatever the degree of suffering of such a man, he will never become clever despite his acute suffering. You need to be pre-occupied by something and also be inclined with passion to find a way out. That is when your mind will start acting like a big magnet to attract ideas from space, and you will then look brainy. But you are not brainy at all. You are simply very worried about something.

"The evolutionists would certainly like to say that man has invent-ed ideas in time 'by mental selection'. This is the kind of vision that Herbert Spencer wanted to vulgarise through what he called 'social Darwinism'. But such a creed is due to the blindness of the evolu-tionists. Ideas are not human inventions. Ideas are spiritual tools that already exist in the space with well-determined functions and purposes as laid down by the Primeval Thought. But man simply dis-covers them by mental attraction according to his passionate needs and aspirations.

"Saint Paul, for example, was very scornful of the Romans for being so presumptuous about their intelligence, as if they were inventors of intelligence, instead of being grateful to God, who had put great ideas in their minds. Paul was absolutely right. Great ideas leading to great achievements already exist in the Primeval Mind. Man simply attracts them into his mind to achieve them. However, what Paul had certainly forgotten when he wrote that letter was that God does not choose a mind at random to put great ideas into it. The Romans deserved to be intelligent because they had a passion-ate ambition: to build a great civilisation and rule over the non-civilised around them. That is what triggered the attraction by their minds of ideas ad hoc from the cosmic mind. They were therefore, in my view, at liberty to be presumptuous about their virtuous abili-ty to be worried and attract great ideas accordingly.

"Ideas exist because space exists, and the Primeval Thought itself did not need to come from anywhere because space does not come from anywhere, and He has always existed because space has always existed. Space is wherever it is, and it is with thought. But the origi-nal thought that existed with the original space before creation is the Primeval Thought. I do not need to go any further in explanations. I do not see anybody trying to visualise the cosmos with no space anywhere, even before creation; and I do not see anybody trying to ignore the – though non-phenomenological – fact that, wherever there is some space, there must be some kind of presence, and that this presence must represent a thought, a mental or spiritual picture, or a law bearing any form of energy that can be activated and realised. Space is, and it contains things even though these things are not observable to us. Even solid objects represent some space, but that space is simply solid, and it contains things that we cannot observe. An orange, for example, is a solid object. But it contains pips that we cannot see before we break it. If we break space in the same way, we will then be able to see what it contains.

"The Primeval Thought was present in space and represented an amalgam of thoughts, pictures or laws bearing energy that was then activated and realised. Will you then ask me the question as to where this energy and these laws come from? Energy and laws are generated by ideas and pictures. Will you then ask me where these ideas and these pictures come from? Ideas and pictures are the products of thought. Is it, then, necessary to ask me where thought comes from? Thought exists because it is the wavy substance that fills the space and moves in the wind. Where does space come from, then? Space is simply authoritatively present at all times. It cannot come from anywhere, since it is everywhere. God is Space, and Space is God, bearing with Him the Thought that is inherent in Him."

It was very difficult to continue the dialogue with Amanoofwom. At that stage, nobody was likely to be able to ask a question or argue at all. Part of the reason was not because the guests had definitely taken Amanoofwom's speech for granted or that they possibly believed it all, but simply because they were off guard. The speech sounded so unusual that you could not know where to start an argument. You could not be pro or con, for most of what was said was too strange and barely understandable. Bekale Be'Nguema, however, as a journalist, always had something to say to tease the participants; thus he asked: "Mr Amanoofwom, the most intriguing thing you said was about the self-creation of the individuals who carry out the Primeval Thought's projects. Who are they in our universe, for example? Is it ourselves?"

"I can say yes, since our mental abilities are in the image of the original forces that were destined to initiate the implementation of the project. But in the very inception of existence, we were not aware of anything about the project. The first steps of our existence are marked by a high degree of unconsciousness. We then needed to evolve, learn and improve throughout experience before we then started understanding and could take conscious and organised actions. That is certainly what the evolutionists call 'evolution by natural selection'. The creationists might call it 'revelation of the knowledge of good and evil'. This is the 'allegedly blind' mechanism of the universe and with it all the creatures that ceased to be a merely unconscious machinery once they learned about the purposes of existence as delineated in the mind of the Primeval Thought. That is where our argument with the evolutionists can come to an end.

If you are unaware of something, this does not mean that there is nothing to be aware of. Richard Dawkins himself, in a reply to Bishop Hugh Montefiore's arguments from personal incredulity, wrote that: 'Even if the foremost authority in the world can't explain some remarkable biological phenomenon, this doesn't mean that it is inexplicable.' If it is true that we have not yet discovered the existence of purpose in the mind of 'the First Cause of Existence', this does not mean that there is no purpose at all. A one-year-old child sees the world around him as an insignificant piece of machinery that has no virtues, nor an end. But the same individual, at 30, will tell you that: 'It is important to respect your neighbours.' But what do you think a neighbour is, if not a sheer heap of funny matter moving upright on the ground, just the way you saw it when you were one year old?

"The external world makes great changes only to improve our perception of it as we grow conscious of its virtues, but it does not change in itself. For example, the world is totally absurd to a cynical man, while it is fully virtuous to a seemly man. And yet, it is the same world; the only difference is that one has a bad perception of it whereas the other has a good perception of it. And you will find that those who strive to have a better perception of the world get the best of it, even though the world does not really change in itself. At least it changes for them. The leading creatures of each universe experience the same transformation when they attain the status of knowing beings. Life then becomes purposeful to them. But they do not invent purpose in life. They discover it.

"When man was still unconscious, he used to walk all naked, and could take notice neither of the moral importance of his genital organs nor of how embarrassing nudity could be, since he was not aware of it. But once he gained knowledge of ethical wisdom, sex suddenly became a taboo, bearing, as an addition, the rest of incestuous processions. That is what is depicted in the tale of the 'Prime Garden', in the Jewish spiritual tradition. Man was still just like an animal, hence his nearness with the animals of the garden as depicted by the addenda of the tale. But once he gained full knowledge of human values, this brought about big changes in his way of looking at himself and at the world around him. And here we go: elevated beings full of principles to be respected.

"Once the Primeval Thought banged off our universe, three different forces came automatically into existence to carry out the functions of the universe as laid down by the project. This is but the spiritual representation of what happened in the beginning when creation was launched by the power of the Primeval Thought, there came first the principle that we call *Nzam* or the thinking force. That thinking force is the mind of our universe. It is that force that thought and conceived the details of our universe as we see it growing. It was called *Nzam* because of the difficulties that man experienced in trying to have a full understanding of it. The Fanghish word *enzamán* means 'confusion'. People got very confused about God's nature and functioning. That force came to be regarded as the Father who had imagined a picture of our universe.

"Then comes *Onohn*, the son. The word *Onohn* means 'swift perceptions.' It is a metaphor of the spirits that come in the form of birds to stealthily drop some revelations to spiritual masters or mystic students. *Onohn* is said to be the uttering, naming or guiding force. He is the one that named the beings of the universe after they were created. Some people will tell you that the famous Swedish naturalist Carl Linnaeus was the one who classified and named all the species of our universe. But my own feeling is that Linnaeus himself had simply attracted the naming abilities of *Onohn* into his mind, the naming force that had already named the beings in spirit. So, Linnaeus' own success in the work of classifying and naming the species of our universe must be held from his – even unconscious – spiritual connection with the *Onohn* principle.

"That uttering force that had named the universe in spirit has often come back to our world and has often spoken to man and guided him through what we tend to call special messengers or prophets, or simply great teachers and reformers. But, before all this, the first task that was given to the uttering force was that of uttering the commands for creation to take place. These commands were then executed by the third principle of creation: *Ñiengon.*

Ñiengon is the modelling or generating force. The word *ñiengon* is a lexical composition deriving from the expression *ñia 'e ngon*, which means wholesome begetter – but, literally, it means mother of a young girl. In this sense, this third principle is viewed as a mother who gives birth to a young girl – the universe – that is meant to give birth to more children – the universe's further creations: human civilisations. It is through that force that the whole internal decoration of the universe was moulded. Everything that had to be shaped as a result of a crafty activity by Nature was shaped by that force; and everything that had to be generated as the result of an engendering labour was generated by the same force. That force is known as 'the Mother'.

"These three forces do not control the existence of our universe, for they reside in it. All they have done is to work out the internal decoration of the universe, and they are the universe's drivers. They are its pilots. But there is something else that sustains the universe as the ground sustains a car. There is something else that sustains the universe just as the air sustains an aeroplane in suspension. This thing, which never entered the universe but is its sovereign sustainer, is the *Outer-Soul* that has always stayed outside the universe. It is the one that has left behind our space-time system. That one is the Primeval Thought. This is not too miraculous to be understood. The Primeval Thought is a huge series of compensatory laws that make possible the equilibration and suspension of orbital bodies all over the infinite space. The Primeval Thought works like a spherical disposition of negative magnets in the middle of which an object with similar charge is placed. There will be no way in which such an object can move out of the magnetic sphere. Because the forces with which the Primeval Thought sustains our universe maintain it together at the same position and pace, the universe is not meant to ever collapse, although there might be some errors and accidents. But this is just natural.

"The three forces that came into existence as our universe was banged off by the *Outer-Soul* – these forces that thought, modelled and uttered the universe – form one single compound that is known as the *Over-Soul* that hovers over human existence, and works through man, its corporeal representation."

"In this case, what do we call God: the *Outer-Soul* or the *Over-Soul?*" asked Bekale Be'Nguema.

"I have already answered that. The *Outer-Soul* is God, but the *Over-Soul* is His active representation within our universe. Every universe that is banged off has its own *Over-Soul* – its representative of God and organiser of the determined universe. However, below the *Over-Soul*, in each universe, we also have different *Inner-Souls* each of them representing a particular way of expressing God's revelations as they are intercepted by different minds – or mindsets – expressing themselves in different ways, using different communication codes.

"Throughout history, in our universe, God has often taken hold of individuals pertaining to different *Inner-Souls*, and has worked through them for the well-being and the elevation of man. Every single man who has worked out a system of thought for the improvement of something real in his nation and the world has been touched by the thinking force that thought our universe and came to him through the *Inner-Soul*. The ones who have brought special messages in our history have been touched by the uttering force that came to them through their *Inner-Souls*. And all men who have created any substantial instruments of labour have been touched by the modelling force that modelled our universe from its beginning and that has come to them through their *Inner-Soul*.

"These three forces have always come to men through their *Inner-Souls*, and have worked sporadically throughout the world. But we have some landmarks of their fuller expression. For example, the thinking force is believed to have reached a very high degree in its expression among the Teutons. The modelling force seems to have been manifested with a particular vigour among the Anglo-Americans. And the uttering force has come to being and had reached its fullest presence among men in the person of *Aduma-the-elect*, a man born among the *Esséna*, but who was regarded as a *Yudi*. Today, his teachings are, as we know, *sui generis*."

Amanoofwom paused to breathe for a while, but Ngwa Beyem was very intrigued by Amanoofwom's conclusion. He had never heard of such a name in his life, and this was almost insulting to him as a historian. "Who is that Aduma-the-elect?" he asked, and Amanoofwom did not complicate the answer.

"We know him by the name of Yésuh, but the world calls him Jesus. He was a man that God Himself used to speak to people. God spoke with him mouth to mouth; I mean, God used his mouth to speak."

Bekale Be'Nguema saw here another occasion to bring about an important debate. "How is it possible for God to use a man's mouth to speak? Either God speaks behind the flames of a burning bush, or He speaks in the clouds. But never in a man's mouth," he proposed.

"Unfortunately, this was the case with Aduma. God really spoke in his mouth. But many people could not understand such a mystery. For example, one day, one of Aduma's followers asked him why he did not just show them the Father straightaway. But, in response, there came a voice that said: 'Since I have been with you, you have not known *Me*?' And the voice continued: 'Who has seen me has seen the Father.' If you look carefully into these two declarations, you will find that there were two different persons who spoke on that occasion. At first, it was God Himself, who gave the assurance of his presence through Aduma; and then it was Aduma, who continued to confirm that he who had seen him had also seen the Father, for the Father was in him. Therefore, there had been two persons speaking from the same mouth. That is even why, one day, Aduma said that "the testimony of two is true". But it was not possible for the non-initiated to understand that two people could use one single mouth to speak. So would they still be wondering: "Where, is that second person whom he is talking about as the second witness, since we see him alone?" Aduma was a true 'double' of God. In fact, God was in him in full. That is why we, who believe in him, do not believe for pleasure or for dogma. But we know that God was with him in full."

Kapla Bikuk-Ebuh seemed a bit shocked at this declaration, though astonished and infatuated in some ways. "I have never heard anything so relevant about God as what you say, dear Amanoofwom.

"But there seems to be a discrepancy with respect to what you explained about the relationship between the *Over-Soul*, the *Inner-Soul*, and men they have often used to express themselves. You said that what is revealed to special men like Aduma comes to them through their *Inner-Soul*. Why do you then say "We who believe in him"? How can you, then, be part of those who believe in Aduma whereas you do not belong to the same *Inner-Soul* as him?"

"I see. But the leading creeds that govern our world today did not come into existence through man's haphazard adaptation 'by spiritual selection'. All truths are generated by God and then handed down onto the *Over-Soul* for man's spiritual achievement. Now, if the *Over-Soul* is revealed to a man A from a certain nation A through its *Inner-Soul A*, other men *b* from another nation *b* can then adopt that revelation if they find truth in it. They will then adapt it to the spirit of their nation *b* so that it can be elevated to their *Inner-Soul B*. The intricate communion between the *Over-Soul* and all *Inner-Souls* will then cause the *Over-Soul* to acknowledge *Inner-Soul B* with respect to that revelation. That is when men from *b* will be able to receive from the *Over-Soul* God all grace in connection with that particular truth. It can be a scientific or a religious truth. Because science and religion are both true revelations of God, they are meant to be adapted to any nation whatever the culture in which they were initially revealed. And, conversely, if you find a revelation that is stuck on one single culture and that cannot be translated into and adapted to different cultures, then you have to make sure that it is a revelation from God.

"To be clear, the revelations that came through Aduma were primordially addressing the *Yudi*. But as these revelations were true, and we find them true, we shall adapt them to our culture to make them ours as well. Henceforth, we will not need to believe in Aduma, but in the truth that came to humanity through him; and we will not believe in that truth as a foreign truth, but as our own truth, for it is a universal truth. Aduma will then be but a symbol of that truth, but not the truth itself, for Aduma did not seek personal glory. The only thing that he sought was to hand over the truth to all nations."

Mr Yans Milo Mi'Mbot, the doctor of anthropology, raised his hand and Bekale Be'Nguema allowed him to speak. "To be honest, I had never thought of such an insight into the creation that sounds so real in almost every aspect, and above all the mystery between Yésuh and God. I mean, I do not really know what to say. I just have one single problem that I have had since I was very young. I do not know if our brother Amanoofwom can say something about it."

"Of course, all our problems should be posed, and, if not Amanoofwom, somebody else can find the response." Bekale Be'Nguema gave an encouraging incentive to Mr Mbot.

"Well, every single Fanghish person has already heard of *Nzam, Onohn* and *Ñiengon* even if only in a superficial way. On that point, I really have to say a big thank you to brother Amanoofwom for giving us such a thorough explanation of these principles. I mean, I am myself so edified by all that brother Amanoofwom has said this far. However, there is something that I have never understood about these three principles. I find that there is a sort of genealogical stumbling block in their line. It is said – brother Amanoofwom must have forgotten to mention it – that *Nzam, Onohn* and *Ñiengon* were begotten by Mebegue, and that is why we respectively called them Nzam-Ye-Mebegue, Onohn-Mebegue and Ñiengon-Mebegue. And Mebegue Himself is called Mebegue-Me-Nkpaa because He was begotten by Nkpaa. My question is: who is then the father of Nkpaa? Why does the line have to stop there?"

"I have already said it somewhat glibly, but you certainly didn't pay much attention. Nkpaa is the eternal energy that had always existed in the dark and that turned itself into Mebegue in the form of a project. I have already said that God is Space and Space is God. It doesn't have an originator, nor a beginning. It is Itself the Root of existence; that is why we call It by the full name of Mebegue-Me-Nkpaa -*Ndzi*. The Fanghish word *ndzi* means the 'root or the beginning of something'. In a very refined way of speaking, I mean in our spoken poetry, we call this *Kenghle*, the first wavy creative sound, or the first cosmic tolling bell. And *Elolongh*, the shiny spectrum braided rope that tolled this bell when creation was launched, is the symbolic Serpent of intelligence in Mebegue-Me-Nkpaa-*Ndzi*'s creation. We know Him by the mystic name of *Mefan*. *Mefan* is immeasurably long. His heavy and slimy two-pronged tongue is the transmitter of knowledge into man's mind. The right prong is the transmitter of the knowledge of good, and the left prong is the transmitter of the knowledge of evil. But at the time of that transmission into man's mind, the right prong lies on the left side of man's head and is connected to the left hemisphere of his brain, while the left prong lies on the right side of man's head and is connected to the right hemisphere, because man is face to face with the Serpent during that mysterious transmission. This is why our brain has to work like a cross. The knowledge of good transmitted into the left hemisphere of man's brain needs to run through the right side of his body; and the knowledge of evil transmitted into the right hemisphere of his brain needs to run through the left side of his body; because good is right and evil is left.

Mefan is, in fact, the tail of God, and its head is the representative brain of the Cosmic Thought. It was the opening of His eyes for the first time that sounded like a bell when creation was banged off. That is perhaps where explanations may be insufficient. You just need to see it in spirit to have the clearest picture of it. However, this image may help you understand and see what it is like."

"Did you then see this?" Eyang-Alouga asked with an apparent expression of doubt in his face.

"Such a question is not very important, because if I tell you, as it is, that I saw it, you will not believe me."

"No, brother. I won't doubt. All that you have said thus far is self-evident enough to chase away my sceptical thinking. I just want to know the whole truth."

"Well, I did see it, of course."

"Where did you see it?"

"I travelled into myself and around, and I saw it."

"How long did you need to travel in order to see it?"

"You can see all these things in a matter of seconds if you are lucky. But breaking them into sequences in order to understand them is the biggest problem that you may face."

"Well, we believe that you saw them and that you broke them into sequences in order to understand them. But, tell us, why it is then said that we are made in the image of God, whereas we are not an amalgam of thoughts and pictures just the way you described the Primeval Thought." Eyang-Alouga posed the paradoxical question.

"I understand that this description does not directly match with the one that we have in the book of the Holy Word. But the fact that we are shaped the way we are does not mean that my description of God is wrong. There is no doubt that we were made in the image and likeness of God. But the problem hinges on the method that God used to create the universe step by step down to man. We are made in the image of God because God's shape is like our shape. Just think about ghosts. They are the same shape as human beings. God is also a ghost in the human shape, but He is the highest ghost. And He created man in His own shape. However, the question remains as to why it is that God is described as an amalgam of thoughts and pictures while the human beings, which are supposed to be made in his image, are shaped the way they are.

"Take a joiner. To produce a chair, the joiner first conceives a mental picture of some device on which people can sit. So the chair is, first of all, a mental picture that the joiner conceives and he can contemplate it in his mind, just the way the school leaver could contemplate his business project. But, to make that chair, the joiner will assemble such elements as wood, nails, glue, tapestry, etc. that exist in nature and stores, made by somebody else by the use of other elements that also existed in nature and stores beforehand, and so on. So the chair is first a mental picture that has to become visible by joining different materials. This is like creating the spirit of the chair first in order to create its physical form. God did exactly the same thing. He conceived the picture of something like a dolphin and then turned it into a physically observable form by joining some elements of nature in the shape of the mental picture of the dolphin, and the dolphin came into being.

"Here, we certainly have two big problems with regard to the way

God made things like dolphins or ants by assembling some materials together as the joiner would do. In fact, there were no materials in nature in the very beginning. One could conclude that God had certainly proceeded like a magician, who unfolds his palm and a squirrel suddenly springs out of it, apparently from nowhere. One would therefore think that God used magic and certainly that the magicians are but little gods. It is probable that magicians are good imitators of God and perhaps that they use the same secret that God used when he created the universe out of nothingness. A magician certainly thinks about a squirrel, and he then activates some kind of spiritual laws that instantly turn his mental picture into its visible form. Different magicians may use different tricks, but this one seems to be the basic one. However, God is not really a man like a joiner or a magician. He is an amalgam of thoughts and images or – say – one big coordinated compound of thoughts linking different images in a certain logical way displaying the picture of the universe. So, what happens? What did God really do?

"God conceived the picture of our universe before turning it into its visible form. But He was Himself the picture that was conceived. In fact, the picture formed itself little by little over billions of years at the time when the notion of year didn't even exist. So, at some point, if there had been somebody wearing the appropriate lenses, a few minutes before creation started, he would have seen a ghost universe in the image of our present universe, and he would certainly have asked himself: 'Where does such a picture come from?'

"If you are a joiner and you want to make a chair, it is true that you have the whole picture of the chair in your mind. But, at the time you make the legs, you tend to forget a little bit about the backrest. This means that you turn all your concentration onto the legs even though they are not the only part of the chair as a whole. In your mind, the chair seems to be limited to the legs only when you are concentrating them But, once the legs are made, you will then turn to the backrest and forget a little bit about the seat; and so on, until all parts are made so that they can be put together to become a chair.

"God was Himself the picture of the whole universe as conceived in His mind. But what He would do to create the universe step by step would be to turn the whole picture into one single aspect or stage, the one about to be physically produced. This simply means that God would turn Himself spiritually into the step to be created, in order to produce its physical duplication. God behaved exactly like the original replicator in the primeval soup, if we refer to genetical evolutionism. In fact, genetical replication itself is but an imitation of the way in which God created our universe. When, for example, God was about to create stars, He turned Himself into a spiritual star so that He could produce its physical duplications as we can observe them today. So, if on day one – which is not a day but a stage that must have lasted some million years – God created light, this means that the first 'shape' into which God turned when He created our universe was that of light; and He then produced a physical duplication of it just the way we can see it today.

"By the same way, when it came to creating animals, God turned Himself into the animal form and produced physical replications of it. Here, it becomes very easy to understand why we are physically the same shape as God. I believe that this was your question. Indeed, not only did God turn Himself into the human shape to produce its replications, but also, as the human shape was the last one into which God turned Himself to produce physical duplications of it, He remained in that shape just like you and me, because there was nothing more to be created after man. That is why we were made in the image of God. God's silhouette looks exactly like the human silhouette, until today and for evermore. The plants, fish, birds, ants, worms, snakes, planets, stars were all created in the image of God too, but once God moved into man's image He remained like that for ever. In fact, if there were anything else to create after man, God would not have kept man's shape. He would have moved to the next shape to be created. And I do not think that He would have come back to take our shape again, for the beings He would have created after man would have been more perfect than ourselves. "This is the

God in whom we believe: the Invisible-Compound-of-Pictures-Coordinated-by-Subtle-Thoughts-and-Fed-by-a-Powerful-Energy that now looks like a man. It is very like a ghost. It is an enormous ghost that fills the infinite space and in which all smaller ghosts reside.

"We are made in the image of God first by shape. But we are also in his likeness by ability. God is a thought, a creative 'machine' by 'mental' conception. That is the ability that He handed over to man. We possess a mind capable of working out highly structured projects that can be realised in a purely material setting. However – I have to remind us of this again – we do not invent thoughts. Our thoughts are attracted from the mind of God. We simply have the ability to organise them, which makes them look like new thoughts. But they are not new. A joiner may design a new type of chair. But the elements that he uses to assemble the chair together are not new in nature. He just puts existing materials together in a different kind of association to make a new type of item.

"So, our likeness with God is mental, or, we can say, spiritual, if we want. I think that here is where it seems necessary to say a word about the atomic combination that the evolutionists had discovered. One might have definitely taken God for a magician by His ability to turn mental pictures into visible forms without making use of any materials. But creation did not start at the level of visible beings. God was a compound of thoughts and pictures. But He used thoughts before using pictures in the creation schedule. He used thoughts as invisible principles to condition the creation of visible beings. Thoughts were turned into laws and these laws became a kind of energy of a variety of forms. These may be what we call the physical or atomic or chemical laws, which are being discovered little by little today. These are the laws that served as the initial material for the creation of the first visible beings. The electrons, for example, had been created before light to make it possible. Electrons are like the spirits of light. But light itself is a combination of different forms of energy. These forms of energy that constitute the whole spirit of light are laws: physical or atomic laws that made possible the material realisation of light. I am not a physicist to explain how an electromagnetic radiation is formed and how it works. But if you simply have it in mind that light is visible to us while the electrons and other subatomic particles that, all together at work, make it possible are not visible, you will easily understand the way observable beings came into existence through the invisible laws that preceded them in the sequential chain of creation.

"Let us imagine that God is now trying to create water. He would not instantly produce water. What he would do is to turn his thought into some invisible laws that would make water possible once the picture of water would be conceived. Here, God proceeds very methodologically. Do not let us forget that what I call God is simply the Primeval Thought of the beginning – eternity. Thought is extremely methodological. The thought would therefore start turning itself into some invisible law (the spirits of water) that, once put together at work, can cause water to be formed. These laws would be the powerful spirits that, once created, would then wait to be mobilised by some kind of command. But that command has to be carefully planned. What God would do is to conceive the picture of a purely transparent, inodorous and insipid liquid whose density would be equal to zero so that it would run for washing. Once this picture was perfect and ready in His mind, a coded command would then be uttered for water to come to existence exactly the way God was visualising it in His mind. Here, the coded command would be thoroughly directed to the hydrogen law and the oxygen law ordering them to get attracted to one another for a massive mating likely to produce water. But that mating would not be haphazard. The modelling force would make very meticulous calculations on the appropriate proportions that are needed for each of the elements in association so that the material formation would be, as much as possible, a perfect duplication of the mental picture of water as delineated in God's mind. (Remember: the modelling force itself doesn't work like a joiner either. It is a thought waving in full energy through space.) Here, it seems that – according to the calculations made by that force after receiving the command from the uttering force which, in its turn, had received the picture of water from the thinking force – hydrogen is needed twice as much as oxygen for water to be almost perfectly made. Then, the modelling force does the job, and it works.

"I took the example of H_2O because it is one of the most popular and simplest. There is a huge range of more complex atomic associations that were required for the formation of the visible materials of our universe; and living beings are not an exception. Plants, insects, fish, birds, animals, and the glorious man were all made just like this. Now, if you look at the complexity of man and start observing that the retina only, which is but a little part of the eye, is made of four different types of layers of cells, some of which are made of huge amounts of cells, like – say – the membrane which has about three million ganglion cells, and there are, for example, 125 million photocells in the thick layer that comes just after that membrane, and that mitochondria cells are chemical cells that possess more that 700 substances, and that the nucleus is a concentration of coded data whose amount can get to billions etc., etc., then you will be likely to visualise the amount of work that was needed for man to be thoroughly conceived in the mind of God, and the quantity and quality of the laws that were created beforehand so that man would be produced by their association. Just imagine the meticulousness of every single particle of man's body and the intelligence and attention and care with which all the billions of elements that constitute it were put together to get such a complex working being made; you will understand how much work and time must have been needed for his completion. And here is where the investigation of the evolutionists begins.

"When beings started to be created, they mostly were not created straightaway. While the whole picture of a determined being would be conceived in the mind of God and the laws that would achieve its creation would start to mobilise for a well-calculated mating, the association process of these laws would be very slow at times. Some laws would start taking shape before others in the form of simple cells or tiny jumbles of simple cells that would then start evolving just like an embryo. This is the first point that makes it clear that the creation and evolution of beings from smaller or simpler forms into their achievement in more complex forms is not without a well-designed foresight. Creation is fully designed and purposeful, and it was not magic. It was a thoughtful and painful job. It was extremely complicated. Time was needed for each conceived being to be completed just the way it had been conceived.

"Look at an embryo. When it starts in its tiniest and simplest form in a womb, it does not ignore that it is meant to become a baby, and then grow as a child, then as a teenager, then as an adult, and then as an elderly person. The embryo knows perfectly where it is going – or shall I say that the mind that had set the laws that connect male and female cells together to launch the growth of an embryo in a womb knows how it is meant to look in its achieved form. It is already programmed to go all the way up as a living being in its form according to its species. It is not by chance that a human embryo grows into a human baby. Otherwise all human embryos would not become human babies. About 99.999% or so would rather grow into something different. We would, therefore, tend to create a new species every time a new baby came into the world. But things don't work like that.

"I know that the genetic shuffling programme in chromosomal combination is set in advance in such a way that the embroys will turn into babies in the image of their parents. But this is exactly what happened in the beginning with the creation of our universe and all that lives in it. The Primeval Thought conceived a universe, created the means to its realisation, and preset the programme of its physical formation and growth. There was no chance, no haphazard or casual achievement, though some errors occurred (I shall try and explain what I mean by 'errors of creation'). But everything was thought, calculated and launched; and this took billions of years for every single atomic association to take shape and grow to its final form. Even though some of us might suppose that none of our species has yet reached its final form, but this does not mean that the thought that conceived and launched creation does not know what our final forms are meant to be in the future. Whatever the degree of complexity of our universe in the future or its degree of simplicity in the beginning, the *intention* that launched creation has never been dumb about it. If one day our universe happens to veer into some lethal disaster, this will simply be the result of some mistakes made by the very God that created it. This will not be the first time God mistakes. Creation, as we see it today, is but the result of a huge series of mistakes. For example, the racial diversity – which characterises our world from the variety between different types of earthworms to that between different species of fish, birds, animals up to men, stars and planets – is but the result of a series of mistakes that God made when He set about creating the universe.

"God made a lot of mistakes, just as anybody – even a great artist – would do. He did not really intend to create such a variegated universe. Let us leave the stars and planets alone and just take a look at the earth. The diversity of species, and, above all, of races within species, does not imply that God had intended to create them differently. He did not turn Himself into every single species that exists to create its duplications. Instead, He would turn Himself into some genera to produce its perfect duplications. But the diversity that came about was held from duplication errors. For example, God did not turn Himself successively or concomitantly into a cat and a leopard to produce their respective duplications. He must have turned Himself into a sovereign shape of the genus *Panthera tigris*, *Panthera pardus*, or *Panthera leo* to produce one single sovereign shape of it: perhaps cats only. But there occurred some duplication errors that resulted in things like panthers, lions, tigers, leopards, pumas, etc. And, likewise, when it came to create the genus *Homo*, God turned Himself into a unique sample to produce perfect human duplications. For example, He would have turned Himself into the Asian shape to produce its perfect duplications with Chinese features only. Then the Brown, the Black, the White and the Red came about as duplication errors. At this level nobody could be 100% sure of which one of these types was exactly in the image of the original replicator-God, and which ones were the errors. Each race can be at freedom to believe that it is the perfect duplication of the original replicator-God. But all this is but a question of affection for one's own nature. For example, in the Bible, as it was originally written by the Jews, they believed that God had created man by means of clay and dust because they saw that clay and dust were the same colour as their own skin. They certainly wanted to insinuate that they were the original men that God had created and surely that the other men were certainly created much later or that they were erroneous: wrong colours for clay. And, today, there is a projudaist theological tendency that believes that the Garden of Eden was located in the Middle East. But all this is not God's business. Man is the one who seeks to pull the cover to his side.

"Indeed, it is natural for man to try and expropriate everything that he seems to be the first to discover. For example, we have been brought up to say 'God the Father' simply because the first individuals to explore the question of God were men. So they tended to discriminate against women by maintaining that God was a father, but not a mother. We have even written a story that accuses woman of being the cause of sin and death, as she was the one that the Devil deceived. That story is quite clever because, in reality, women are really vulnerable and gullible enough to persuade without much effort. Suffice it that you mirror them something that looks beautiful to get them to succumb. Presumably, if Jesus had been a woman, he would certainly have accepted the kingdoms that the Devil offered him on the mountain and he would, consequently, have given up on his mission.

"But – I have already said this – all this is not God's business. God Himself is not male or female. The energetic principle that we call by the name of God is sovereignly bisexual. But, behold, what I am saying here is not biological or erotic. It is a metaphor. What I mean is simply that the creation of the universe is the work of a thought that played both roles at a the same time: the role of conceiving mental pictures and that of turning these pictures into material realities. So, the instinct that haunts every human being in trying to erect its shape, nature or colour as a paragon of perfection or the genuine type in the image of God is simply a matter of selfishness and narcissism. The way it is difficult to tell whether it is the cat that is the most likely duplication of God in the *Panthera tigris* shape is exactly the same way that it is hard to decide whether it is the Chinese who are the most perfect duplication of God in the *Homo* shape. Moreover, this is not really important. There is one good reason for this to be of no importance.

"In fact, there exists no perfect duplication of God among the beings that were created by replication from God in the different shapes that he took to create life. All beings that are created are duplication errors of the very original replicator - God. The reason is simple. There is no way in which material beings can be as perfect as their mental conceptions or spiritual representations. We often say that 'perfection is not from this material world'.

"Let us take a photocopier (I am not saying that God is like a photocopier, but God's work in the framework of creation can be compared to that of a photocopier). If you want to make 30 copies of a one-page document, it is likely that the ink will falter on a line, a word or a character. And you may find such errors on ten copies, and it will certainly not be the same line, the same word or the same character that will falter on the ten copies, which will have one or several duplication errors. However, each copy will still give you the same information, but that information will have some corrupted points with respect to the original copy and will be, at the same time, different from any other copy bearing a different error or different errors. You will then have 20 identical copies and ten different ones. This will make it 11 samples. But if the machine is really defective or that the paper type does not fit the loader, it is more likely that the ink will falter on the 30 copies, which will then all bear different errors. In this case none of them will be a true likeness of the original copy, even though they will all give you the same information, each of them bearing errors that will be different from those of the other copies. You will then have 30 samples, all different from the original copy, and also different from each other.

"Given that our material world is very different in nature from the spiritual world, all materials might have been imperfectly adapted to the image of the original replicator-God. Therefore, neither the cat nor the lion, neither the leopard nor the jaguar, is a true likeness of their spiritual replicator, but they are all nearly in its image, while each of them bears an error that makes it different from the others and different from the original replicator. And, likewise, it is more likely that none of our human races is a true likeness of God in the human shape. But each of the copies is nearly like the original picture while bearing its own error that makes it different from any other copy as well. The point I am trying to make here is that we are all duplication errors of God. It is true that we were made in His image, but we are not basically equal to Him, nor are we basically equal to each other, because we do not all bear the same errors.

"So, when God created life, it came out as errors, and some of the errors might have appeared to be more grave than others. Well, let us take written mistakes in our writing systems to explain the point. A phrase in which a word is missing is more difficult to understand than a phrase with a word in which a character is missing. However, it would be more appropriate to fill in the word gap by browsing through a lexicon than through an abecedarium. What I mean is that, if the approach is appropriate, a bigger problem can be more easily solved than a minor one. So, the solution is not too hard to find. However, how did God cope with the errors He made when creating living beings?

"Our universe itself appears to be very diversified in matters of geology, climatology, meteorology, etc. This diversity of conditions was also due to errors. God did not really intend to create colder or hotter regions in our universe. There should have been one single climatic condition for the whole universe. But, as errors occurred at that level too, diversity became undeniable. Ideally, God would have created one single perfect climatic condition matching one single perfect sample of every species. But the errors that occurred ended up corrupting that intention. However, the environmental diversity turned out to be fitting to the diversity of species, and all the species that couldn't match with any of these conditions simply vanished away. They disappeared. The dinosaurs are not the only species to have faced such accidental extermination. Many more species beyond our knowledge died for such reasons. So, this was not a coincidence. God simply faced some laws of physics and logic that He couldn't transcend. For example, if one single sun came about to illuminate our solar system, it would be practical that, if the earth is round, the sun's rays would not hit the earth with the same intensity on every spot at the same time. No miracles could be achieved at this level. God does not fight logic. The errors that occurred in the duplication of species fell into the same category. It is not easy to produce the same item several times alike with no errors. Even the most perfectly tailored system of production would not achieve a zero-error probability over several items. I am convinced that, if we check out on a series of brand new Ford Sierras spot by spot, we will not find them perfectly alike.

"The problem in God's diversified creation by errors would have been to pour all different species together into the same conditions while they would not have the same adaptive features and abilities. Take this hypothesis. If you catch different species of fish from different backgrounds and pour them into one single fishery condition – say, salt sea waters – it is obvious (even though this may not happen in the end) that those caught from river waters will have big trouble surviving in there. However, if they end up surviving, they might not be able to develop as efficiently as those caught from sea waters, which are used to such a condition or are meant for it. On the other hand, if you set up different aquariums with different water conditions matching different fish species, it is more likely that each species will be well adapted in to its environment and grow with similar efficiency to any other species in a condition matching its body features and surviving capabilities. It will be like saying that they are 'separate but equal'. They will surely grow and enjoy their different conditions equally. This is exactly what the divine intelligence did too. Each error was carefully identified with the earthly conditions that could rightly match with its body features and surviving capabilities, and it was thoroughly dropped thereon. All errors were therefore disseminated all over the face of the earth in such a way that each error was dropped in the part in which it could be better adapted and developed. I am not borrowing from evolutionism. I said that there had been an atomic and evolutionary sequence in creation. I would have said this even if evolutionism had never existed because it is simply true. But it did not happen by chance. The reality is that it was very hard for any being to survive in an environment that would not match with its own type and abilities. Shuffling mutations of species between different environments that are not originally appropriate to them is now made possible thanks to our level of achievement, which has made us capable of fighting hostile conditions.

"Let us take again the example of an embryo. If a pregnant woman drinks too much alcohol, it is likely that the embryo will suffocate, and it may collapse and die. But the same embryo now as a 30-year old man will be able to drink the same amount of alcohol, and even more, without dying, because it will be now more developed and stronger than it was in its mother's womb.

"Life evolves and gets richer and stronger. That is why it is now possible for an Arctic Eskimo to move down to the Amazonian hot jungle and fight the heat until he gets used to his new environment. And, likewise, a tropical African Negro can now move to Siberia and survive there until he gets used to his new environment. But such mutations were certainly not possible when man was still evolving throughout his simpler and weaker forms several million years ago.

"However, there are two levels of diversity in life: the racial level, which concerns all living beings and which came about by duplication errors; and the cultural level, which is – allegedly – the property of the genus *Homo*. It is this second level of diversity that is important to look into here. What are the reasons for humanity to be culturally diversified? Why do all peoples not have the same habits? Why do all nations not observe the same traditions? Why do we not simply speak the same language?

"Let us start reminding ourselves, once again, that environmental and racial diversity is a mistake. That is why it has no substantial objective with regard to the work of nature and, especially, the advancement of human life. The fact that a mammoth is different from an elephant, or a wolf from a dog, or a blackbird from a crow, or a humpback whale from a dolphin, or a python from a boa, does not play a major role in life. We have nothing to lose, nothing to gain, in the difference between a cat and a tiger. It is just like that. It is but a mistake. It has no aim. And, likewise, if we leave the beasts and turn to the genus *Homo,* we will meet the same vagary in racial diversity. The fact that the Indians are different from the Chinese in biological terms does not play a major role in life. It has no role at all. It is just a mistake of creation. It is due to duplication errors. Being brown, yellow, black or white cannot help humanity comply with any special tasks. Colours have no determined ambitions to fulfil related to the fact of looking the way they look. Colours can be mixed up and mistaken one for another, and this will not endanger anybody. For example, some people who suffer from what I may call 'conceptual chromatopsia' tell us that pink's white and that brown's black. But this bothers nobody because it is not important. What I mean is that racial diversity has no end. It is just a mistake.

"Cultural diversity, on the other hand, has such a consequence that men bearing identical racial features can have diametrically opposed perceptions of life, and this can shake the world. For example, the English drive on the left side of the road while they are the same colour as the French, who drive on the right. Such an opposition is cultural and it can shake the world. It is equally possible for different men from different racial stocks to thoroughly be assimilated into one identical cultural world, and this can result in historical overthrows. For example, some people with a Negro skin texture have been so thoroughly integrated into the Anglo-American culture although they are so different from their fellows of European, Asian, or Indian extraction. Such people 'stand together as one' to defend one cultural and national cause while being biologically different. They can burst into war against China, Germany, Pakistan or Zaire while some of their fellow citizens look very like those against whom they will be fighting in such a war. Here, race is of no importance. It is just a mistake. 'I fight for my nation' has nothing to do with 'I fight for my colour'. Nobody can ever fight for his colour. If you try it, you will soon understand how aimless such a fight is.

"Race has no future, because it is a mistake. If two men belong to different cultural backgrounds and national identities they will have nothing to defend in common even though they are very similar in matters of colour. And, likewise, if two men belong to the same culture and nation, they will have to stand shoulder to shoulder whatever their racial differences. I hope that you get my point. My intention is not to try and urge people to neglect racial differences within their nations and stop racial discrimination if they are allergic to all that looks different to them. I am simply explaining the motives of creation. However, why did God intend the genus *Homo* to be culturally diversified?

"I said that our universe is like a business project. It is a company in its actual form. And, as potential workers in a company, the divine intelligence needed to diversify the human world into hundreds and even thousands of sections needing hundreds and even thousands of different skills and jargons to efficiently fulfil the different tasks involved in the work of the company. Just take a look at a modern clothing company like Marks & Spencer, and see how diversified it is. The weaving section uses textile skills and jargon; the sewing section uses tools and machinery skills and jargon; the sales section uses marketing and commercial skills and jargon; the accountancy section uses statistics skills and jargon; etc. And yet they all serve one single business project. These different sections work separately and sovereignly, like the *fingers,* in matters of their individual achievements; yet interdependently, like the *hand,* in matters of their mutual assistance for the fulfilment of the project as a whole. I believe that you can follow me.

"God caused cultural diversity so that each group, using a particular language and having particular skills, would achieve its microproject and bring it forward as a contribution to the fulfilment of the whole project. And each of these groups of men that uses a particular language and has particular skills is inhabited by a leading mind, that is known as the *Inner-Soul.* The *Inner-Soul* is a kind of trans-individual system of visions, conceptions, beliefs, observances and methods within a group as they are expressed in the group's way of speaking. It is also observable in the group's modus operandi. We call it a 'tradition' in its primary manifestations. It becomes a 'culture' as it improves in quality. A group of men who observe the same tradition and work out a culture together may be regarded as a tribe in its primitive form, but it is known as a 'people' as it grows bigger and stronger. And we call it a 'nation' as it stands as a social and political force. Its final form in a well-defined and well-organised unit is a 'country'. Some call it a 'state' if viewed as a machine.

"However, at this level, the question may come up as to the way in which cultural diversity came into existence. The aim in such a question is to try and give a historical answer. We would not try to retrace the history of cultures from their earliest manifestations in the human world. The best way to put the question is to ask why God created cultural diversity

"Cultural diversity is not a blind outcome of random or cumulative adaptation 'by tribal selection'. It is not the result of a series of hazardous trials for men to get adapted to their different worlds in their struggle for communicative survival. Cultural diversity already existed in the mind of God by the existence of different *Inner-Souls* in God's pictorial composition even before creation was made observable. In the mind of God, *Inner-Souls* represented the different visions and approaches [departments] of the universe machine just as they are manifest today in the way of life of each human group, known as a culture. But an *Inner-Soul* is first an expression, a way of communicating. It is a language; and the visions that come to a people through their language are meant to be turned into abilities and powers. And this can shake the world."

Eyang-Alouga was about to say something else, maybe ask another question, when Bekale Be'Nguema apologised, saying that the programme was nearing its end, and that if any participant had anything more to say the speaker would unfortunately have no more than 45 seconds. This is what seemed to have discouraged Mr Eyang-Alouga, who thereafter put his hand down. Mr Eyang was undoubtedly going to ask for clarifications as to the way Amanoofwom travelled into himself and around to see the mysteries. Alas!

A moment of silence reigned at the rostrum during the remaining 40 seconds, at the end of which Bekale Be'Nguema got up with his microphone, smiling to the camcorders. "I deeply apologise, ladies and gentlemen, as we have come to the end of this programme in terms of the time allotted to us. Thank you for watching *Questions about God*. If you have any queries related to today's debate, please do not hesitate to write to *Questions about God*, PO Box 150, Messanza. We will forward your queries to today's participants so that we can answer your questions if we have any elements of response. Please send your queries with an addressed and stamped envelope. Ladies and gentlemen, see you on Sunday."

Everybody was visibly disappointed to be cut off from Amanoofwom like that while expecting to get more revelations. A lot of people were waiting to hear more things about Aduma. Amanoofwom was certainly going to tell people the truth about that phenomenal character from the East that nobody really knew.

Perhaps he was going to settle the case around the controversies over the imperial system of faith that Aduma had created, and which was being disputed by some local factions.

Moreover, the story of Aduma himself as a person was bizarre. Aduma was said to have lived for 33 years. But he was known from 1 to 12 years old, and then disappeared, only to reappear at 30 and definitively vanish at 33. Which means that, out of 33 years, he was known only for fifteen 15 years and unknown for 17. Therefore, he was less known than unknown. Nobody had given the followers a reliably itemised account about what Aduma did from the age of 13 to 29 inclusive.

Equally, Amanoofwom was certainly going to say much more about *Elolongh* too, that bizarre character that he might have seen in spirit when he travelled into himself and around to meet God, and perhaps define the real purpose of creation. Somebody might have well understood that there was a mind behind creation and that this mind had set purpose to its work. But what is the purpose of that work? What are we here for? Where are we going? Was Bekale Be'Nguema not aware of the great importance of the debate? Why did he stop it?

That is what is disgustingly aberrant with TV. The journalists stick so much to time limits that they overlook the pith to be drawn from the programme. A debate is like a mathematical function. You cannot just get away with it before you draw the line. If a case is not exhaustively debated, if an all-embracingly informative conclusion is not reached, why get away with the debate for the sake of the time limit? Why not ask the participants to take a break, have lunch or a cup of tea for a few minutes, and then get back to work?

Bekale Be'Nguema had definitely spoiled a golden occasion on which Amanoofwom could have contributed to helping phase out a good amount of blur around the phenomenon of creation. Anyway, the debate was over and Amanoofwom, the unknown guest, gained sudden credibility from the public and became very well known and famous from that Sunday.

The programme received hundreds of letters from the public over the week. But most of them congratulated Amanoofwom rather than asking questions. Some others asked for his personal contact details. In fact, Amanoofwom had given Bekale Be'Nguema the contact details of Ebongué, as he did not want his mother's PO Box to be overloaded. Anyway, he was sure that he would receive some letters. And, above all, he could not remember it. The fact that he had been absent for nine years had made him forget the contact details that he had used as a boy. In fact, even Ebongué's PO Box he could not remember. When the question about his contact details was asked to him after the programme, he said to the journalist that he would send them to him later. Fortunately, as Ebongué turned up just a few minutes after the programme to give him a lift back home, so could he give his details in person to the journalist.

CHAPTER 4

OF FEELINGS AND BELIEFS

Ebongué was fired up with the letters and phone calls he received in the following weeks. He even received a letter from the ministry of culture that proposed a position for Amanoofwom as internal councillor. Amanoofwom accepted the offer and started the job two weeks later, under pressure from Ebongué. Unfortunately, he found his functions so superficial and worthless that he ended up resigning three months afterwards. He then started busying himself in his house, preparing for nobody knew what. Amanoofwom could no longer go out for a drink with his friends. Every time he was invited, he always replied, "I am sorry; I am too busy at the moment."

"But, what are you doing like that night and day?" You are going to destroy yourself. Look at you! You are worn out; tired; your eyes are reddish. Are you going to kill yourself or what? First of all, I do not understand why you left your job. Do you know how many people in this country would like to have that position? Your old man, who has reared you for these nine years, has really killed your human sense. You say beautiful things; you're super-intelligent; you are a open guy; you are a specimen; you are so lucky to be like you are. But you do not dare care about anything. You prefer shutting yourself away to prepare for I do not know what. Are you not fed up with shutting yourself away? You have been shut away for nine years and you want more!"

That was the way Ebongué, Ngule and Bifun would complain to Amanoofwom. But he would never respond, nor even tell them what he was preparing for. They remained good friends, however, and the three kept on assisting and cheering up the fourth. They loved him so much, but just could not understand what was going on. They became like the parents of a mentally ill child. They would provide for as much as they could to support their friend, and kept on trying to find out how to heal him; how to change his lifestyle;

how to bring him back to life.

About four months after the debate on TV, however, Ebongué received another important letter. It was from the dean of the faculty of humanities. He wanted to offer Amanoofwom a position as an assistant lecturer in the department of anthropology. He would start assisting a tutor in his lectures for a period of 18 months before receiving his appointment as an official lecturer. But Amanoofwom turned down the dean's proposal on the pretext that he was too busy. But nobody really knew what Amanoofwom was busy doing. Neither his close friends nor even his mother could tell what Amanoofwom's activities were for him to decline golden offers like that.

Ebongué wanted his friend to take advantage of the propositions he was being offered and become a man just like other young people of his age. He increased his visits to try and convince Amanoofwom, until the day he had a talk with Mbeng, Amanoofwom's mother, a few weeks after Amanoofwom refused the offer from the university. He found his mother sitting on the veranda and greeted her, asking if Amanoofwom was in.

"I don't understand Aman," said Mbeng, alarmed. "He spends nearly 24 hours a day locked up in his room. You can see him out only if he is hungry. Please, Ebongué, try to give him some advice."

Toc, toc, toc. Ebongué knocked at Amanoofwom's door, and, as he heard him, "who is it?" he just broke in to create a funny surprise for his friend; but the real surprise was in there. He found Amanoofwom sitting on a mat with his legs crossed, wearing just a tiny piece of clothing around his hips.

"Oh, sorry, man!" Ebongué was shaken to his core and tried to shut the door back.

"No, no, no! Come in. Don't worry; I was just finishing my prayer."

Amanoofwom got up and grabbed Ebongué's sweating and trembling palm to shake it.

"What is on in town?" Amanoofwom asked.

"Rightly, I received another letter (this was about a month and a half after the first letter). But this one is from my boss. He is asking me to ask you if you would not like to join our office. It would be great if we worked together, would it not?"

"Oh yes. That is really the ideal. But, you know that I cannot take up any job at the moment. I am very busy."

"What are you busy doing, man?"

"Ebongué, listen, we will talk about this later. I haven't had my breakfast yet. Will you join me at table? I am going to ask Mum to cook something quick."

It was half past two in the afternoon. Ebongué had already had his breakfast at a quarter past eight in the morning. He had been in his office until 12. He had been in his house for lunch. He had had a short rest until a quarter past two, and now he was going to university to give a two-hour lecture starting at three o'clock. He wanted just to drop in and see if his dearest friend was OK, and also talk a bit about the job offer. But Amanoofwom was offering him a breakfast at half past two. What a delay!

"No, thanks, Aman. I can't even sit down. I just wanted to see you, and tell you about the offer. What has happened to your telephone? It hasn't responded since last night."

"Nothing. It is OK. I think I just forgot to switch it on. Anyway, you are going to be late. We can talk about everything later."

"When?"

"I don't know. When do you prefer?"

"This afternoon, after my lecture."

"OK."

"So, I come back to pick you up by half past five. We can also go to Pope's Avenue for a drink, if you don't mind."

"No. I don't mind. But I think that you will not need to come here. I need to stretch out my legs a bit. Just ring me once you have finished, I will be not far from the university.

"OK, à tout à l'heure."

Amanoofwom got to the university too early for the appointment. It was still about half past three. And he took advantage of the extra time to visit the student union while waiting for Ebongué. And, coincidentally, he found a young female student being booed at by a crowd of male students.

"What is going on here?" Amanoofwom asked.

A young male came forward to him saying that the young woman had been suspected of having three boyfriends in the same university.

"That is a shame, man!" exclaimed the young student.

But once the young woman too saw Amanoofwom, she ran to him, saying, "No. They are bugging me off for nothing."

But Amanoofwom was already aware of the issue. He then asked her: "Young woman, is this true that you have three boyfriends at a the same time?"

"I cannot lie to you. It is true. But it was cidental. I did not mean to keep them all together."

The ragging grew louder at that answer. But Amanoofwom said, "I understand that this can happen, but how do you yourself feel about it?"

"I feel terrible, teacher. I do not really want to go on in such a mess."

"What are you going to do, then?"

"I don't know; what do you think I can do?"

"I think that you have to choose one and dismiss the others. But you will have to choose the one you love most, so that you do not bemoan your fate."

A long pause ensued while the young woman has kept her face thoughtfully down as she made an exact calculation about the one she loved the most. But, in the end, she suddenly looked up and turned to Amanoofwom to reply: "No. I really can't choose the one I love most so that I do not bemoan my fate. I prefer the one who satisfies me best so that I would have no regrets."

That was a courageous answer. But it caused the students to kick up a row again. But Amanoofwom held up his right hand to calm them down.

"Young people!" he started. "None of you is more truthful than this young woman. She really said the right thing. Because, I tell you, if somebody says to you 'I love you', make sure he means 'I like you'. For love is more an acceptance than a satisfaction; and, most of the time, it is induced by external pressures rather than personal feelings. That is why it is easier to give up with love than with satisfaction. A man who can cling to love alone is barely still a man. He is a bit more than a man. But this young woman is very truthful in that she recognises that she is not yet more than a man. She is just like you, and doesn't want to pretend otherwise.

"I understand that it would be most perfect to seek love rather than satisfaction. But, if you are not up to it, then cling to satisfaction, and you will be faithful by satisfaction."

There was Mr Bursar, who had come for some financial checking in the student union. Once he heard Amanoofwom say these things, he came over to say: "My friend, I bet you are one of those cynical types that cause people to think that the most amazing justification for how exalted our humanity is today resides in the fall of taboos and the subsequent death of nobility. Are you trying to encourage debauchery among these young people? What is this incentive to pleasure rather than to true love? Just look at the TV and you will see for yourself. It is a shame that, at the dawn of the highest exaltation of our humanity, stripteasing ends up supplanting the art of sounds. Some time ago, we loved to see the brisk and neat moves of the magical fingers of Jimi Hendrix on his electric *solid body*. But today we seem more inclined to visualise Whitney Houston's rump twirling around to awaken our wildest instincts; and Shaba Ranks is the champion. What is the end of this? And you encourage such an indulgence in vulgar appetites. What an immorality!"

"No, my friend. I am not encouraging immorality. The point is that morality is mostly for other people's eyes rather than for personal well-being. The eyes of the society have made up a set of attitudes that they want you to adopt; and, if you fail to satisfy them, you will soon be rejected. And yet, you know that the very eyes that rebuke your attitudes are not very much different from your own. Tell me, then, what is more criminal: to commit a crime or to watch a criminal in action."

"I do not know the contradiction into which you are trying to take me. It is obvious that committing a crime is more criminal than watching a criminal in action."

"This is, of course, the right answer. But you just did not take notice of the implications of such an answer."

"What do you think the implications are?"

"What you mean by this answer is that a man who makes love with his wife is more criminal than a man who does not make love with any woman, but who watches pornography. Is this not true?"

"No, man. Your trap seems quite well put, but pornography is something that deserves condemnation. We do not need to argue about it."

"No, my friend. You are simply reacting by the psychosis of preestablished condemnation. You do not have time to look into things carefully and judge by yourself. How can you justify the fact that a man who watches a sexual scene is generally repressed while a man who does it in person is not?"

"Your question is not complete. The repression does not start with the one who watches pornography. It starts with the ones who perform it."

"But what is the difference in the act of having sex between a man who does it with his wife and a man who does it in front of cameras?"

"No, man. Making love with your wife is legal because you do it in the framework of marriage. Sex within marriage is legal because it is allowed by God Himself."

"In this case, if marriage is your problem, will you regard pornography as legal if only performed by married couples?"

"Oh, my God! What do you want me to say now? Do you want me to say *yes?*"

"No. I am not trying to force you to say *yes* to me. I simply want you to understand that our moralistic system is not always tenable with respect to God's will. You said that sex within marriage is legal because it is allowed by God Himself. But this is not true. There are two main reasons why it is not. First of all, the idea of marriage has nothing to do with God. Marriage is not a spiritual alliance. It is an existentially legalistic contract. People get married in front of law for social security, and the documents that are signed are part of public authority records, not God's records. Secondly, sex and marriage are not linked in any way. Sex is a physiological act by which two bodies enter into contact through hormonal reactions, while marriage is a social contract by which two persons agree to live together and take care of one another. Moreover, the word 'sex' is not mentioned anywhere in the marriage contract. That is why it is normally possible to have sex with somebody who is not married to you; and, likewise, you can marry somebody who will never have sex with you, because sex and marriage are not linked in any compulsory way possible. We just put them in the same box because they fit; and we use them as a common rule because we need them linked for the purpose of designing norms and regulations to control the functioning of our societies; which has got nothing to do with God. Because, if it were true that marriage comes from God and not from man, then those, like you, who want to believe that marriage is more godly than manly should have started rejecting the use of such phrases as 'brother-in-law' and perhaps say 'uncle-in-god' instead. What I mean is that we can't just play around with contradictions like that and brag high that we are right. If you believe that marriage is an *in-God* commitment, how do you manage to say 'my daughter-in-law' instead when referring to your son's wife? How do you justify this? Is it just a lexical mistake made by our academic legislators? No! The reality is, rather, that marriage has nothing to do with God's will. God Himself does not even need living beings – including men – to be married to meet the purposes of life.

"If two people have good reasons to love and trust one another, they can live in that condition for life. They are partners 'in heart'. And if they are sincere enough, they will not need a legal procedure to confirm their sincerity to one another. They will care for one another just like that, and even achieve great things in life, until one dies before the other, or they die together in an accident or by coincidence. This doesn't matter, really. The point is that marriage has got nothing to do with God, otherwise pagans and atheists wouldn't be practising it, and some believers wouldn't be celibates. Marriage is simply one of the ways by which people who need a common identity can get it. It is about the search for a joint identity. But why search for a joint identity?

"People need a joint identity for business. But it is not only via machinery that you have business. Anything you can build or found in life is business. However, you won't found a business without giving it a name in the first place. It won't be a legitimately recognised business. It will be but an informal activity, and you will not get it to expand and prosper until you give it a name and get it registered for it to have a legitimate and legal status. And this is what marriage is about. People don't get married because God needs them married – any more than God needs men to found a tobacco company – but because they need to found a family for social purposes. A family is like a business. It is a business. It is something into which you put a certain amount of investment as you expect it to produce something in which you, your community or your nation can take pride in the future. But you will not get it working properly until you get it registered for it to operate legitimately and legally. A child itself, which is one of the products derived from the family enterprise, doesn't need a birth certificate because it would fail to be a human being if not registered, but because it needs to be a legal being for it to operate in the world. It is itself a further business.

"The need for a joint identity between people united in a business – or the need for a common name for the business itself – is the reason why people need to legally register their sexual partnership in a certain name 'X' in the prospect of building the kind of business that we call 'family'. Most conveniently, it is the man's name that takes over. However, it can also be the woman's name in some circumstances, or…"

"No, man! This doesn't exist anywhere. You're not gonna tell me that you want to encourage women to start claiming such a right!" somebody shouted in the room, interrupting Amanoofwom in his explanation. It was probably a student.

"No. This is not my point," Amanoofwom replied calmly. "What I am saying is that there may be circumstances in which this would be more appropriate."

"My God! What are your circumstances now?"

"They are not mine, if there are any. They are but realities of life. Imagine a Spaniard marrying an English woman and the couple decides to settle in England for good. It would be more appropriate for the woman's name to take over in such a family, as the children, in this case, are meant to be English. I understand that modern political liberalism and democracy have led to the freedom of nationals to bear foreign names as their likings and origins go. But my own personal feeling is that we have to be a bit careful here; because, if – for example – your name is Castillo, I do not believe that it will be very easy for you to be an appropriate symbol to epitomise the English identity as a political representative. Even in a so called 'melting pot' nation like the USA, being Anglo-Saxon in essence it will not be very easy to find a leader there bearing a Spanish or Japanese name even though such citizens may be powerful athletes, singers, business moguls, professors, etc; they will not be able to represent America in political terms.

"What I mean is that an English child who bears his father's Spanish name will surely have contrived some social barriers to his own progress in his society. Even the right to defend his nation and fight for it will appear somehow awkward for him, as he will rather be viewed as a foreigner by his name. I am not saying that I am in favour of such an iconoclastic purism in political integration. But it is, rather, a reality in sociopolitical psychology that men feel better represented by those bearing names that mean something to them through the symbolic expression of their cultural universe as perceived in their authentic and historical names. This is not a dogma. Things just work like that.

"This is the kind of circumstance in which the woman's name would certainly be more appropriate to take over on the couple's registration form. Some people may even use a hyphenised form of the two names, or even a side name chosen or coined on agreement by the couple for the same sort of reasons. This doesn't matter. The essential thing is to get a registration number and name for your business.

"Marriage is also looked at by a number of people as a social parchment, a qualification, a diploma to impress the neighbourhood with, and also to enjoy the socioeconomic privileges from certain pieces of legislation. A barren couple, for example, will not get married to build a child-bearing business. They will do it for the status, and maybe for different undisclosed reasons.

"There are, equally, people who get married for reasons of security. Indeed, human beings can be very devious at times. It is not very easy to trust a business partner if you do not start making sure that he is bound by some sort of agreement through which you can pursue him for abuse in a legal court of justice. But you will not be entitled to take him there unless you have a formal proof that you are partners in such or such a business line. This is what marriage is about too. It lies in the search for artificial trust where natural trust proves hard to establish.

"If you are to build any kindred business with your mother, you will not need to get married with her to trust her as a business partner. Somebody may say, 'well, you are married to your mother through her marriage with you father'. But this is just like saying that a bastard wouldn't trust his mother, which is not true – and you will not expect her to cheat on you in any way, because there is already that natural trust due to your natural link with your mamma. But you will not be able to establish the same kind of natural trust with an unknown individual coming from a different family, and sometimes from a different nation, so naturally linked to different people surely having a different education and certainly defending different interests. This is not an easy peace. That is why you will need some legal agreement with such a person to get him somehow frightened by law in case he is tempted to overstep the limits.

"These are some of the different reasons why people get married. There may be more, but none of them will have a very substantial deal with God. It is the business of a human life turned into legal life. And I personally find nothing aberrant about it. It is just that there is first a problem of comprehension. Our religious and political legislators want so much to attribute the idea of marriage to God and convince people with such a fallacious vision as though God Himself had celebrated Adam and Eve's marriage in the first place for them to be permitted to mate and have children, some of whom were even very blessed by God. It may be mentioned that Adam himself had expressed his joy at having a beautiful and helpful companion by his side, for whom he then coined the name by which he would be pleased to call her. But this doesn't say that God Himself uttered any words to unite them in any formal way; no less obvious than the idea of having them sign any form of record. The idea of signing a record should be irrelevant here if we suppose that writing facilities wouldn't have existed at that time. But God's own discourse about something like 'marriage' is totally absent.

"I am not saying that marriage is a bad thing. I myself have a great admiration for married couples, not because they are married in the formal sense of signing registers, but because two people who commit their lives to care for one another deserve to be admired. But what I am saying is that God did not institute marriage in person. The idea of marriage came to men much later for social reasons: the need to set up regulations to control, and maybe improve too, the functioning of human life. However, what strikes me is that these regulations – which we want so much to attribute to God and the Spirit of Good Morals – are mostly irrelevant. No wonder if they are always prone to amendments whenever we need to change them to fulfil further interests. For example, the French society has made concubinage something legal, which they call 'union libre', as though things that are united could stand detached at the same time. This is not even a contradiction. It is but a shocking aberration in the history of civilised legislations. Our English society too has allowed public use of cannabis that, some time ago, was as illegal as pornography, while they have kept pornography in illegality. That is where I often say, Who knows what comes next".

"You are very hard to cope with, my friend. But you have to understand that cannabis and pornography do not have the same implications. Cannabis destroys only those who take it, while pornography affects even those who are not into it. Pornography is something extremely shocking by sight; it is embarrassing; it is simply immoral!"

"This is exactly what I wanted you to understand. You are saying this because somebody has advised you that pornography should be perceived as something shocking. But you should be more shocked by your own sexual intercourse with your woman, because it affects not only your sight, but also your own body. I believe that you can get my point. If a married man performs pornography with his wife, the only difference is that he is seen by a large public whereas you are not seen while doing exactly the same thing with your woman in your room; which means that the real foundation of morality is 'embarrassment'. You said this for yourself. People condemn others because they are embarrassed by what they do. Yet, there are only two reasons for you to be embarrassed by something: either you do not do it and disparage those who do it for being different; or you do it in secret and are simply shocked by those who do it in public. Here, you do not hate them because what they are doing is bad, but because they are giving away something you would like to keep secret. This is what immorality is all about. If you are secretly immoral, you will be condemnation-free, because your immorality does not shock or embarrass anybody. That is why the only difference between a man who makes love in his room and another who does it on a pavement is that one is hidden while the other is in total disclosure. But they are doing exactly the same thing, and perhaps they are both married with their partners. Here, the one who does it in his room is simply like a culprit that the police have failed to detect. Does this mean that he is not a criminal?

"The true purpose of morality is essentially to control human freedoms, but equally and most often to make criminality rather secret, but not to eliminate it. This is the reason why morality has nothing to do with God's will. God's own Word is not moralistic. It is impulsive, full of explosive energy and free will. For example, in the Holy Word, God commands man to *multiply*. But because the world would view it as unhealthy for a woman to have 20 children, even though it is totally feasible, many people, even believers, have committed themselves to limiting the number of children they are naturally able to have. What I mean is that real believers should normally abhor the idea of family planning and contraception, which were, obviously, invented by our worldly civilisations as opposed to God's free multiplication command. I know that many believers are fighting abortion on the grounds that it is against God's will. But if destroying an embryo is criminal and sinful because an embryo is meant to be a human being, is it then not also criminal and sinful to neutralise an ovum by means of contraception as an ovum is equally meant to be a human being?

"However, I recognise that, if a woman needs to abort for reasons of health, this would be a special circumstance in which contraception or abortion would have a good excuse. But this is not going to be the case for most women. They are just civilised and, for this, they fight against God's free multiplication command. My intent here is not to go heretic. All I want is for you to understand how our civilised morality – which involves pagans as well as believers – is fighting God's tree values, because restriction and secrecy do not apply to God's values..."

"Look! You are being too contradictory, my friend," The bursar interrupted Amanoofwom.

"How?" he queried.

"If you think that restriction does not apply to God's values, why would you then allow a woman to practise contraception or abortion for any reasons if she has the ability to mate? Is this not an irrelevant restriction? Either she can make love and bear children or she is not well and should stop making love."

"Look! This is just like saying that blind people should be up to playing football since they've got healthy legs, or that if you are blind you should also be in a wheelchair. You don't stop making use of all your faculties because there is just one that's been withered by accident, do you? All the faculties that your God put in your mind and body are consistentsly and absolutely free for use for your fulfilment in life. Man is the one that sometimes invents repression and, especially, when he doesn't like his brother doing something, he will tell him that it is God that doesn't like it, to credit his own personal plea. Here, those who, for example, tell you that God would prefer to see you mating rather in your room than on a pavement forget that, if you mate with a woman in your room, you are doing it in front of your God just the way you would be doing it in front of Him on a pavement. Thus, it is not God that you fear in nominating specific places to perform specific deeds. It is man that you fear, for if it were God that you feared you should have started fearing Him in your room, since He is there too with His eyes wide open onto you, because He is everywhere. He is fully and energetically everywhere. His presence and power fill our infinite space in its entirety, including the space occupied by solid objects and living beings at all times. Hence everything we do is public before Him wherever we do it. But most people still look at God as if He were living far away on a Middle Eastern mountain, because they have no idea of who God really is.

"I remember one day I was reading *Beyond Good and Evil*, a masterpiece produced by Friedrich Wilhelm Nietzsche, a German prophet with loads of Christian education. In the book, the prophet wrote, somewhere, that 'Man is dishonest towards his god [because] he is not permitted to sin', as though we could tell lies to our God after sinning behind his back. But, what Nietzsche failed to see is that you cannot lie to the very one who accompanies you in every single crime you commit. Your god is in you and you are in him. Being dishonest towards your god is like saying that you are dishonest towards yourself, which is not feasible, since lying to yourself would mean that you were yourself absent while committing a crime. Is this possible? I don't think so. Anyway, I understand the reason why Nietzsche made such a mistake. Somebody might have convinced him that God was absent when Adam and Eve sinned. But this is simply a general mistake that was made by those who translated God's Thought into human languages. Because there is no way in which God can be absent. God has always been intricately and constantly connected to all His Creation even before creation was made observable.

"On the other hand, the truth is that 'Man likes darkness more than light because he is not kept out of other men's eyes.' And that is what morality is all about: it is about other men's eyes. And, lo, individuals' freedoms are being repressed in such a cruel fight against 'evil', not because we want to get rid of 'evil', but simply because we want 'evil' to be secret. And not only that, there are a lot of things that we regard as evil, not because they are evil, but because we have been blinded by our senseless moralistic system that, in addition, is so corrupt that it can be amended at any time, to satisfy man's whimsical interests. I have already reminded you that cannabis has been made legal whereas it was illegal some time ago. Even a demeanour such as kissing in public, which was offensive some time ago, has ended up gaining the consent of our moralists. Some time ago, a transvestite was an abomination for his gender; but, nowadays, you see them on public TV channels telling their fascinating stories. Who knows what comes next?"

"No, man. These are but the deeds of a sinful world in total decay." It was Mr Bursar again.

"Oh, right! Do you not know that, some time ago, remarriage was not tolerated in the Church for being regarded as sinful too, but that, today, some venerable bishops stand in favour of it for the interest of our princes? Now, tell me, if the Church also performs the deeds of the sinful world, who will perform those of the holy world? Is it the police, the nurses, or the teachers? Who will be part of the holy world now?"

"I told you, my friend, you will never know what comes next. Even our Church will grow more and more sinful in the search for something more realistic in the light of God's will as opposed to the idyllic dream-like world that they desperately sought to create in the beginning. And this is what I want you to see, not to make you a heretic, but to make you wise.

"Those, like you, who despise Shaba Ranks are not aware that sexual immorality is the virtue of a man who finds spiritual sublimation too speculative to fill in his somatic voids and that, if you want to help such a man, condemning him is the worst thing you can do. Instead, give him in abundance what he needs, and he will soon understand that he needs something more virtuous. If you still can't understand this, just consider the wisdom of the bottle. 'If you force an empty bottle into water, it will pop up brutally in you face. But, if you fill it up, it will sink.'

"Behold, brothers, he who hates *Evil* is more evil than the *Evil* that loves *Good*. And, likewise, if a demon is good to you, why then trust a careless angel?

"It may be a good thing to stand against debauchery, as we say, 'There is nothing as loathsome as harlotry.' But what surprises me is that it costs money. Tell me, then: who has ever paid for something he finds so disgusting?"

"Of course, it may not be disgusting. But you have to pay for it because it is not love; and yet, as you know, love is not something you pay for," Mr Bursar spontaneously stated.

"I understand this, my friend. But I just wonder whether you have ever met a woman who would be very happy with a husband who doesn't know how to buy a present; a husband who doesn't know how to pay the bills; or a husband who doesn't know how to build a home. Is this not another form of love payment?

"In fact, what you are not prepared to see due to your moralistic education is that love – as well as any other relevant factor for man's satisfaction and well-being in life – is something you will always have to work and pay for in some appropriate ways. But you are at liberty to choose your payment options. Do you want to pay for an hour's service, or do you want to pay for some years' service? The choice is yours. Sexual services exist in our society just like any other services company. But, if you do not need them, you are free to reject them just the way you would reject flaxen trousers for blue jeans. And, if your colleagues from the office repress you because, as an office worker, 'you gotta be in a wicked flaxen suit!', you will reply to them: 'No, man! I just prefer my San Francisco blue jeans style!'

"Now, they may condemn you because, as an office worker, you will be breaking some kind of moral principle – the office comprehensive dress code. But do you really think that you are evil because of your blue jeans offending office morals?

"Those who know that blue jeans are not formal enough for an office worker will burden themselves with their flaxen suits; and those who know that sexual services are not healthy enough for a virtuous man will burden themselves with their wives. But none of them shall despise another. None of us shall be rejected as long as he contributes to the well-being of his nation by performing any helpful act, for none of us is purer than another. Do not forget that what is extremely impressive about very healthy people is that they fall sick at times.

"Those of you who are keen advocates of *true love* as opposed to *love by satisfaction* do not take notice that the way in which we love our world and everything that exists in it is not very straightforward. We love our world through some special things that we particularly lust for. Imagine that you like money. In fact, you don't like money. You need it. The bother in your need for money is that you will not get the money that you like until you take up a job. And yet, a job is an array of obligations that you will have to put up with because you need the money that will come through it. It is not always pleasurable having to get up at five every morning, drive ten miles away from your place every day, remain seated in front of a computer for hours and hours, prepare a presentation on a new package, etc. If you are a teacher, you will have to embrace and interact with your students even when you would like to sit back, relax, and talk to nobody.

"The process is the same when it comes to loving people. Imagine that you like a girl because she's got very beautiful lips. The trouble at this point is that the girl you like is not only a pair of lips. She is also a pair of hands, eyes, legs, buttocks, a neck, a tummy, a vagina, a nose, a single mother, a professional, a dancer and the rest of the things that you may not fancy about her. The problem here is that you will not get these beautiful lips that you certainly visualise kissing you sensationally until you agree to embrace the whole thing that yet bears plenty of aspects that you have no liking for. What do you choose in this case? Either you lose the lips, or you have to carry the weight of the whole compound just to get the lips through which your genuine satisfaction will come in your relationship with such a woman. Remember, if you choose to lift the whole thing just to get the lips, you will never say: 'I love my lips.' You will say: 'I love my wife;' and this is not hypocritical. The reality is that, because one single aspect of the compound is satisfactory to you, you are held to love the whole compound; otherwise you will lose what satisfies you about it by losing the compound. Do not forget that, as a teacher, if you do not love your students, it is likely that you end up getting sacked; and you will lose your job, and the money.

"If a woman is about to lose her life in a ghastly fire consuming her house and an unknown man braves the fire to save her life, she will not be far from loving him. She might even end up marrying him, not because she loves his nose, his eyes, his lips, his bottom, his shoulders, his penis, his pectorals or his career, but because she will love what the man has done for her: saved her life. Her own salvation to life from death will be her main satisfaction in her relationship with such a man, but she will not say: 'I love my salvation to life from death.' She will say: 'I love my husband.'

"The believers of the Christian line of credence say that they love Jesus. But this is not because they love anything about him as a man – for I am not quite sure that they have ever met him in person – but, rather, because they were taught that Jesus had saved their lives for heaven; which gives them great satisfaction. Here, what they love is what Jesus did for them, not Jesus himself. And they say: 'I love Jesus.' Of course they love him.

"Brothers, atoms and genes did not create pleasure and satisfaction in the building of emotional organs in man's body through some kind of adaptation 'by sentimental selection'. Feelings were not created as a result of some kind of purposeless response to some blind, neurotically exciting reactions in man's body as it was growing more and more complex. I do not feel like attacking evolution any more. But what the evolutionists don't know is that the Thinking Force that conceived and launched life was fully aware that pleasure and satisfaction would be the foremost factors to bring about the feeling that we now call by the name of 'love'. Thus, the statement of this young woman is no way near immorality. The truth is that she definitely likes one single satisfactory thing in the one she is going to choose between her three incidental boyfriends. But she will love him as a whole, because there is no way in which she would get the satisfactory aspect that she needs until she agrees to take him on as a whole; and she will love him in the end; and this is exactly what we all do in everything we love. We look upon what we like, and we take up the burden that we then love. Who does otherwise?"

There reigned a silence of astonishment. People were stricken dumb with admiration. Everybody was turned towards Amanoofwom. Students forgot their drinks and games; employees stepped out of their posts; and visitors were diverted from their touristic interests. Amanoofwom was the centre of everything that existed in the room.

A woman, probably in hers, working for the student union as a cashier, left the till wide open behind as she suddenly approached Amanoofwom in a pretty frenetic attitude to ask: "Young man, who are you?"

"Who do you think I am?"

"I don't like guessing. Just tell me who you are."

"I am Amanoofwom, Fridio Wúlyem."

"Where are you from?"

"I am from Messanza."

"No, that is not my question. Where do you come from?"

"I come from where I said I am from."

"No. That is not true. There is no school in Messanza that teaches such things as the things you talk. Tell me truly where you come from."

"Is this so important?"

"Yes, it is."

"Why?"

"My husband has just died, and, coincidentally, our daughter gave birth a few hours after his death. It is a boy that we named after him. I love that baby so much so that I want him to be like you. You are the only model I would like him to follow. Please tell me where you got you knowledge from."

"God gave it to me, mother. Send your grandson to God and he will be like me; just like me."

"Where is He? Please tell me where God is so that I can send my grandson to Him. Please tell me," the woman begged desperately.

"Mother, I have just said that you cannot lie to the very one who accompanies you in every single crime you commit. God is in you, and all around you. You move with Him wherever you go and whenever. Everything you do, you do it with Him. God is in your grandson, and your grandson is in God. Send him to himself, and he will meet his God."

"Is this the way you met Him?"

"Yes, mother. I met Him just like that. I travelled into myself and around, and I saw Him."

A young man, probably a student, interrupted the conversation between Amanoofwom and the woman to ask: "Is it true that you saw God?"

"Yes, I saw Him with my very eyes."

"How is He?"

"I already said on TV how God is. I do not want to repeat myself. The only thing I can't tell you is that He is wonderful."

"No, no, no. This is too easy. God can't be wonderful just like that, with a rotten, putrid world as ours – filthy, crammed with evil – unless He did not create it or He does not care about it."

"No, young man. He did create this world and He does care about it."

"But what is evil doing here, and why does it have to dominate a world created by a wonderful God?"

A student hoping to gain a Ph.D. in anthropology broke into the discussion to try and give a response to the young man's question. He started to smile in a very sarcastic way so as to play on the worries of – certainly as he was – his mate. "You could have asked me this question beforehand," he said.

"Shut up, boy! What do you know about God?"

"Will you just give me the chance to tell you my stupidities, and then judge for yourself?"

"Oh yes! You are really going to tell me sheer stupidities! Anyway, go on."

"Thank you! Well, the reason why *Evil* is more dynamic than *Good* in our world is because the face of a man of good is smiling, whereas that of a man of evil is wrathful. We are always attracted by the smiling face of a cheerful benefactor, and remain so stuck to him that – as 'all that is ingested shall be retched' – when the time comes to repay his hands are the nearest ones to receive. As a result, *Good* is made static. By contrast, the wrathful face of a torturer repels us so far away from him that, when the time comes to retaliate, we pour out the retaliation onto the nearest someone else. As a result, *Evil* keeps moving. Should we, then, do good in a wrathful mood to make it move too?"

Bemused, Amanoofwom burst out in laughter, saying: "Yes…that is not wrong…your vision is really genuine, but your last question is simply too cynical! Of course, evil is dynamic because we tend to always retaliate against the wrong faces. We are very often like a woman who, vexed by her wrathful husband, fails to give proper care to her needy child. But this does not mean that evil dominates the world. No. It just moves around. All men who have seen the Very High have also seen the master of evil. For no man who has a revelation shall see the Very High without seeing the Very Low as well. If you are given the knowledge of good, you will be given the knowledge of evil too. But you can just choose to use one, and this does not mean that you do not know about the other. It is a rule that you should see both, and never one alone. And all those who have seen both will always tell you that the Very High is, by far, greater than the master of evil, and this disproportion works in everything all over the universe. So, there is no way in which evil can dominate, anywhere. We are just too much concentrated on evil that we do not consider the presence of good, even though good is dominant. So, believe me, the Very High is wonderful, for I saw his wonders."

But the philosophy student put his hand up again to ask: "How do we know that you saw Him, or even that He can be seen? Why should we believe in something that you are the only one to have seen out of millions of us?"

"You know, brother, when I still was a mere little boy, I met a very wise man called Mvé Mb'Essa. The first time Professor Mvé Mb'Essa said to me: 'My son, you have to believe in the Very High because I saw Him and I discovered how wonderful He is,' the answer that I gave him was: 'No, professor. Let me see Him with my very eyes in my turn, and then believe.' I answered like this to Professor Mvé Mb'Essa because I did not believe that he had really seen the Very High, nor that the Very High could be wonderful while our world suffered so much evil, nor even that He was visible at all. But once I saw Him for myself with my very eyes, I finally understood that Professor Mvé Mb'Essa was right and that the Very High is really 'something' visible and wonderful. Now that you have *two testimonies*, will you still need to see before you believe?"

"Teacher, I really believe. But would it not be interesting for every single man to see, just for the sake of enjoying the marvel? Besides, I must be honest with you: we all know that the Very High is a spirit. How is it then possible to *see* Him?"

"If your spiritual eye is occluded for any reasons, resulting in it being impossible for you to see Him in spirit, then you will, at least, see Him at work in your life," Amanoofwom reassured the young man.

"What kind of work?"

"Well, for example, if you ask your God to achieve a miracle in your professional life, you will soon receive a promotion, for he who asks receives."

There was an old woman, surely in her 80s. She was a very devoted believer and a faithful member of one of the oldest churches of the town. She couldn't help breaking into the discussion to say to Amanoofwom: "Young teacher, the god that you are teaching to your fellows sounds more like the 'geist' rather than the 'I am'. This is the god that created materialism rather than salvation. Today, spiritual salvation is no longer very different from *satisfactory convictions*. That is why testimonies of faith have rather turned into testimonies of success. For example, if a man turns to God in the wake of his divorce, he will not feel liberated until he finds a new wife. So, he's got a conviction to be topped up with a satisfaction; which gives him the assurance of being acknowledged and saved by God, and he will praise the Lord for that very reason; which leads to the nullification of salvation beyond life. But if true salvation is postmortem and spiritual, as it is written, it will then follow that a real believer is the one who believes in God but not in life. Should he then live?"

"Mother," Amanoofwom started timidly, "your worries are legitimate. But you have to understand that what puts traditional prelates at odds with levity is their belief that God only smiles at the dead but never at the living. But, truly, I tell you, if you are saved in heaven, then you will be saved on the earth, because…"

"What is wrong with you, young teacher?" the woman interrupted Amanoofwom before he could finish his sentence. "How can you first be saved in heaven and then on the earth? What is this chronology? Are we saved in heaven to come down here into such a muddled place?"

"No, mother. We are not first saved in heaven to finish on the earth. What I mean is that we are chosen to enter the upper realm while still living down here. And, if a man is chosen to enter the upper realm, he shall start flourishing in the lower realm as a result of his salvation promulgated in heaven *while* he is still living on the earth. That is why he who sees the Very High at work in his life can be sure that his spirit has seen Him in his heavenly form and that he has been saved. And he can praise the Lord for that very reason. The 'I am' Himself was followed by the people of Israel, not because He killed them on the earth to save them in heaven, but because He got them out of earthly slavery in Egypt and gave them freedom and prosperity in life. Is this different from the 'geist' at work?"

While the woman hesitated at this question, Amanoofwom continued: "I tell you, mother, if you hear a wise man say: 'Happy be the poor, for the kingdom of heaven is theirs,' do not get him wrong. For it is far better for a man to be poor than to possess riches that do not come to him as a result of his salvation in heaven. But no man who has received salvation will perish. He might lose battles at times, but he will be the victor of the war."

Amanoofwom's mobile phone suddenly rang in his pocket, and: "D'accord, d'accord," he said into it. Ebongué was already standing outside in front of the university main entrance, trying to check out where Amanoofwom was as he had told him that he would be around. And the teacher instantly waved goodbye to the crowd, saying: "Je suis désolé, mes frères, que je ne peux pas rester plus longtemps; quelqu'un m'attend dehors. Je reviendrai très bientôt."

"Oh non, non," the crowd grumbled with disappointment.

"Je suis vraiment désolé. Mais ne vous inquiétez pas. Nous continuerons prochainement."

The automatic doors opened in front of the teacher and he swiftly popped out to join his friend. But the woman who wanted her grandson to meet God followed him to get more details about the real method that Amanoofwom used to see the Very High. She looked so worried and even desperate about her grandson's spiritual future that she would not let Amanoofwom go. To this, Amanoofwom advised: "Mother, let the boy grow up. A time will come when he will receive a complete picture of everything he is meant to achieve. He might not be exactly like me. He might be very powerful, even more powerful than you think I am. But just pronounce one single sentence to him as many times as you can. Tell him that 'passion is the key to everything."

CHAPTER 5

OF THE WILL OF THE SPIRIT

About six weeks after the chat in the student union, Amanoofwom went to church that Sunday morning. Almost everybody recognised him as he entered through the front side entrance near the altar. The priest also recognised him and discretely acknowledged this by his expression as he greeted him. Amanoofwom turned slightly to nod at the priest in response.

After the service, a lot of people went to greet Amanoofwom in person. The priest was the first to descend from the altar to shake his hand. Anyway, Amanoofwom was a star; not a musical star, but a star of wisdom. He was very young, but was not very different from a priest. His personality was not very far from matching the category of the clergymen, the politicians, the teachers and the local noblemen. They were his friends, his sympathisers and his admirers. So, was it not awkward for the priest to descend and shake his hand.

"I listened to your intervention on *Questions about God* with great attention. I also read some articles about other speeches you gave afterwards."

"I am sorry, Father; maybe I said something inappropriate."

"No, no, no. You are brilliantly relevant. We find that the things that you teach might be true. But, just be careful, because the Church is the first institution in charge of questions of God. It would be better if you consulted the clergy before speaking. We might find some common points upon which we would like you to lay much stress in your speeches. The public admires you very much. Nobody can deny it. And the truth is that you say nothing hurtful. We just want to assist you and work together in wisdom to educate our people. You know, we, who are ordained, are not allowed to speak in a certain way. But you are not ordained. So, we can work together and teach certain things to people through you.

This can work perfectly."

"Father, I am really willing to work with you if you allow me to speak in the church from time to time."

"Of course, it is possible. You might not be allowed to speak at the main Sunday service. But I can convey special meetings on Wednesday or Friday evenings in which we can both speak alternatively to the congregation."

"I thank you very much, Father. just I know when we can meet."

"It is all up to you. I am happy for you to choose the day on which you are free, either Wednesdays or Fridays, because these are the days on which I myself have some free time."

"Er, I think Friday is better; it is the beginning of the weekend, when most people are free too."

"No problem. I will let you know when I have made the necessary arrangements."

"Thank you, Father."

The believers kept waiting for the priest to finish with Amanoofwom so that each of them could also shake his hand, and maybe exchange a few words with him in person. That was the only possible thing. Amanoofwom never signed autographs.

The following Sunday, after the service, Father Armah stood in front of the horde to make an announcement: "Brothers and sisters, I wanted to announce that this coming Friday evening, at half past six, our brother Amanoofwom is going to be our guest. So I would like you to come and attend the talk with him."

Father Armah was a Fanghish boy from central Odzab. He was running a syncretistic church in the town. The church was named St Michael's Sword Christian Alliance. Father Armah's close relationship with the locals made him tolerant enough to allow an an unusual and charismatic layman, such as Amanoofwom to speak in the church. Very few, or nobody else, would do that.

The news broke that Amanoofwom was going to speak in a church. This did not sound very strange. People had already heard Amanoofwom speak in the name of God. The only thing that was different was the setting. Speaking in a church sounded more clerically formal. Was Amanoofwom going to read the Bible to people? His knowledge of God, judging by his speeches, did not seem to have a biblical basis, even though a great many things he said could be justified in the Bible. How was he going to reconcile both? But these questions were not a major preoccupation. What was more important for the people was to listen to the teacher.

On that Friday, at half past six, all seats were occupied, except two chairs placed near the altar and facing the audience. And double the number of those seated were standing behind and all around. Amanoofwom and Father Armah appeared from the presbytery, where they had been waiting together. And people acclaimed them as they came down to take the seats in front of them.

As they sat down, Father Armah just said a few words to introduce Amanoofwom to people, after which Amanoofwom looked up and asked: "Who remembers what Father Armah said last Sunday morning during the sermon?"

Amanoofwom's question was a very interesting one to start a valuable chat with the congregation with. But the question was too surprising. Five days after the Sunday sermon, the absolute majority of people had forgotten about what the sermon was about. Not only that, almost three-quarters of the attendees had been absent that Sunday morning, or they had simply never been to that church beforehand. They went there that Friday evening exclusively because the teacher was there.

People were stuck, but the meeting promised to be good fun. People sensed that the encounter was going to be miraculously interesting because there could be an exchange of views. Amanoofwom could ask questions, and people could answer and ask questions as well. It was going to be a special 'service'. This had never happened before in a church. We do not put questions to the priests sermon. We just listen to them. We therefore have no chance of filling in our comprehension gaps. Even the Bible studies are but sheer dogmatic ingurgitations of a particular theological philosophy. No wonder if they practise the MCQ method. But, here now, with Amanoofwom, things were going to be drastically different. It was going to be a conversation, a chat. How amazing!

"Who remembers?" Amanoofwom resumed his question, looking cheerfully at the audience.

A very stunningly gorgeous lassie, certainly 18 years old, smiled at Amanoofwom, putting her hand up shyly. What was this? Was this real? We knew, in principle, that only off-track flotsam finds shelter under the gospel shade. In general, the people who would be interested in the gospel would be quite old, ugly and miserable, seeking salvation in heaven after missing the beauties of life. It was, however, true, according to papers and magazines, that there were some surprising nations, such as the kingdom of the English, where you would see sparklingly beautiful and wealthy young people devoting their lives to the worship of the Spirit. But this was an exception that still had a very long way to go to become a rule. The majority of followers remained authoritatively advanced in years and stricken with a high level of indigence.

It was thus obvious that such a ravishing piece totally in her springtime and so lavishly vested would not have time to listen to the gospel, and, worse still, memorise it. She had so many edibles and refreshments to ingest; she had, due to merit, carte blanche to share in the exciting fun games of life. The gospel was the food and the drink of the dead. What was she doing there? Was she going to open her mouth and say something plain and idiotic just to show off? Maybe she wanted to seduce the teacher. That was the most obvious possibility.

She was indescribably glamorous. Those who were sitting or standing behind her and who missed a face view of her could judge by the stylish haircut, the thin neck, the flat upper back, and also the gothic designs of the satin hem of her collar lying smoothly on her padded shoulders. Those who were at the flanks could judge by the side view. They could admire the modestly salient eyebrow, the round and lifted cheekbone under her radiant eye, her straight and fine nose, her puffy and slightly hanging lower lip; the straight furrow that linked her nose and her upper lip, making it a bit pointy and lifted in the middle, her triangular flat cheek outstretched down to her chin. Then, the visible outline of the clavicle bar, and, above all, below the clavicle, the bulge under her plastron was remarkably protuberant. She was simply artistic. She was magic. She was extravagant. Amanoofwom himself was unspeakably shocked and throbbingly moved from inside at the sight of the dazzling creature. What a babe!

Amanoofwom was himself aroused. But the teacher battled physically and mentally to escape his feelings. He put his left hand, in discretely, where appropriate, and sent his thoughts, where necessary, to force things down. Amanoofwom still had fresh recollections of that picture that only memory can describe, but not words.

And, the teacher, now somewhat down, allowed himself to say: "Yes, young lady? You remember?"

"Er, yes. I think…" She started with an angelic voice. She had certainly worked it out. You cannot speak like that naturally. The voice caused extra emotions in the public's heart as well as in the teacher's, and Father Armah was not exempted at all. He was himself an indisputable runner. The year before, a clerical scandal had burst out around his name. Two girls from Nzeng-Meyong district were said to have fought for him. And the worst was that one of the girls was already engaged with a young Igbo guy from Abia (in Nigeria) named Raphael Ugochukwo, who was working as a fitness instructor in the Messanza County Leisure Centre.

The room was simply flabbergasted by the Venus; and the goddess continued: "Er…last Sunday, Father Armah read the second epistle of St Paul to the Corinthians, eighth chapter, verses 7 to 14. It was a picture of the example of Christ that we have to follow. Through these verses, Father Armah developed three main points. namely, Excellence, God's Will, and Equality. Through verses 7 to 10, Father Armah laid stress on our Lord's recognition that we are well performing excellence in almost everything – namely, knowledge, utterance, faith, and all diligence in our activities. But also that it is far more important that we always seek to go beyond so that we can achieve greater things that our Lord likes and, especially, we must love each other. Father Armah then moved to verse 12 and said that nothing can come to achievement but through good will. If our minds are not willing to achieve great things and share them between ourselves for common well-being in our society, we will never achieve anything great, however brilliant we may be in our souls. Sharing is therefore our Lord's command so that there will be equality and happiness between us. To illustrate the point, Father Armah remarked that, if some brothers perform good deeds and share them with others while the latter languish in total idleness, there will never be equality, for the lazy will be a burden on the active. On the other hand, we have to be willing to work all together so that no one will be anyone's burden.

That is where Father Armah introduced the equality principle subsumed in verse 14; that is to say, our abundance must be a supply for our brothers' wants and their abundance must be a supply for our wants. And Father Armah eventually concluded that, by giving what we have in order to supply for the wants of our brothers, we will become poor like our Lord Jesus, who, though he was rich, became poor to enrich his brothers and the world in the knowledge of the Father. However, Father Armah assured us that, as Jesus made himself poor by giving, and became rich by being proclaimed king of kings as a result of giving, neither will we be poor by giving. Our brothers also will supply for our wants in their turn, and that is when we will all be rich and equal." She stopped for a second. "This is what I can remember. I hope that I did not omit too much or commit too many errors," the young girl said, smilingly, after the exposition.

"Alleluia!" the room echoed, not only to approve of the message, but also to express admiration for the girl. And applause rattled all around for about half a minute.

"This is impressively brilliant!" Amanoofwom exclaimed, petrified after the cries and the clapping had died. "This is the Will of the Spirit in all its splendour! I just find that I have nothing to say at this meeting. She said it all perfectly. I really have nothing to add."

Amanoofwom kept staring at the girl, shaking his head in extreme admiration. The admiration had gone beyond the visible beauty. She was spiritually beautiful too. She was not simply attractive, but magnetic. She was something that words could not describe. And, after a few seconds of astonishment, the teacher said a few more words, if not to partially rephrase this advocacy of his. Thus spoke Amanoofwom: "The Will of the Spirit wants you to outshine and illuminate the world so that your brothers can see light. The Will of the Spirit wants you to create and distribute so that your brothers will be filled up. The Will of the Spirit wants you to love and respect your brothers. That is what we have to do if we want to be in a perfect relationship with the Spirit and live in a world of beauty and harmony."

There was a young man standing not very far from Amanoofwom on the left flank behind a few people. He raised his hand while making his way through to be seen by Amanoofwom, and maybe the audience as well. Amanoofwom nodded to allow him to speak. "Teacher," he said, "you know that the laws of wolves are like the rights of a taxi driver."

"What do you mean, young man?" Amanoofwom asked.

"A non-smoker taxi driver will always wave a 'no smoking' sign in his car while the non-smoker passengers are not allowed to wave their 'no smoking' sign to smoker taxi drivers. Is this fair?"

"Who is the taxi driver, and who is the passenger?" Amanoofwom enquired again.

"Teacher, our leaders rule over us just like a taxi driver smoker. They are obnoxiously unfair over us, and we have nothing to say, nothing to do about it. We are doomed to submit to their orders. And they afflict us with severe ill treatments if we try to stand against whatever they do wrong. Is this too the Will of the Spirit?"

Father Armah was deeply concerned. He was very worried about what Amanoofwom would say, because it was not acceptable for Amanoofwom to make any pronouncement against the leaders in church. The Church, and especially the Catholic denomination, has always been the winsome girlfriend of political systems. It has never stood against even the most abject rulers. While some people have often rejected the Church where they find it appropriate, the Church, on the other hand, has never been capable of rejecting anything, even where appropriate. Maybe this is due to the message of overflowing love and unconditional acceptance that is so prolific in the Church. You have to love even your enemies.

But before Amanoofwom could answer the young man's question, somebody else instantly began to make a blustering attack on Father Armah's gospel: "All this is the responsibility of God. God only knows why He gave to some people the authority to bully others at will. Anyway, equality does not exist, not even in mathematics, for if 2 = 2, 2 is simply 2. But if a = b, a will remain different from b while sharing some conventionally representative features with it. The notion of equality that the Bible is trying to promote is but a fairy tale."

Amanoofwom turned to him slowly, trying to think about what to say. The questions put by the two young men were both relevant and, above all, hard to tackle. The teacher started a quiet reply to the latter first, however. "I agree with you, brother. But if you are inferior to somebody, you are yourself responsible for your weaknesses, not God."

"This is absolutely stupid, teacher. Everybody is not going to become a president!"

"Of course, no. But you do not need to be a president to be equal to the president. If you start rejecting your oppression to set up a fairer ruling system in you nation, you will have the same rights as the president."

"No, teacher. You are wrong. All those who have tried the rejection option have had their heads under the guillotine. Is this the fate you want us all to take up? And not only that, inequality seems to be inherent in life itself. If, for you, it is possible to reject political oppression, inequality remains mercilessly expressed everywhere in nature in a very irrevocable way. Just take somebody who has lost one of his lower limbs in an accident. How can he be equal to you again? This is just impossible, and it is the work of God, and it is simply unfair."

"That is true, brother. But you have to stop accusing God in matters of man's destiny. Disability is not really meant to diminish man. A disability can, rather, encourage the disabled to create something stronger than the limb he had lost and have a more fulfilled destiny than he would have had with all his limbs. Do we not always say that the crippled have stronger arms than the valid? What I mean is that if you lose something substantial you shall get something else more substantial to replace it. A disability is really a disability. But the way in which we look at our disabilities can make us more valid than the valid, or simply more disabled than our disability. Those who are disabled have to look at themselves as being fully valid and live their ability in their disability, and fulfil themselves through it."

After these words, somebody in the room put his hand up to ask Amanoofwom: "Is it not true that the evidence of a fact is not in what man wishes the fact would be, but in what the fact itself proves to be? How can the simple fact of looking at one's disability as an ability help sway away his wholesome handicap?"

"Your statement can be relevant only if the disabled person just keeps looking at his disability as an ability without taking action to make it wholesome. For example, if human beings were winged beings, a man like you would think that he is disabled and that he would never be able to travel across oceans and visit remote places, for he would not be winged like those who are *normally* winged. He would even envy the winged ones. And if he simply kept thinking that he was not disabled, he would never travel across oceans. But if he thought that he should be able to travel across the oceans and set about inventing an aeroplane, then he would be able to fly just like the winged ones. He would even be better off than the naturally winged, for birds are wet if they fly in the rain while men are smartly safeguarded from meteorological intemperances in an aeroplane. And men can now fly in a better condition than the birds. And yet, the birds are flying beings by nature. Can we still envy the birds?

"Brothers, destiny works as if it were trying to maintain some kind of horrid balance to create a diabolical excitement between risk and benefit, between danger and opportunity, between loss and gain; but for destiny, risk and benefit both play exactly the same role in our lives; danger and opportunity too; as well as loss and gain. They are all catalysers of man's fulfilment in life and global advancement. Risks are like a bleeping alarm that warns you to get out of your house and save your life from an impending fire. Is it not beneficial for one to save one's life? Dangers are like your house being on fire, which makes you start thinking about finding a new home. Is it not a good opportunity for one to seek a new home? And losses are like your house that has been reduced to ashes and that you have replaced by a brand new one. Is it not a gain to get a brand new house?

"I tell you, brothers; if you are wise, you will turn your risks into benefits, your dangers into opportunities, and your losses into gains. Consider your destiny carefully, whatever the circumstances, then break the bone to draw out the marrow, and you will see what happens next."

"Teacher, I do not doubt that the harder you work to turn you tragedies into triumphs the more you will be likely to change catastrophic conditions into good fortunes. But how can we justify such a natural injustice in which some people have to experience misfortunes in order, perhaps, to possibly rise while others go smoothly?"

"Young man, destiny comes from on high, and we are held to execute it willy-nilly. However, we are always responsible for everything we go through. We are responsible for our destiny. We cannot really blame anybody else for it. We create it; we programme it; we project it; and we trigger it. It is weird. It is nonsense to sustain that a man who loses his limb in an accident is himself at the origin of such an atrocity to himself."

"Of course it is."

"Yes, it is. But that is what happens. I have already said on TV that God created our universe by the power of mental picturing; and I said that we are in the likeness of God because He gave us the same power to create by mental picturing, just like Himself. Anything that we achieve in science, arts, architecture, philosophy, political organisation, labour – we start it up from a mental picture. We start conceiving a picture in our mind, and then we seek the means that can make it material and observable. Every single dream that comes true in our world goes through the same scheme; and destiny works exactly the same way. Even those who do not achieve anything in life have dreams. But every single dream is a picture that is meant to be turned into a creative energy to trigger its materialisation. I do not really need to explain myself any further. Let me just put it this way: human beings have pictured dreams that are sent to some kind of cosmic transformer that sends them back in the form of projects likely to come back to us as realities exactly or very much in the way in which we conceived them. Can you understand now?"

"No, teacher. I cannot understand that. A man cannot dream of himself losing his limb. This is no way near anything realistic. There must be something wrong."

"You are right. But destiny, once formulated, does not come down to meet its targets in a totally random way. If you have an enemy and dream of him having an accident to result in the loss of one of his limbs, your dream will be turned into a real accident that will happen; and when this accident is dropped down, it is simply dropped towards our world. It comes down to hit our world, not necessarily a particular individual. And, as it comes floating down on a trajectory into our world, you cannot be sure that it will not be your own son or even yourself this is the one who will be in the wrong place at the wrong time. The atrocity might also hit somebody you do not know at all, or, if you are very lucky, your very enemy may be the victim. But nothing is very sure at that level.

"What this means is that we are all somehow shuffled in the eyes of the hidden organiser of our universe in terms of who deserves what as an individual. If you wish a man to be destroyed, you simply wish the destruction of our world because you can't tell who is going to be the actual victim. However, even if the victim is not precisely predetermined, it is more likely that the victim will tend to deserve his misfortune, for whatever the reason.

"The cosmic mind is not very stupid, young man. Imagine a plague hitting our humanity – say, Aids. The dream of the majority of people is to find a cure for that disease, and you may happen to possess the intellectual capabilities to become a medical researcher and develop the right cure to defeat the virus. But you know that, in general, men of science and artists have often had trouble fostering a family as they do not have enough time for this. Or else, if they try hard to build a family, this may affect their commitment to their projects. In this case destiny will make it very difficult for you to meet a woman because your mission is not compatible with family responsibilities, unless there exists a very wise woman who can understand that her husband needs to be in his laboratory night and day. You will yourself need to be very wise and stone-hearted enough to leave your woman and your children for long hours, days, weeks, months or years to concentrate on your job. But you cannot lie to destiny, for destiny knows you better than you yourself do. This is how it works."

"Now, teacher, if it is true that you might end up destroying yourself if you wanted to destroy somebody else, is this equally true in the positive sense?"

"What do you mean?"

"I mean, if your dream is to become a pilot, you might rather help somebody else become a pilot."

"Exactly. That is what I have been trying to show you; if you want something good for yourself, you simply want it for the whole of humanity, for you do not know who will actually deserve it in terms of appropriate ability and disposition."

"So, there is no way in which you can be sure that you will be the recipient of your dream?"

"Yes. That is possible too. Dreams can indeed be achieved in a very precise way. But this demands very much work, both technically and spiritually."

"What kind of work?"

"You will first have to train very thoroughly in the fields that involve the skills needed for the achievement of your dream, so that you will be an appropriate recipient. Then you will need to be so wedded to your dream to such an extent that it will have to become an intensive activity in your mind. It will have to become like a religious belief to you. You will have to be very constant in contemplating your dream, visualising it mentally, meditating about it, and praying for it; then it will come straight to you. You have to have a clear picture of your dream, work hard for it, and strongly believe in it, and it will come true.

"Be wise, brothers. If you work hard and strongly believe in your dreams, then they will come true. If you are wise, you will understand that human beings, who are not winged, are flying today in a better condition than the birds, which are winged by nature. This is the principle of excellence that Father Armah taught last Sunday. And, if you start flying, always seek to fly better and better. Do not forget that what is impressively particular with a genius child is that he goes to school. Always go further than your possibilities, and you will soon fly without wings; for, I tell you, he who can fly without wings he achieved far more than he who uses his wings to fly. And, likewise, even though you have no wings, you will always need to prove that you can fly.

"As you go further than your possibilities and start flying without wings, do it with passion and you will be an excellent flyer, for passion is the key to everything. Be passionate, and you will fly. But, if – unfortunately – you have no passion, then do it with rationality and it will work for you as a sound result of rationality. Be rational, and you will fly. And, if – again – rationality is also something that you do not have, then let it be an obligation to you, and it will work for you as a fair compensation for your obligation. I tell you, brothers, be very committed, and you will fly."

There came a silence, but it was soon interrupted by a charismatic young pastor who was running a new church, called the Siloam Apostolic Centre, in Angône district. He asked: "Teacher, our latest alliance with the Spirit has killed law to the advantage of free devotion, and this is the route all men should take. So why, according to your teachings, do we still need obligations towards legalism, or whatever, compelling us?"

"I tell you in truth, brother, free devotion is for those of you who have had a revelation from the Spirit. But law needs to be rigidly unfolded upon the rest; because, without law, they will be like wolves and will devour the world. That is a reality. We have to give law its rightful place on the right subjects.

"You who bully your children and ask them to smile at your visitors, do you want happiness to be something we feign? Do you not know that we say: 'Happy Christmas! You need to be happy before Christmas'? Do you not know that 'a hypocritical smile is not very different from a skimpy skirt: short enough to display the legs, but quite long to mask the essential. And the funny side of it is that we always know what is hidden'?

"You who spend your time feigning happiness to please your impostors, do you not know that we say, 'Loèñ'e mbok é ne dzu'e ossón,' I mean, 'If you keep laughing to keep from crying, you are just crying in a very stylish way'? And those who see you laughing will say, 'Here you have a happy camel.' What a pity! Did you look at the camel's back and see how massive the burden is?

"Brothers, if the cows knew that they were reared by men for the sole purpose of being slaughtered and eaten, they would stop procreating. But I suppose that they know everything and, therefore, conclude that they are very generous. And if you attain to such a level of generosity, I will crown you as the epitome of wisdom in the midst of the beasts.

"Some spiritual teachers will tell you that you have to turn your right cheek to somebody who has just hit you left cheek, as though somebody who really intends to get you estropiated will give you time to think about turning your right cheek to him. He will break it even before you think about your teacher's silly wisdom. And, likewise, the wisdom of those who tell you that 'if you do harm to your neighbour, you are doing harm to yourself' is not the least wanting in our secular spiritual teachings. David (Paul) Yongi Cho is one of those whom I think of. In *The Fourth Dimension*, for instance, he wrote, somewhere, that 'you cannot smear somebody's face without smearing your own hand'. 'Wow! What a heavy revelation!' a friend of mine suddenly shouted while reading the Revd Cho's sentence. But what my friend, and even the author of that sentence himself, had failed to see is that, if you smear your hand to smear somebody's face, you are not too silly, because you can put your hand in your pocket when walking down the street, and nobody will see the shit on your hand, whereas the one with a smeared face won't be able to hide his face if he wants to take a walk around. He may get hooded so that nobody would sees the shit on his face, but in this case he will look like a terrorising Ninja; which means that all passers-by will run away from him. Thus he will not be able to wave 'hi' to anybody, smile to people and maybe have a drink with them.

"What I mean is that a man with a concealed blemish is far better off than another with a visible defect. And this reality can even go some what further. Imagine that you want somebody dead. You can cleverly make up some good excuses to kill him, and you may go to prison for murder, and then be released after 10 or 20 years of imprisonment. Here, you will be well alive while the victim will be dead. Now, are the two of you in the same condition? No. I, however, recognise that some believers may say that the victim will be in heaven, which will make him much better off than his murderer in life. But not only do we not have any evidence of this, since we can't see it, but also, if the believers are so sure that life is much better in heaven than on earth, why do they not simply kill themselves then? Why insist living in a muddle while they know that a better condition is just a few seconds away? What I mean here is that the easiest thing you can do with your life is to lose it. Why then keep it, and even fight for it, if it is so mean?

"In fact, what disappoints me with spiritual literature is that most of it is poetic. But life doesn't work like poetry. Life is not an idyllic, dreams like, magnificent universe. That is where many prophets got it wrong in their writings, and most of their messages do but take the believers away from the understanding of real life and even that of the Will of the Spirit.

"Real life works through observable beauty. For example, ugly cars wouldn't have a buyer if beautiful cars were not too expensive, because nobody is prepared to seek defective things.

"Some people will tell you that invisible spiritual beauty is more virtuous than observable material beauty. But this is not because spiritual beauty is predominant in life, but because the only way in which ugly things can be beautiful is to turn to spiritual beauty to be desired in some way. But this doesn't apply to the majority of cases. If you are ugly, you are ugly. Whatever your attempt to be spiritually beautiful, this will not be visible at first glance. You will have to work 100 times as much as a visibly beautiful individual, or you will repel as many observers as he will attract.

"I am not trying to belittle spiritual beauty. But what I am saying is that spiritual beauty is not a rule for beauty in life. Spiritual beauty is like a prisoner. It is locked up in a concealed environment, and most of the time it doesn't help very much. For example, a lot of people will sing praises to some primitive societies in our world that they believe to have some sublime spiritual values. But these primitive societies – with such a spiritual record – can't avoid falling under the rule of materially sophisticated civilisations that are mostly regarded as having no spiritual values, and these primitive societies are even enslaved by these material civilisations. At my level of understanding, the most obvious question that comes up here is as to what is then more powerful in life, spiritual beauty or material beauty. Tell me, then, who out of the two is the master, and who is the servant?

"Brothers, some people who've got a negative perception of real life have tried to vulgarise a chaotic picture of our existence so much so that they have turned the Will of the Spirit into something unwholesome in order to shirk life. But this is a commodity dogma. Real life is not polite. It is not dodgy. It is not consolatory. Real life is sensibly cruel, because it is true; and this is the Will of the Spirit. The Will of the Spirit is not in poetry. It is in real life. The Will of the Spirit is not in Israel; it is not in Egypt; it is not in Palestine; it is not in Rome. The Will of the Spirit is in your society with your neighbours; it is in your office with your colleagues; it is in your house with your family; it is in your bed with your woman. The Will of the Spirit is not in your mind; it is not in your heart; it is not in your soul. The Will of the Spirit is in your mouth with the words you say; it is in your feet in the places you go; it is in your hands with the deeds you perform. The Will of the Spirit is not in your wishes; it is not in your desires; it is not in your ambitions. The Will of the Spirit is in your observations; it is in your findings; it is in your resolutions. If you can solve your society's problems as a lorry driver, then go for lorry driving. If the best way to avert horrendous disasters in you world is to be president, then go for presidency. But do not have the ambition to accumulate honorific titles that won't solve any practical problems in your world.

"Be wise, brothers, and you will understand that the Will of the Spirit is not in the psalms; we do not just sing it. It is, rather, in our lives; we just do it.

"Tell me: who is the more obedient among the two sons who, after receiving a request from their father, the first says, 'I will do it,' but does not do it, and the second says, 'I do not have time,' but ends up doing it?"

Amanoofwom stopped so as to wait for an answer from the audience. But nobody answered the question. And this was not because the riddle was too hard to undo, but because not only the answer was too obvious and even popular, but also because of their amazement. It seemed that it was not necessary to make any noise to give the answer that everybody was supposed to know. And the teacher continued: "Be wise, brothers! If you cannot do anything for yourself, then do something for somebody else and you will lose nothing. But, remember: you will not do anything for somebody else until you are up to it. If you do not have something, check it out; you will find that you do not deserve it, or you do not deserve it yet, or you did deserve it and you have lost it. Because there are two main reasons for a man to desire something: either he is still looking for it, or he has lost it.

"Be wise, brothers! If you do not have something, then love whatever else you do have. Love it with passion, and it will be far more beautiful and powerful than what you do not have. Do not ask other people to give you the good things that you know you do not deserve, but help them find those who deserve them. Be wise, brothers!"

The teacher paused again, and the room remained deadly silent. After a few seconds, however, somebody whispered from far away, asking his friend who was sitting next to him: "Is it realistic that a man can refuse the good things that he does not deserve and then volunteer to help find somebody else who deserves them?"

Amanoofwom intercepted the question and suddenly blasted: "This is what you have to do, brother. There is nothing unrealistic in it. It is wisdom. You find wisdom unrealistic because you are not wise. If you are a married man and you randomly meet a very charming girl who offers to give you the beauties of her body and heart, then tell her that you do not deserve her, for you are married. Then help her find somebody who deserves her: a single man of your knowledge who can take care of her. Is this not realistic? I tell you, brothers, be wise and you will understand the message that our dear brother Armah brought to us last Sunday. Impoverish yourselves –

just the way Jesus impoverished himself – so that other people can be enriched through your poverty. And this is exactly the principle of Equality that Father Armah taught you last Sunday. The fact that you refuse to take that extra woman makes you poor for you lose her, but it makes your friend rich for he gains her. And, lo, your friend and you become equal to one another, because you are both married. For I tell you, brothers, be wise and you will understand that a man who is married is richer that a man who is single for the former possesses something that the latter does not possess, and he is superior to him in that very respect. And, if you are wise, you will fight inferiority and inequality amongst you by giving others your extras. Thus, your abundance will be a supply for their want, and their abundance also will be a supply for your want. Then, there will be equality between you, as it is written: 'He that had gathered much had nothing over; and he that had gathered little had no lack.' I say, be equal to each other by your devotion to mutual assistance, because, if somebody becomes very useful to you, you will have to make sure that you are not too useless. Be wise, brothers!"

It was already nine o'clock and the tropical night was heavily dark outside in such a town, where the main roads suffer from insufficient electricity supply. You could walk in the dark for half a mile long before you came across a lamp-post in a good condition. It was risky for those who did not have a car, or any money to take a taxi. Aware of this, Amanoofwom gave an instant and unexpected conclusion to his speech, saying: "I recommend you to be wise, brothers. Be very wise, as you are going back to join your families and friends. Be wise! Amen."

The following morning, the news broke on in the papers and on radio and TV bulletins that the teacher had spoken at St Michael's the night before. But very little was reported about the good things that he had said. The journalists rather concentrated their approach to the event on the fact that a pantheist had been allowed to speak in a church. Who had given him permission to do so? In any event, the young teacher had spoken and the people were happy with his message, and many articles appeared in the local press talking about what they generally called the 'theological revoution'.

CHAPTER 6

OF THE LIGHT OF SALVATION

The 150th anniversary of the arrival of a French layman called Bessieux who had laid the foundation of one of the most respectable Christian missions in the town was being celebrated about seven weeks after Amanoofwom spoke at St Michael's. A prominent high school had been built and named after Bishop Bessieux in Mekie-Me-Kwule, to far from Pope's Avenue. The school's premises were to be the place to host the countless guests, lay people from all over the world, where they and the believers were to attend the celebration and enjoy the feast.

Several Christian workshops were organised, including a huge exposition of the works of Bishop Walker, a famous Myènè-English-born priest who had faithfully rehabilitated and followed Bessieux's work. It was on Sunday. The main Sunday service had already taken place between ten and twelve in the day, and the manifestation in Bessieux's High School was to start about an hour later.

The venue was flooded with people. All classrooms and special meeting rooms and wards were open to let the visitors in to appreciate the efficient work of the French missioner and his followers. The sunny yards were full and crammed with the rabble. Bessieux was a great man of God who had come from so far away to show the true way to the people of lower latitudes. He had loved them and gifted them with that spiritual education that they could not have got by any other means than his eventful advent in Messanza a century and a half earlier. What a holy man!

By two o'clock, the horde had gathered before the main court, where a memorable speech was given by Bishop Anguilé, another Myènè citizen who followed Bessieux and Walker's trend of credence and who was chairman of the town's most influential Christian association.

Bishop Anguilé appeared on a first floor balcony facing the

court, where people were fighting the solar rays heating the top or of their heads. For many, their palms would do for kepis and sun-glasses as they tried to look up at the balcony to see and listen to the special words of God's representative in their town on that particularly historical occasion.

Bishop Anguilé coughed to clear his throat, but it turned out to be a bad cough for a few seconds before he could start his allocution. This was not very surprising. The man was known to be a heavy smoker. He had even undergone throat surgery. Sometimes he would stop preaching for a while on Sundays, as his voice would fail in the middle of the service due to his smoke-damaged lungs. Anyway, the bishop got there at last and delivered his holy speech to the attendance. It was highly spiritual, full of good morals and healthy intentions for the people of God to unconditionally follow and keep.

After Anguilé's speech, people were invited to go off enjoy the event. And people began to wander around in the rooms and courts, and under the tents where workshops were being held. Amanoofwom was there too, with the people. It was not the kind of event he would miss on; and he was with Ebongué, Ngule and Bifun. It was true that Amanoofwom's friends were not believers. But he was a good friend. And not only that, the occasion was not for the believers alone. It was a public event. The banner proclaiming '150 years of Christianity' was not the only reason people flowed down to Bessieux's High School that day. Some went there to play kermis games, have a laugh with friends, meet a smiling face or a beautiful body, have a good conversation, make a romantic appointment, and so on. Anyway, where you find people, you find all purposes.

But soon after the tumult started on the site, some sharp eyes in the mass began to recognise Amanoofwom, and people began to approach him to exchange a greeting and maybe share a meaningful phrase. Many people who had never met him knew him through the visual and written media due to some articles and the publicity about his speeches, and – especially – from the day he went on TV to discuss the Beginning. They approached in twos and threes where he was standing with Ebongué, next to Bishop Walker's library to have a look at the clergyman's publications about his personal experience as a man of God and of his people. Some of his books were written in local languages, including the Fanghish, even though he was not Fanghish and certainly could not have produced a good work in that language. But almost everybody, and even Amanoofwom himself, was fascinated by the man's attempt to be so prolific in literature and to hand over such an enriching inheritance to the next generations.

Bizarrely, Amanoofwom started to get taken over by those who came to greet him. None of them went off after greeting him. They kept standing around, maybe to try and ask some questions. But nobody attempted to ask any question, and nor did anybody leave. They stood still and silent, as if waiting for something, and the numbers increased as the seconds strode past. The library attendant started panicking, fearing some bad hands that would surely begin to lift his books free of charge.

"Step off the tables, please," said the library attendant to the increasing crowd, meaning that the customers would need some space around to see the exhibition, as he was quite reluctant to push people away in front of somebody respectable like Amanoofwom, and continued, to conceal his worries, "Here you have the *Rapido-langue* for 2,300 CFA; the *Dictionnaire Mpongwè* for 4,200 CFA; *Souvenirs d'un Nonagénaire* for just 3,000..." Nobody seemed to care very much about his marketing cries, however. People wanted to hear a different cry, from someone different, selling something different. Obviously, they were looking forward to buying *Souvenirs d'un jeune Maître* instead, and Amanoofwom was the one from whom they wanted to get something new and different. They knew, for sure, he had something to give out for the occasion. But what could it be: the description of a mechanical God, the alienation of morality, or the promotion of equality? What could the young teacher sell out that day?

Ebongué began to feel quite awkward about the people surrounding him and his friend. He almost said: "Let's go, Aman." But all ways out were already blocked by the mounting crowd; and Amanoofwom sensed that he needed to say something to content and relax the people, and maybe get them away by doing so.

Thus, suddenly, he turned round and unexpectedly asked: "Who among you hopes he will go to heaven?"

Those who were standing nearby were startled briskly by the abruptness of it. It was obvious that they had heard the question clearly, yet they looked extremely confused, while those standing far away began to enquire: "What did he say?"

A long pause animated by a huge commotion in the crowd allowed the question to be transmitted on from man to man, mouth to ear. But it seemed that nobody had got a clear understanding of the question, and Amanoofwom resumed: "Brothers, I asked: 'Who among you hopes he will go to heaven?'" But the meaning of the question was still incomprehensible. Nobody could tell what Amanoofwom really meant by that question. Had he received from God the power to send people to heaven? Was he himself about to go to heaven and would like to save those who would follow him? How would he go to heaven then? Would he ascend in flesh and take the chosen ones with him, or would he have to die with them and then take them to heaven in spirit? It seemed quite hard to give the right answer to the question as the conditions in which the teacher would take his followers to heaven were yet unknown.

Suppose, then, that the teacher would not need to die to have access to heaven, and that he could send people to heaven alive. How could he do that? It was already taught that the illuminated Yudi had ascended to heaven in flesh, even though this did not sound feasible. The believers say that God is a Spirit and that His realm is a spiritual realm. But how had it been possible for a man to access such a realm in flesh? How does he live in there? How does he feed his body in a spiritual world? Does he often have to come down in high secrecy to eat some food every time he is hungry? If he does not need to come down for food and drink, however, how then can we explain the case of a body that has ceased to live on food and water? Perhaps *David Blaine* is a good example. But for how long?

On the other hand, if death were a sine qua non condition for man to access heaven, would then all those who would say 'yes' to the teacher have to die with him? Was the teacher, then, staging a collective suicide? Or would he just register all those who would say 'yes' and die alone, and then wait for them until they would die one by one? The majority of people didn't react because of the impossibility of understanding the way in which the teacher was going to take the people to heaven. A great many people, however, as usual, who did not have time to stop and think, burst out into a widespread chuntering of "me, me, me, me, me", putting their hands up to express their desperate desire to go to heaven.

"Listen very carefully to my question," Amanoofwom suddenly remarked to draw people's attention to something important in his question. "I did not say, 'Who wants to go to heaven?' I said, 'Who *hopes* he will go to heaven?'"

This quick remark resulted in a surprising drop in the number of hands up, by almost 100%. Was this because they needed to think a bit or because they had suddenly realised that they did not have a genuine hope that they would go to heaven? There was, however, one stubborn hand left up. It belonged to an old man, probably in his 70s.

"Yes, father; you hope you will go to heaven?" Amanoofwom questioned.

"Yes, I firmly do."

"How?"

"I believe in God."

"Oh!" Amanoofwom seemed pretty surprised by the answer.

"What! Do you want me to believe in the Devil to go to heaven?" the man enquired, confidently.

"No, no, no. I was just a bit hit by the punctuality of your answer."

But Amanoofwom instantly turned to the crowd to ask, "Is there anyone who identifies himself as an atheist here – I mean, anybody who does not believe in God at all?"

Some seconds passed until it seemed safe enough to conclude that there were no atheists, since nobody put his hand up to say yes.

"Oh!" Amanoofwom seemed surprised again. "Can you see this, father?"

"What?"

"There is no one who does not believe in God. But you are the only one to hope that you will go to heaven among all these believers. Tell us, then, what you do in particular to be the only one among all these people who yet believe in God just the way you do."

"Listen, young teacher, I don't need any tricks. I believe in God and I hope that I will go to heaven for that very reason. I am not responsible if somebody else who yet believes in God just the way I do *doesn't* hope he will go to heaven."

"Father, if two men do the same job, how can you justify that only one of them gets paid?"

"Young teacher, I don't need a technical justification for this. God's grace is spiritual. It is not strategic. I hope that I will go to heaven because I am a believer, period!"

"Be careful, father." Amanoofwom gave a hint of a lurking warning, and stopped for a while before resuming: "You cannot get anything special if you do not start doing something special. This rule is both material and spiritual. Just take a look at those who have been canonised throughout history by our holy popes. You will find that they have really done something special to deserve to be canonised. Do you think that this is nonsense?"

"My God! Are you trying to tell me that I will not go to heaven because I have not done anything special like the canonised ones?"

"I do not have the power to say so. But you have to be very careful. Hope is not an expectation. Real hope is a procedure. You need to follow a sound rule in order to hope that something will happen. In *Shawshank Redemption*, Morgan Freeman tells us that, if you receive a life sentence, you can still look upon freedom. But you will need to make a hole in the wall. Do you think this is nonsense?

"Success does not hold from an individual's expectative conviction that something will certainly happen. Success is methodical. You have to apply a formula that works to succeed in some line of activity. Imagine a number of students who have to take an exam in mathematics; and they are required to find the hypotenuse of a right-angled triangle. One of the most delinquent among the students sums the squares of the other sides of the triangle and finds the square root of this result; and one of the most serious among them multiplies the other sides of the triangle and divides the result by pi. Which one of these two students do you think can *hope* to get it right?"

There was a young man standing there who had been struck by Amanoofwom's words. The young man had just finished a university degree in psychology. He courageously approached Amanoofwom to say: "But, teacher, if the student gets it wrong by mistake, what can he do then?"

"There will be two possibilities," replied Amanoofwom; "either he will be dismissed, or he will be given another chance. But he will never succeed until he follows the rule, for willingness itself is nothing if it is outside of the right procedure. I tell you, my brothers, do things the way they work, and they will work for you. No child will love its adoptive parents the same way it would love its natural parents, unless it is not aware of being adopted. However, as funny as it may appear, they always end up discovering the whole story. Who would like to be an adopted child?"

"Teacher, tell us clearly what you mean," asked the young psychologist.

"What I mean by what?"

"If you are aware that we are at stake and that you know the right procedure to be tackled to ward off our impending destruction, then say it straightaway."

"I have already said it somewhere. Just bear in mind that you will find two types of men who will appear to be very dangerous to the common man: the one that ponders upon a collective suicide after being stricken by cultural alienation; and the one that plans to withdraw from life when affected by sexual impotence. But, according to you, what is the link between sex and culture? Why do you think that they are so important to incite a man's voluntary death?"

"I think that one has a generative power and the other has a creative power," the young psychologist answered after some seconds of reflection.

"That is right!" Amanoofwom approved with satisfaction. "We are here to create and be exalted, absolutely exalted into superhumanity, kind of gods. But we have to live very long – billions of years – to get there. Yet, our corporeal support cannot live that long. It needs renewal to continue the work. And when we achieve the highest point of our creative abilities, we will then be proclaimed legitimate sons of the Very High, for we will have become like Himself, the leading creative principle. And, after that, we shall be allowed to move on."

"Is this to say that a man who has not initiated any work to be continued after his death does not need to have a child?" asked the young man.

"No, brother. There is a difference between running a family inheritance and continuing a work of inspiration in the march of a civilisation towards its fulfilment. If you have no inheritance to be run after your own death, someone else might have initiated a work of inspiration to be continued after him. And you cannot be sure that your son will not be up to it. So give life. Maybe your son will be the one to top up the last toil that will give us permission to enter the upper realm."

There was a young evangelist from a congregation newly settled in the town. He bowels began to boil up inside with disappointment as he heard Amanoofwom talk about "the last toil" to "give us permission to enter the upper realm". And, as he could not help it, he raised his hand to say: "But, teacher, we do not need great works to enter the upper realm, we rather need the Father's grace, which is not a reward, but a gift. What kind of upper realm are you talking about which needs great works to be rewarded for?"

As Amanoofwom turned to him, he said: "I tell you, my brother, our languages are sometimes more poetic than prosaic. That is, we tend to indulge more in the words than in the images they convey. The word 'gift' exists for the sake of beauty in our languages, but the concept itself does not exist in our world. There is always a criterion, however unnoticeable or overshadowed, upon which you get whatever you have. That is why you will always get what you deserve; but if you expect so much from grace, you will be rewarded by pity instead. You will be rewarded indeed.

"If you do not achieve great works to deserve a seat in the upper realm, then you will need to confess and worship to keep from creating. And, for that very reason, you might be saved for your faith though not rewarded for your works. Now, imagine that in your life you have not achieved any works, and you have never confessed, and you have never worshipped. Will you tell me that you can expect to enter the upper real in that condition?"

The young evangelist shook his head in puzzlement. But he eventually avowed: "I find it quite difficult. But it is possible if the Father wills so."

"That is the point, brother," Amanoofwom said lightly. "The Father has a general rule that we know and by which we are required to abide, and through which we can be sure that we will see the upper realm. However, He might sometimes supersede His normal way of working if He wills so. But this is incidental, and such incidents are not a guarantee. You cannot be 100% sure that the Father will do so out of the rules that He revealed. That is why there are always some duties to perform. That is the rule, and that is what you are doing as a minister. Now, is this absolutely free as a gift?"

"Er…I don't know. It might not be absolutely free, but we have to trust the Father."

"Dear brother, if you want to trust the Father that way, then stop

ministering and renounce to your confession. I will then understand you. But I know that you will not do this. Besides, even trusting, in a very pragmatic sense, is still a duty. Trusting is laborious.
Trusting can make you spend sleepless nights. Trusting can make
you sweat. Trusting is a draining internal activity. Trusting can make
you very worried. A man who trusts is not as idle in his mind and
heart as another man who does not trust at all. If trusting were not
a hard work, disappointment by those whom we have trusted would
never be a hard blow to us. A man who trusts is like a man who has
invested all his money and energy in building a business. If the business goes bankrupt, this can cause him to die. As a matter of experience, some people commit suicide after being disappointed by
those whom they have trusted. Do you think that this is a joke?

"I tell you, brothers, while I was travelling around the world, I met
a great 'teacher of the Word' in Britain. His name is Virgo. I liked
his way of picturing God as a husband, and man as the wife of God.
Now, if you look at that picture and see the number of tasks that a
good wife performs to please her husband in order to receive his
love, care and protection, you will understand that, if grace were not
something that we deserve, nobody would expect to receive it at all.
Or else, it would be offered to all living beings in the same proportions."

The young psychologist was struck again by the words of the
teacher, but in a very shocking way. He grew a bit cynical and even
agnostic when he then said: "I find that we are just God's slaves in
this world; and, if I were to make up my mind, I would choose not
to live at all so that I would not need to be rewarded or saved."

"Oh!" exclaimed Amanoofwom. "That is really tricky! You want to
get away with your responsibilities by choosing non-existence. But I
tell you, brother, in the last moments of existence, even nothingness
will be either rewarded or saved, or left aside in total desolation and
tribulation. Where will you be then, if you choose in non-existence,
to escape your duty to create or worship?"

"But why do we have to be so obligated?" the young man persist-
ed.

"It is true that we are obligated in a sense. However, you have to understand that life is like a crucible. But riddling it is a shame, for all that can be sieved is tiny. We have to take up our duties. The Very High Himself took up His duty to create. If He had got way with it, where would He be today?"

The crowd nodded in total approval. But the young psychologist still seemed worried about something, and this was the occasion to bring all his questions into the open. The teacher had just said that we needed to "achieve great works and worship" to have salvation in the Father's realm. The young man then asked: "Teacher, logically, I find it quite convincing that we will certainly need to perform some works to enter the upper realm. But what annoys me is that the theme of creativity in our world mainly – if not always – revolves around science. Yet, as you know, science and God do not walk side by side. How can you then justify that creating and worshipping can both take us to the same realm while they are opposed?"

Amanoofwom directed a gentle but affective smile at the young graduate; and thus he spoke to answer: "Brother, there might come a time when you will be free and permitted to build your nation. Truly, I tell you, you will have to hold creativity with you right hand. And, if some of you choose to worship instead, do not mock them. And, likewise, do not let the worshippers despise their brothers who will be into creativity; for your will all be on the same train going to the same destination, though sitting in different wagons.

"Let me tell you this story. One day, while I was travelling around the world, I heard somebody pray against what he called 'the strongholds of science'. I tell you in truth, that prayer gave me the impression that medicine had been revealed by Satan to save human lives while God Himself wanted them slain. Only those who will withdraw their registration from their dentists and stop consulting GPs will prove their claim that science is from Satan. Only those who will stop using automobiles and refrain from taking airline flights will justify their stance. Only those who will step away from computers and reject academic education will be sincere to their anti-scientific God.

"Brothers, are we trying to give Satan the chance of becoming the master of all that the Father revealed to us for our well-being in this world? Are we trying to let Satan think that he is so wise as to reveal medicine, psychology, scientology, cosmology, masonry, chemistry, mathematics, electronics, physics, astronomy, bacteriology, architecture, genetics or whatever else is made to improve humanity?

"Satan has created nothing; he has revealed nothing. He is an outsider. We should not give him the opportunity to reign over our beautiful revelations. If man makes bad use of God's revelations for personal, selfish interests, this does not mean that Satan was the creator of his ghastly plans. God is the only one who reveals everything we know for us to improve our creative abilities to better our existence. Satan is not the master of science. Science is from God. We have to create our own means for a better existence through science. This is God's own will."

"My goodness! Everything is 'create, create, create'. But what is the end of this?" a man in the crowd asked truculently.

"Brother, I have already said somewhere that only those who have never been born can have a good reason to keep from giving birth. The Creator Himself has already worked very hard to produce something beautiful like you. What would then be your reasons to refuse to do the same in your turn? And not only that. If you believe that you were made in the image and likeness of God, how would you justify your reluctance to impersonate Him? Well, suppose that you do not believe that the Creator had worked hard to create you, nor even that there is a creator at all, and – consequently – that you are not in the image and likeness of any form of creator. Nevertheless, we can still look at the matter from a purely existential angle. And, accordingly, the question I will ask you is the following: will you be happy to be somebody's slave all your life on the grounds that he is more creative and, consequently, more powerful than you; or will you just have to kill yourself – like many of the slaves that have committs suicide in our history, wherever this has happened – if you fail to be creative and powerful by chance; or will you just take your enslavement on board and wisely understand that you deserve to be somebody's slave for failing to compete with his creative abilities?

"Brother, humanity is an explosion of creative forces; and this has a virtuous end. We have to create for our material salvation, which leads to our spiritual salvation. I have already said somewhere that a man who fights for the improvement of humanity cannot fight against cloning. Somebody who wants to say 'no' to cloning has to start saying 'no' to his GP and dentist and surgeon, and pharmacist and car manufacturer, and airliner designer, etc., in the first place, for we cannot go halfway and be consistent. Imagine your lungs destroyed by a horrendous cancer, and you are given a few months to live. But somebody comes over and says to you: 'I can produce a pair of lungs in good condition for you that can work for more than 50 years.' Will such a piece of news make you happy or miserable? We can still suppose that this will sound horrible to you. But why did you first accept the artificial fillings that your dentist put in your mouth for effective dentition while you knew that these were not God's teeth – that they were but science's teeth?

"Brothers, the improvement of our material existence by the power of our creative abilities through science is the condition of our mental and spiritual improvement; and this is God's own will. We shall be able to save man's life from horrendous diseases to fight discomfort in humanity. We shall be able to produce human spare parts to effectively fight disability. We shall be able to correct calamities of nature. We shall be able to protect our planet against cosmic errors. We shall fight suffering to make 'happy believers' in God with a genuine and assertive hope that they will go to heaven. Because, do not lose sight of the fact that the greatest believers are the happiest ones. Or let me put it this way: the happier a man is in his material condition the more confident he will be about being loved by his God and the surer he will be about being part of God and going to heaven in the end. Some believers may fight such a vision for the sole sake of pertaining to some old theological philosophy. But this is the way things work in life. It is not very easy to believe that God is by your side when you suffer. And the more you suffer the more you are tempted to get involved in criminality, as a rebellious reaction to what you would then tend to call "the injustices of destiny" and the more your relationship with your God – if you already had one with Him – will deteriorate.

"One day, a very clever woman said to me that she did not understand why testimonies of faith had become very much like testimonies of success. That's right, of course. If a man who suffers sets out to believe in God, he will do so only in the expectation that God will heal his pain. But, if this does not happen, he will soon be stricken with disappointment, because it is not very easy to give honour to the very one you suppose may be the cause of your pain; since we believe that God is the cause of everything. That is why he will easily be tempted to turn to evil and betray his relationship with his God, which a happy man would not do. A happy man does not have any reason to betray his relationships. That is why friendship is the business of decent people, because a miserable man in his battle for survival cannot avoid being devious, even towards his best friends, for the sake of survival. In our culture, we say that 'ngue o abomanne à ngaga á mbú ô se à fôn, o ke hlè ñe ná otog'. Imagine a very rich man who starts setting up charities everywhere to assist orphans. But the same man in a very poor condition would rather be tempted to rob such a charity. Is this nonsense? I really don't think so.

"I tell you, brothers, believe me, we can increase the number of future heaven-goers by improving the condition of our citizens through good politics and, above all, good science. Because the improvement of man's material condition will lead to the improvement of his spiritual condition, and this will improve God Himself, not only because God will be happy to see man happy but also, and above all, because man is the very factor that is meant to improve God. Once again, I have to note that I am not being a heretic by saying that our God is mean to be improved thanks to man's efforts.

"Our God is a subtle Thought. But that Thought is not completely achieved yet. We are the machines that He created to help Him improve Himself for His achievement. Somebody may say, 'This is the God of the Fanghish that is not achieved yet!' I do not care about such a reaction. But those who believe that their God is already complete will have to justify their imperfect condition while they are in the image of a perfect God.

"Around 1,000 years ago, before man conceived and created cars and aeroplanes, his condition was less improved than it is today. Man's ambition, in creating such sophisticated machines as well as inventing more and more different refined devices, is to improve his own living conditions. And the improvement of man's condition is expressed through the improvement of the machines that he conceives and creates. God had exactly the same ambition when He conceived and created human machines. But the difference is that the machines that man creates to improve his own life cannot set out to work by themselves to improve their creators, because they are mindless. Human machinery, on the other hand, was gifted with full consciousness to work for itself to improve its creator through its own improvement. Some billion years ago, before God conceived and created man, He was less complete than He is today. And though we have already marked a very big step to improve our God through our own improvement, our duty is to carry on helping Him to improve Himself though our own improvement. It is true that our life was created, programmed and launched by God Himself with, of course, a high degree of wisdom. But He put great intelligence in it so that life could go further and further for its improvement and exaltation in Him.

"In *The Selfish Gene*, Richard Dawkins wrote that God had certainly programmed orgasm for sexual satisfaction so that this would play an important part in man's happiness in life, but that He might certainly not have been prepared for masturbation to the same end. But this is like saying that, if God knew that the chemical substances contained in vegetation would possess medical properties and virtues likely to cure man by absorption, He might certainly not have been prepared for surgery. But this is not true. God is a huge fuse of thoughts – good thoughts as well as evil thoughts – that man's intelligence can attract to sort himself out. But the problem is ours if we prefer to take up evil thoughts instead of the good ones to create horrors rather than beauties for our lives; because God does not impose His will on man's choices.

"I have already said on TV that man's mind acts like a magnet to attract thoughts that already exist in God's mind – good thoughts as well as evil thoughts. Masturbation itself is not man's invention. It is part of God's intelligence. And man is free to take up between the evil part of God's intelligence and the good part of it, and everyone will pay the price and receive the reward for the options taken up. Sometimes, I am most likely to say that our intelligence has to go beyond God's own intelligence so that we can go further and further, in our own improvement as well as that of our God. But this is not really what I mean by this sentence. The reality is, unfortunately, that, if you have an accident and lose one of your legs, God will not be able to provide a replacement. It is true that God's mind is full of solutions, and it certainly has a good solution for your amputated leg. But because of His 'inability' to perform in life by Himself, you will be doomed to be disabled for life after such an accident. But medical science, as performed by man, can make you another leg and get you walking again, because man has the power to take over God in life thanks to the Spirit of Science. And this is where our march towards perfection lies.

"When the Spirit commands to man 'be ye perfect', this does not solely concern moral perfection. It is not just about being polite and gentle, or thinking positively, or giving some clothing to the poor, or drinking only a few drops of wine or no beer at all, or being a vegetarian, or praying for our salvation in heaven. Man's perfection in life, and in the prospect of approaching God's perfection and hauling Him to a higher perfection, is a full command. It will make no sense to us who are aiming at spiritual perfection if our material condition is depraved. Spiritual perfection results in such qualities as bounty, compassion and inner joy. But you will not ask somebody to be good if he does not have the material means to help his needy neighbours. How will he help them? Neither will you expect somebody to be joyful and thankful to his God if he does not feel fulfilled and satisfied in his existential condition. What will he thank Him for?

"To understand this, just take a very simple case. A lot of people will tell you that most disabled subjects that they have met tend to be aggressive and odious if they are not sad. This is not a mere wicked coincidence. The behaviour of these subjects is due to the frustration they endure in being unable to effectively use their body in a certain normal way. And, I have to tell you this: the minute you mend a disabled person's limbs he will unconsciously start thanking his God even though he is well aware that it was, rather, a surgeon that did him the wonderful favour.

"What I am trying to tell you here is that you can't ask a miserable subject – stricken by any kind of unfortunate condition like, say, illness or destitution – to smile at you or at whatever god you preach to him before you help him up. And science is one of the most obvious tools we can use to help humanity up.

"I am aware that, today, medical advancement has even led to this impending possibility: for women to bear children by themselves with no need for male semen. And somebody may think that I am being contradictory if I say 'no' to such an aberration. But we have to understand that the objective of any scientific advancement should be to save lives and improve the quality of human existence, but not to defy and destroy the principles of life. I will not comment too much at this point. Just bear in mind that, according to the principles of life, beautiful things are meant to be *shared*. A child is a beautiful thing just like, say, a good meal or a glass of wine. I don't see anybody being so happy to take a walk down the street towards a modern restaurant and sit there in front of a sumptuous meal, all alone. This is simply miserable, not because social psychology looks at it as being so, but because it really is. Man is most happy about what he possesses when he shares it with someone else. However, nobody would like to sit and share a sumptuous dinner with a terrorist. Nobody would be delighted in going out to share a delicious drink with a criminal. And, likewise, nobody would consent to share a child with a remorseless heartbreaker. But the problem, here, is not about sharing. The problem is about finding *who* one can trust to share something beautiful – like a good meal, a glass of wine, or a child – with. Those who work hard to bear children by themselves will soon understand that it is much better sweating blood to find a perfect shareholder than risking millions to be a selfish sole trader.

"Brothers, I want you to hear me carefully. I am not personally intending to promote some kind of superhumanity. Humanity itself is inclined to transcendence in all senses. If, in the year 2000 AD, a modern Czech went 5,000 years back in time and met a primitive Bohemian, and said to him that men would fly across the seas, the Bohemian would certainly charge him with heresy, because, in his primitive percept of God's will, only birds are meant to fly. And yet, we really fly across the seas today, and this does not appear at all heretical to us. And, likewise, the achievements that we will have made in 5,000 years' time forward for the improvement of man's existence may sound ungodly today, not because they are demonic in essence, but simply because they are not practicable yet. But they will be familiar and even very reasonable to us once they are made practicable; and – no doubt – our God will approve of them at that very time. Do not forget that the Roman Vatican, which fought science 1,000 years ago, is now the owner of one of the biggest research panels in the world, whose job is to investigate theological facts – by means of science. 'What a ghastly contradiction!' one may say. But this is not a contradiction. The truth is simply that, 1,000 years ago, the Vatican personnel were surely not aware that our God needed science to express and prove Himself.

"God is an amalgam of subtle thoughts and images whose 'ambition' is to get more and more dynamic and improved. There shall come a time when our minds will have attracted all thoughts and images that exist in the mind of God, but we will still have to improve them to make them more and more subtle, reaching to infinity, until they become a light. This might take millions of years, but we have to get there, because man's creative abilities are the only machines that will help the Cosmic Thought improve itself to become a light: *the Light of Salvation.* This is the great work in which every single human being has to participate, either materially or spiritually, for the infinite achievement of our God. However, we have to understand that creativity has only one ladder leading to it: the ladder of cultural improvement. We have to turn our culture into a powerful instrument of improvement so that we are able to participate in the improvement and the achievement of our God; for, I tell you, all those who will fail to participate in that work will be left in oblivion and desolation when the time of human assessment comes."

The teacher suddenly began to walk away without adding a word to that ultimate statement; and his friends immediately followed him as he walked off out of the crowd and straight to Ebongué's car. He looked so wrathful that nobody in the crowd dared attempt to stop or follow him for a question. And, soon after, Ebongué's Trooper hummed off.

CHAPTER 7

BEHIND THE LEADING WALLS

Amanoofwom started some kind of normal life once he agreed to lecture at university, after Ebongué had sweated blood to convince him. It was about four weeks after the Christian event at Bessieux's High School. Ebongué might have received a huge amount of pressure from behind the leading walls to urge his friend to join the formal academic board, where he could teach more "Catholic" stuff, instead of lecturing in the agora. In fact, a lot of people in the intellectual and political arena had agreed that Amanoofwom should not be kept out of the circle. He was thenceforth, to lecture at President's University, in the faculty of arts and humanity, and – more precisely – in the department of anthropology.

President's University was a modern campus, with some impressive lecture theatres newly erected at the front view of the site next to its main gate on Normal School Road, one of the most popular streets in the town. The name of the lifelong-elect president of the country was displayed on the gate in gleaming colours to mark his unfailing presence among "his people". A few years earlier, his name had just been marked in blue paint on a large sheet of plywood. But a student union strike centred on the rejection of the president as the patron of the university resulted in the incineration of the plywood sheet showing his name at the main entrance to the university. The strike was part of the popular protest that took place after the president cheated the general elections at a time when almost nobody in the country wanted him back in power. So the muscular regime behind the leading walls found no other solution than to erect a powerful gate on which the name of the president would be carved in reinforced concrete. That job was done under the surveillance of hundreds of troops to protect the masons, at work night and day. Anyway, an inscription carved in reinforced concrete would not be that easy for unarmed students to destroy!

And there it goes. The name of the everlasting president remained, irrevocable, at the university gate.

Amanoofwom's appointment at President's University was not without some ethical controversy. Nobody really knew where he had come from. It was not likely that he would meet some standard requirements as a lecturer. For example, he was certainly not a Ph.D. holder, as befitting a lecture theatre. But he was appointed anyway. Maybe his nomination as a lecturer derived from his public speeches, even though nothing that he said rang any bells in the academic world. Most of his contentions sounded more like spiritual revelations, though sometimes they were viewed as heretical. It was, therefore, most probable that an outstanding curriculum vitae had been made up by some brains behind the leading walls to get the young teacher onto the academic panel. But why? Why did they need him there?

The brains behind the leading walls might have seen Amanoofwom either as a tool to be utilised in some wily way, or as a threatening weapon to be deadened in some strategic manner. But the young teacher did not bother being exploited or muzzled. He knew nobody that could shackle him in any possible way. He knew perfectly what he was up to. And he slipped into the Trojan offer quite heedfully.

The young lecturer was shown his office, where a young man in his 20's was introduced to him as his secretary, and he had an induction of about 60 days with Mr Yans Milo Mi'Mbot, the head of department. And he started lecturing the following week. But Amanoofwom soon—only three months after joining the academic world—began to fret about the inadequacy of the curriculum delivered in his department. Despite the title designated to the department in which he had been appointed as a lecturer, the officially approved curriculum instead told a totally different story. To begin with, the curriculum in the department of African anthropology was, miraculously, not exclusively African. It was a browse through countless uncivilised traditions the world over, from the rituals of exotic tribes in Papua New Guinea to the hunting techniques of Bakongo pygmies; from the warfare strategies of the Nguni people to the hallucinogenic initiations of the Amazonian Ashaninca; from the eccentric visions of the Aboriginal Ayapatu chanting celebrants to the Morimó visits of the dead among the Bioko Bubiè; from the young women's clitoral excision observances among the far west African Wolof to the traditional ceremony of the nomination of the Maffo among the Bamiliké, etc. The remit was wide and vague, but mostly cryptic and purposeless due to the lack of appropriately experimental knowledge of the subjects under study, and especially the impossibility of tracing a significant and beneficial connection between the different traditions.

The visible syndrome of such an academic approach to scientific subjects was psittacine. The students would be required to produce no more than a merely parrot-like demonstration of their knowledge of the subjects. For example, none of them would be likely to be able to describe with any degree of precision the clinical and spiritual effects of the Ayahuasca potion to a new student, or the witchery secrets of a Bakongo hunter, or the mystical criteria upon which the Maffo was nominated. They would make but mere folkloric recitals of the traditions overviewed. But where would such a poetic approach to scientific facts lead them? To knowledge? What kind of knowledge?

Amanoofwom was a 'practicist'. His search for knowledge and truth was more pragmatic than theoretical. But the battle against the theory rule of knowledge at President's University wasn't going to be an easy mission to complete. It wouldn't even be completed. This was the first litigation that put Amanoofwom at odds with the rectorial authority.

To try and solve the problem, Amanoofwom suggested the organisation of official invitations to some renowned Ayapatu celebrants, Ashaninca practitioners, pygmy hunters, Nguni warriors, etc. – all of them being trained to speak the French language that was in use at President's University – to properly explain their traditions in kind of seminars and workshops, and even initiate some of the students who would volunteer to experiment the different traditional sciences. Or else, what could alternatively be done would be to organise expeditions of groups of students who, with respect to their own choices, would visit the very places in which these traditions were practised, to gain a deep insights into them.

But Amanoofwom's suggestions were flatly rejected by the university authorities, on the grounds that such projects would require huge amounts of money for the fares, accommodation and medical safety of the students, or for the guests' training in the French language. This would take too much time and investment – even though it would end up producing a good knowledge of the subjects under study in the department of anthropology, and maybe result in something efficiently useful for the future of the community. The benefits that could be drawn from Amanoofwom's suggestions did not seem to be of any importance. Saving the state's funds was the prime preoccupation of the authorities in their negative response.

In a meeting convened by the rector to discuss a letter that Amanoofwom had sent to him two or three weeks earlier, the young teacher turned round to changed direction somewhat and put forward a more economical alternative to his proposals. Instead of sending tens of students abroad, he proffered the nomination of two or three lecturers who would be granted a sabbatical leave to spend nine months or so with the masters of the traditions under study, which would give them more practical insights into and greater authority in the subjects they lectured on. He even noted that he would not personally need to be one of the lecturers to be nominated for the sabbatical leave, because, as he advised, he had already been practically trained in the Buiti tradition, on which he was prepared to lecture exclusively.

But delivering Buiti teachings at university was another shocking idea to the authorities, on top of all that had already been rejected. The Buiti – a mystical tradition revealed among the Tsogo and then adopted and developed by the Fanghish – was primarily regarded as a demonic credence by the historical alliance between academic institutions and the institutional clergy. Taking the Buiti tradition to university was like taking Satan to church, even though it was true that Satan himself would often meet with the sons of God in God's own temple to discuss the future of Creation, and even have a sensible conversation with God, through which he would be given carte blanche by God Himself to complete some historical missions on the earth. But, in the case of the Buiti tradition, such a correlation wouldn't make sense.

Amanoofwom formulated some questions of practical logic related to his claims, which the authorities refused to answer. For example, why was it that such remote traditions as the Ashanincas, the Ayapatus, the pygmies or the Ngunis were accepted for study while the authentic Fanghish tradition wasn't? What was the end of a shallow theoretical study of an aboriginal tradition for the practical future of the people of Odzab? What could we gain in the study of an Amazonian culture that we could lose with the study of the Buiti tradition? How can we justify the fact that the Buiti tradition was refused on the grounds that it was demonic while Amazonian non –Christian traditions were accepted for study? How true was it that the Buiti tradition was opposed to God's Will? Who could make a relevant and truthful demonstration of such an assumption? To which extent would the study of the Buiti tradition be destructive to the youth?

Amanoofwom's proposals were unconditionally dismissed, and the university authorities refused to continue the debate with him. The young teacher didn't feel like stopping his fight, however, even though it would certainly take him nowhere.

Amanoofwom was a nationalist, not in a political sense, but rather from a cultural angle; and, for him, the word 'culture' had more crucial implications than anyone could imagine. Some people think that the word 'culture' is confined to mere folkloric imagery or some straightforward and superficial observances within traditions, or even a set of communal rules established to run groups of people in a sociopolitical framework. But culture wasn't just that for Amanoofwom. Culture was a powerful instrument upon and through which a nation could erect a mighty civilisation. But the first point to set clear in such a weird definition of the concept of culture was its role in the world. On TV, Amanoofwom had said something remarkably important when explaining the purpose of diversity in Creation. He had said that,"God caused cultural diversity so that each group, using a particular language and having particular skills, would achieve its microproject and bring it forward as a contribution to the fulfilment of the whole project. And each of these groups of men that uses a particular language and has particular skills is inhabited by a leading mind that is known as the *Inner-Soul*. The *Inner-Soul* is a kind of trans-individual system of visions, conceptions, beliefs, observances and methods within a group as they are expressed in the group's way of speaking. It is also observable in the group's modus operandi. We call it 'a tradition' in its primary manifestations. It becomes 'a culture' as it improves in quality. A group of men who observe the same tradition and work out a culture together may be regarded as a tribe in its primitive form, but it is known as 'a people' as it grows bigger and stronger. And we call it 'a nation' when it stands as a social and political force. Its final form in a well-defined and well-organised unit is 'a country'. Some call it 'a state' if they view it as a machine."

If one went back to review the argument preceding this statement, one would find that Amanoofwom had made use of a practical example to illustrate the point. Marks & Spencer was the typical case he quoted to explain that cultures are departments of the human enterprise to make the world move. This was not sheer spiritual poetry. Cultures are meant to be studied and exploited exhaustively until they can be more and more efficiently utilised by the human machinery for man's improvement and advancement. Cultures are instruments for man's exaltation in life, which will unfailingly result in his exaltation in spirit.

The trouble is mostly that some cultures seem to be satisfied with a certain static level of mastery of the arts of living and knowing so much, so that they unnoticeably play the failing part of the human enterprise. Because if, in a company, there is a department that fails to follow the rhythm of outside technology and market requirements, this will make the whole business fail. And the unfortunate fact is that this is not something we can see now. We will certainly see it in the remote future. And it will surely be too late by that time.

Let us take a very popular political fact that governs our world in these present times of 21st century AD. The most advanced nations of the world very constantly spend their time expediting huge amounts of food, clothes and money to save the lives of those that can't afford surviving by themselves all around the world. And some citizens of these advanced nations are caustically pouting such a senseless largesse. And some people think that they lack some sort of human sense. But this is not true. They are absolutely right, because nobody should be there to constantly help others. The Will of the Spirit does not recommend any one-way assistance between men. Exchange and mutual assistance between men advancing at almost the same pace is the 'voie royale' for a dignified human enterprise in the eyes of the Spirit. Thus, the modern political fact that some have to constantly help others is but a remarkable premonition of the future failure of our enterprise.

What is regrettable is that many people don't like to stop for a minute and ask themselves the question as to what really happened for some department of the human enterprise to be so advanced as to have the power and the means to constantly help others; and, conversely, the question, too, as to what happened for some to be so unable to get up by themselves. Is it equally an error of creation? Are some brains naturally more likely to get the most of it effortlessly? Could the Creator make such a horrendous mistake with such implications for the future? Is there anything missing somewhere? If so, is it a natural miss or a 'nurtural' failure? If natural, why that? But, if 'nurtural', where does the failure stem from, then?

If you are a normal human being, frustrated by the oddness and unevenness of the world, you won't fail to come across such questions one day in your life. It is, however, true that some methodologists in some bizarre trends of modern philosophy think that questions are more important than answers. But, if an answer can eliminate an important question, it is unlikely that one will be too disappointed by such an unusual event in philosophy. Many people will surely see where such an idea comes from. Philosophy is not a demonic art. But you cannot spend all your entire life producing questions to which you do not expect to receive a practical answer, unless they are not questions in essence. For example, if somebody puts Anaximander and Anaximenes to the challenge and asks you, accordingly, whether it is water or air that is the prime cause of the creation of the universe, you will not be likely to give any answer to such a question, not because there wouldn't be any answer to the research for the origin of the universe, but because the question itself is wrong. Such a man wants you to say whether it was the dog or the cat that gave birth to chicks. But you won't choose either, for the answer is not there. In front of such a dilemma, some people may recommend you to rather choose air, because God, the Creator, is in the space and they confuse air and space. But air doesn't equal space. Air is some matter that occupies space just the way water occupies it. You can easily have space with no air. For example, each water molecule or oxygenic atom that is part of water's components is surrounded by some space that looks like a spherical shield. But that space is not airy. It is oxygenic.

So, philosophical questions do not remain everlastingly important because it is more beneficial to keep questions as they are to keep philosophy alive, but because most of them are not questions at all. And, therefore, it is not likely that a productive philosopher would wish to keep posing the question as to what really happened for some cultures to be in a position to constantly have to help others up in a world intended to give the chance to each cultural department to keep pace with the moving requirements of the cosmic mind for the human enterprise to grow richer and stronger evenly.

Probably, all this may have seemed to be too nonsensical a wrangle to cling onto. For example, Eyang-Alouga, the head of the Nguess language department, who soon became one of Amanoofwom's close friends at President's University, would propound some eloquent contentions about his vision of 'the sense of history' to calm Amanoofwom down, if not to try to prove him wrong in a certain way. Dr Eyang-Alouga would expound that our world is meant to grow unevenly, and even alternately. His opinion derived essentially from the fact – as he loved to quote it – that, once upon a time, one of the continents that is towed today by human advancement was the prow of man's pride on earth. That continent is called Africa, and the people that did that job are the Egyptians. At that time, the people of the pink world would come down to the subcontinent to learn how to live among the brown genes. The conclusion of that short account, which subsumed thousands of years of human history, was in fact, that – one day – things will surely come back the other way round, and the subcontinent will take the lead back again. History alone will decide when.

Here, one could easily notice that Dr Eyang-Alouga believed in history the way Christians believe in the God of Redemption. They say that "you do not need to work hard for it; God Himself has already done the whole job by shedding His son's blood for your sins". But do things really work like that? Is it truly through some sort of historical providence that our human civilisations come to existence and flourish?

Amanoofwom grew sleepless, unnerved by the inability of the university authorities, and even a huge lump of the intellectual panel, to understand his worries. He was not alone, however A few among his colleagues, including Yans Milo Mi'Mbot, the head of the anthropology department, also paid great heed to the young lecturer's concerns: the need to thoroughly study and exploit the local genius in a university curriculum. But, unfortunately, many of the resolutions to be taken did not depend on their free will and disposition to reform and innovate the academic world for the benefit of their nation's future. It was a political issue. But how could they get on with politics?

Fourteen months had already passed since Amanoofwom embraced the academic milieu, which he had spent lecturing some of the time on the folklores of some primitive societies of nearby regions, but mostly negotiating something here and there, as he was bothered by the issue of studying and exploiting the local genius at university to give the students the chance to improve their lives through the exploration of their intrinsic values. What to do? How could Amanoofwom make himself audible to the authorities of the university and, especially, the policy makers of the country?

This was, coincidentally, the time for another session of general elections to take place, about seven years after the previous exercise. The president in power was the eternal candidate of his 'democratic' party, though grumblings were expressed here and there against his candidacy, surely the fifth time he presented himself after something like 30 years of rule.

Amanoofwom got into the protest movements against the president's candidacy, not so much because he didn't like him as a man, but because he thought that someone else would certainly legitimise a thorough study of local values at the university. Anyway, everybody always has his own personal reason when going for or against something. Amanoofwom may have had some other reasons for protesting against the president's succession to himself, but they did not seem to be essential to him at that point.

Nonetheless, the president stood by his candidacy and the elections took place in horrendous circumstances. First of all, schools and universities were shut down a few weeks before the elections due to social agitation. Even industries and administration and information agencies faced closure. The only public institutions that were left open were churches and mosques, maybe because they always think that they are not concerned by worldly fights. The whole country was dead in terms of economic activities, but blasting in brawls and gunshots. The presidential guards had to defend themselves against the invading protesters in all places at all times; but, above all, they had to defend their sovereign.

The economic recession, the agitation, the brawls and the gunshots continued till D-Day. No comments. The president was even elected before the electoral activities were completed. It was bizarre; for example, you are standing in a queue looking forward to casting your vote in the ballot box, and you see the doors of the premises closing in front of you. You would then think that the officers certainly must be knackered and that you could maybe come back the following morning to cast your vote. But then, you see somebody surely more informed than you instantly throw his ballot paper away, and you first think that he is just discouraged after being kept on his foodless, meagre legs all the day for nothing. But you hear him say "This is impossible!" using a different tone to convey a different message. Then you approach him. "What is the matter?" you ask. "It is over," he answers without even looking at you. "What is over?" you ask. "The elections," he replies. "How's that?" you ask. "The president's won it," he says. "Shit!" you shout, and then collapse. You don't even have time to ask yourself the question as to whether it is possible for the president to win it before you cast your vote. You just take it as it is, and burning anger wells up deep inside. Then you just start walking home, straight to your bed, in search of some peace, maybe after wolfing down a good mug of bibuss.

Things got worse in the wake of the president's self-proclamation. Public buildings were smashed. Monuments were hacked off, men were burnt alive by other men. The town smelt of human barbecue everywhere. Some people in bad taste say that the "best meat is human flesh". This may be true. But it wasn't very easy to eat those ones. They were people you knew. People you used to say "hi" to in the streets of Messanza; and, sometimes, mates, friends or relatives. Some who may not have known them might have been tempted to cut a bit off a thigh. But they might have been too afraid of being assaulted by an irascible band of next of kin.

The situation continued for about three months after the elections, during which the political activity in the country reached boiling point. Amanoofwom soon even joined a coalition of political parties that then set out to nominate a parallel government to defeat the president in a different kind of fight. The elections were definitely not the best way out. But even this way didn't turn out to be very promising. The president had men and guns, and powerful friends in some powerful nations of the West. You didn't need to be a genius to see the dead-end in the struggle. In the meantime, human barbecue sessions continued in the streets of Messanza, reaching a level that seemed to have started worrying some Western investors and exploiters in the country, who might then have pulled the president's ears for cowardice before the vandals.

The president ended up appearing on TV screens to say that "the revolt was over", and promised severe treatment to anyone who was suspected in the future of disturbing public tranquillity. Meanwhile some tensions and schemes continued in the dark, though with no hope. Anyway, if you fail to beat somebody you can at least beat yourself, or at the least bite your lips.

Economic and public activities were ordered to reopen under a strict curfew. Amanoofwom was wrecked. He had spent too much of his energy fighting and, above all, hoping. And, two weeks after the university reopened, the young lecturer had still not been seen on the site for any purpose. The university authorities sent him a warm-toned letter inviting him back with a prearranged appointment to discuss some matters with the dean and the rector. But the day Amanoofwom presented himself there, what he brought them was a resignation letter instead. This was outageous to the authorities. Amanoofwom had not been taken in to university only to leave it, even though he turned out to be unable to produce a good lecture. Such must have been the tacit agreement signed by those who wanted his presence there.

The authorities approached Ebongué, advising him to speak to his friend. And Ebongué took up the challenge.

"Are you mad, Aman! How can you resign like that?" Ebongué was blazing with rage.

"Please, Ebongué, try to understand me. I can't just continue like that. I need to do something else."

"What?"

"I don't know yet. But I can't work in such a condition."

"Which condition are you talking about? What is wrong at university? Politics is politics, man! What is done is done. Now, you have to take care of yourself. You've got a life, haven't you?"

"No. That is not me, man. I won't have a life like this. Not just like this."

"Aman, you know, you make me suffer too much. Do you know how many hundreds of young people like you in this country would like to be in your position?"

"No. The position is not my problem. There is something wrong somewhere that you can't see. And I need to do something different from lecturing at this very time."

"But can't you do that while lecturing? Listen, many of us have got side activities. And you are not going to give up with your job because you want to do something in parallel."

"Don't worry, man. A good player is never short of teams. Somebody else will certainly make me an offer once I have finished what I have to do."

"This is really shit, Aman. Listen, you can't do things like that with these people. You don't know how things work here. You can't fight the Matrix, can you?"

"Whatever you call it, I am not here to fight. I am here to teach."

"Indeed, that is exactly what you're doing at university."

"Listen, man. You can't just understand me. Let us talk about it later."

"Later, but when? Do you even have any idea of what you are getting into by doing this?"

Indeed, Amanoofwom's resignation had not been taken calmly. The 'republican' institutions had grown quite bothered about his case. And, even before that, some complaints had already been lodged against him behind the leading walls. Most of the allegations were supported by the clergy, not only for the simple fact that he spoke of God without being an ordained member of any formal credence, but also because of the kind of God he spoke of, which had nothing to do with the formal clerical God. Now, the political arena that had defended him against the clergy's plea on some intellectual grounds had equally gone haywire about him. Ebongué naively reported to the authorities that his friend had definitely decided to quit because, apparently, he had something to do. The bothersome question was, then, as to what he would do after quitting the intellectual square.

A few days after Ebongué reported his conversation with his friend to the authorities, he had a conversation with one of his boss's closest councillors, who came over secretly one morning to tell him that his friend was surely risking arrest, and that, if there were anything he could do to escape, it was high time he did it.

Ebongué rushed to Amanoofwom's house to warn him about the situation. But the only thing he found was Mbeng, Amanoofwom's mother, crying. Aman had gone.

"Was it the gendarmes or the president's guards?" he asked, panic-striken

"No, he went by himself."

"Where did he say he was going?"

"I don't know. He just calmed me down saying that he would be safe, and that he would be back quite soon."

"That is incredible. We need to know where he is."

"I really couldn't achieve any miracles to get him to say where he was going," Mbeng replied desperately, in sobs.

Amanoofwom was gone. But where? Nobody knew, anyway. And not only did nobody know where he had gone, a lot of people also started to ask themselves an important question. Who was

Amanoofwom in reality? Where had he really come from? His birthplace was not part of the quandary at all. The question as to whether he was a normal man was not necessary either. People knew his mother and some had an idea of who his father was. There was a prolific debate, rather, about the things he would say in his speeches. Nobody had any idea of where he could have learned such things. The only information they had about where he had got his knowledge from was in the sentence he had uttered to the old woman in the student union. He had said that he had "travelled into himself to meet God". But this was the kind of sentence that you could find only in the speeches of mythological characters. Moreover, the day he went on TV, Bekale Be'Nguema, the young journalist, had said that Amanoofwom had been studying abroad. But where? In what kind of school? Bekale Be'Nguema had said that it was modern anthropology that he had been studying; but the trouble was that no link could be established between his own speeches and any known tendency in the history of modern anthropology – if such a science even existed in the first place. In fact, nobody could really understand what was going on. Who was Amanoofwom, really?

CHAPTER 8

THE TRUE AMANOOFWOM

Amanoofwom was born in Messanza, the capital city of Odzab, a vast country located in west central Mboga. He was the first-born of his father and his mother. Ongongora was 29 and Mbeng, his wife, was 18. But Amanoofwom's father vanished when the boy was only seven days old. Nobody knew where he had gone. He had said to his wife that he was going to visit one of his friends. But he did not get to his friend's and nobody else saw him. Amanoofwom was then reared up and nurtured by a single mother.

Mbeng was a very beautiful woman. She was also kind, caring and intelligent. Anyway, she couldn't help being kind and caring, particularly to Amanoofwom, who was like a substitute for her late husband. The son was the only thing that could fill in the void left by his father: the mother's most cherished being. For Mbeng, Ongongora had been like a gift from on high. Nothing else was so perfect! The young man was a beautiful bloke, bright and intelligent, hard-working and caring. And he was a fantastic lover on top of everything wonderful in him. He was a kind of dream-like body that you could not find on the earth. But he miraculously happened to be there; and a very lucky, chosen girl had met him and had shared loads of marvels with him. But now he was gone, and his only son had to take over.

The love that the young woman felt for her son was so extreme that her psychosis and paranoia were made openly expressive in her way of protecting him. Amanoofwom didn't go to nursery as a baby, nor did he start primary school at six as recommended by the national education cabinet's scheme. The boy grew up a in the special protective custody of his mother, who was obsessed by a singular affection. However, it seemed that the mother had succeeded in acting as a teacher to her beloved son. Mbeng taught Amanoofwom how to read and write at home in a very effective way. She started buying a huge range of reading books and then expanded to elementary natural sciences, mathematics and geography course books. They would work together almost every evening. Mbeng found educating her son herself more instructive and exciting, and she definitely resolved not to send him to the lousy and heartless teachers of the public education system. Indescribable was the pleasure they experienced in living together and sharing meals, drinks, games, jokes, discussions, work and so on. But Amanoofwom started to come under some pressure from his school-going neighbour-friends, who wanted him to be with them at school.

Amanoofwom had very good friends in the vicinity. There were three of them: Ebongué, Ngule and Bifun. Ebongué was the nearest in terms of neighbourhood distance, and also in feelings. Ebongué was about three years older than Amanoofwom, and Ngule and Bifun were almost the same age as him. Amanoofwom started to sneak out of the house for a few games with Ebongué, and some rare times with Ngule and Bifun, when he was seven. They were the ones who started to pressurise him about going to school with them. They believed that he would be a genius. They could not understand how he, who had never been to school, could talk perfectly with them as if they had been taking the same lessons together. And he even taught them certain things at times. Amanoofwom's protective mother had to yield to the pressure that her son started to exercise on her in his turn, not to hurt the most precious thing she had.

Unfortunately, the day Amanoofwom first went to school under his friends' pressure he was nine years old. This made him mucholder than his classmates, who would scathingly call him 'big brother', not because he was fat, but because of his advanced age among them. Luckily, however, Amanoofwom was not large for his age. He had only a moderate physique; which helped him fit in a bit among his younger classmates. Fortunately, too, he was so well trained beforehand that he was allowed to jump on classes and catch up. Amanoofwom went up five classes over the three years during which he stayed in Ebôna Primary School, at the end of which he was dismissed in the wake of a series of incidents that gave him a reputation as an evil child.

It seemed that Amanoofwom showed signs of losing interest in education near the end of his third year in the school. He was accused of repeatedly having acerbic arguments with the teachers, and addressing them very arrogantly, of repeatedly missing classes, and of having contaminated more than a third of the pupils with his rebellious behaviour. He was very like opium: a weed in a fertile land.

Amanoofwom's problem at school was, as he explained to his mother, that the teachers never paid any attention to his preoccupations. They would never answer his questions. They would even bluntly ignore him and shout at him. Thus he could find no alternative other than to get off and think for himself. "You know, Mum," he said, "when you have something that you want to understand, it gnaws you up inside like a bacterium." But what could such a little boy seek to understand that could gnaw him up inside like a bacterium?

Amanoofwom was dismissed from his school when he was twelve years old. From then on, he never more studied in a formal educational institution. But Amanoofwom and his mother really loved one another. Very often, when a child is dismissed from school for a misdemeanour, his parents rather make it a felony, and punish him severely. But, in the case of Amanoofwom's dismissal, his mother instead cried bitterly for three days and three nights, and Amanoofwom had to console and cuddle her with extreme tenderness. Definitely, Mbeng had to act the teacher again and give as much care as she could. Life restarted as before. Meals, drinks, games, jokes, discussions, work and so on were shared again with delight between mother and son, and this lasted about a year, until a strange revelation from the realm of the unseen came to Mbeng recommending her to send her son to Mikolongo, to the north of Messanza, where he would be taught by an old man called Meyaba.

It was Biyeyem who came to deliver the message to the woman in a strange dream. In the Fanghish theogony, Biyeyem is the messenger of the spirits to the living. He reveals himself to men in visions. He can sometimes come in the form of an ancestor or in any other form: animal, bird, fish, unknown mysterious ghost, to deliver messages. In the vision, Biyeyem came to Mbeng in the form of a huge white rabbit.

Here is what he said: "Woman, we have seen your devotion in loving and educating you son, who is our representative among the Fanghish in this new world. We appreciate very much your efforts in such a toil. But now, your task is over. We want you to help your son to go to Mikolongo and meet Meyaba, the old master who will guide him in his mission. We have already seen Meyaba, to announce to him the visit of Amanoofwom in his temple, and he is ready to work with him. In seven days, the seventh day from tomorrow, at the third hour of the day, take your son to Mekie-Me-Kwule motor station, and, from there, send him north to Mikolongo in the village of the old Meyaba. Let him go by himself. We will be with him over the trip, and never visit him. Just wait until he comes back by himself."

It was nine o'clock in the morning when, on the seventh day, Amanoofwom pitifully set out for Mikolongo, memorising cautiously the instructions that his mother gave him as instructed by Biyeyem. Amanoofwom got to Mikolongo by midday. After being misled and lost several times on his way up, he eventually found the hairy old man sitting in the shade of a big mango tree some 20 metres away from a huge temple.

Amanoofwom was thirteen years old when he arrived in the old man's village. He was young and barely prepared to pay proper attention to the marvels of the world in which he was now living. But his curiosity about the striking mysteries of the old man's spiritual empire grew in time. The first thing that started to impress Amanoofwom was the temple. The Holy Temple of the old Meyaba was, surprisingly, a sumptuous masonry and brick edifice. The temple had two front entrances separated by a massive pillar, which made a picture of Moses' Tables. You had to take your shoes off to get into the temple through the door on your right, and get out through the one on your left; never the other way round.

The essence of the interior decoration was banners of different colours, which were hanging all around the walls – mainly red, yellow, blue and green. In the middle of the temple were two pillars: one physical, with a massive staircase around it; and the other was imaginary or simply spiritual. You could not see it with your eyes, but with your Eye. The altar was a fenced stage with three entrances: one at the middle front, and one at either side. Behind the altar was a kind of spangled banner wonkily stuck on the wall by kind of drawing pins nailed at each of its four corners. The presbytery was behind the altar and gave out through two doors, one on either side of the altar. And that presbytery served as a room of spiritual retreat for students of a certain category.

There were also some compounds of the temple outside. For example, in the centre of the yard, straight in front of the temple, there was planted a massive crucifix, followed by a little triangular stage made of reinforced concrete. And far behind the crucifix and the triangular stage was planted an isolated vestry with the same kind of double door at the front and two similar doors on either side. And behind the vestry was the garden of meditation, in the middle of which a massive mango tree had been planted to provide shelter.

Four things surprised Amanoofwom. The first thing was the temple itself. He could not understand how a traditional temple could be built in brick. He had thought that he would be hosted in a hut built in clay and straw, or the bark of some special trees.

The second surprise was the crucifix. Amanoofwom had not expected to find a crucifix in a traditional temple, even though the rituals were said to have been revealed by God. It was true that the crucifix had ended up representing the modern god taught by the Western invaders, but it was not a traditional symbol of God.

The third thing was that it seemed that the prayers said in the temple were addressed to a unique God, and not to several local gods. And yet, if the Fanghish tradition was not animist, or pantheist, it would be – at least – henotheist in some respects. But none of these aspects was perceived in Meyaba's system. What was going on?

And, eventually, the fourth thing that astonished Amanoofwom was the genius of Meyaba. Amanoofwom had expected to meet a kind of Stone Age, illiterate old villager who would spend his time telling him about the social aberrations of the Fanghish forefathers. But, ironically, Meyaba was an all-knowing man in the classical and modern sense. Amanoofwom did not know if such a man had existed anywhere else in this world. Meyaba knew everything. He knew about the history of powers; that of peoples and nations; that of religions and secret societies. He knew about the West, the East, the north and the south. He even knew about the unknown histories. Meyaba knew about the traditional features of peoples and cultures wherever they came from. He could explain their differences and similarities. He could tell you how different traditions started and evolved, as well as the principles that underlay their philosophies and practices. He could tell you about all these things in one single, coordinated discourse. Meyaba was erudite.

Meyaba even knew about the human body. He could explain the functions of the brain, and the circuit of information transfer in the spinal system. He even knew about the double helix, and could describe the working scheme of the chromosomes, the genomes, the ribosomes, and the amino acids, and he could define the precise role of each of the catalysing enzymes that invigorated them. Meyaba even knew about energy. He could give you a very technical account of the roles and the movements of the neutrons, the electrons, the protons and the photons.

Meyaba was even a philologist. He knew about modern and ancient languages. He could tell you about Latin, Greek, Aramaic, Chinese, etc., in their ancient structures and meanings, and he could speak with different people in their different languages when they visited him in his temple. One day he had a bilingual conversation with Mr Chessial and Mr Gordon, who came from two different nations of the West. Another day it was Romero and Hungenberg, who also came from the West and who had a long conversation with him in their Western languages. This was too amazing to be true. Meyaba was a subjugator who could make you excellent by the very fact of admiring him. He could easily get you to say, "I ought to be like him." Amanoofwom never understood how the people from the West knew about Meyaba, who was not very well-known in his own nation, though he was so erudite.

Meyaba also knew about the realm of the unseen. He knew about God and the Devil. He could tell you about the angels, the archangels, the thrones, the cherubs, the seraphs, etc. But he also knew about Nguíl, Melahn, Biyeyem, Mimbará and Mefan. The old man also had an excellent mastery of Eyano.

Let us just have a glimpse of these local principles. Nguíl was the order that was in charge of defeating negative witchcraft.

Melahn was the rite by which young people were initiated to become great warriors, powerful politicians and important public figures. Some people even thought that Melahn was the secret of the successful and wealthy people.

Biyeyem was the messenger of the spirits to the living. He could sometimes come in the form of an ancestor to deliver a message to man about his personal concerns; or in any other form – animal, bird, fish, unknown mysterious ghost – to deliver other kinds of messages.

Mimbará was a protector. He was the one who could divert your enemies' bullets and preserve you from destructive attacks. The functioning of Mimbará was quite complicated to explain. It was primarily expounded that Mimbará was a superior self, because the human being is a kind of superposition of several selves graduated in the form of a ladder. The human spiritual substance moves up from the lowest step to the highest one as a man grows spiritually mature. If a man's spiritual level is located at a certain step 2, his Mimbará would be at the following step 3 on the ladder, and would keep an eye on him to protect him. Mimbará is, in fact, some kind of guardian angel, but it is simply the man himself at a higher level. At birth, a man's Mimbará is inactive. That is why one needs to be initiated into the Mimbará ritual line to activate him in his favour.

Mefan was also an important principle. He was a peculiar godly archetype that transmitted knowledge to man. He was the guide of teachers, inventors and prophets.

As for Eyano, he was an adopted principle borrowed from an extinguished nation that had lived near the southern borders of Odzab. These people were said to have possessed the secret of the spirit known as the holder of the keys of the heaven's entrance. A man who desired to visit the holy place needed to be initiated into the Eyano to see what was on up there.

Meyaba knew and worked with all these principles; and, on top of all this, the old man possessed a magical secret. He could send you to the spirits and get you to see them and speak to them face to face. He could open your Eye and get you see the unseen. Meyaba was a God fallen into flesh. Amanoofwom would think that Meyaba deserved to live as long as our universe existed, because, if such a being died, where else could we find a similar knowing spirit? It was true that Aristotle was said to have been a *global* scientist. He was a philosopher, a physicist, a mathematician, an astronomer, a medical practitioner, a geometrician, a cosmologist, a sociologist, etc. Amanoofwom still wondered, however, if Aristotle could really face Meyaba in an intellectual competition.

Meyaba started teaching Amanoofwom as soon as the young student arrived in the temple and was shown his room. And, surprisingly, the Master of the Holy Temple also made arrangements for Amanoofwom to be enrolled on a part-time course in a nearby private school, and the old man himself volunteered to pay for the tuition. Amanoofwom never knew where Meyaba had found the money and, especially, why he paid for his education when he wouldn't do this for other young students in his temple. Nonetheless, Meyaba started teaching Amanoofwom in his science.

The initial sessions began with body cleansing and senses open-ing rituals. The student had to be clean in body and open in spirit to have a full understanding of the teachings and a full perception of the visions that would come to him. Everything would start in the afternoon, at five o'clock. Amanoofwom would cleanse himself, and then have a short talk with the teacher while having a family dinner or sipping a cup of special infusions, the constituents of which were known only by the old man. Amanoofwom would then go to bed at nine o'clock in the evening, where he would then be taught by the spirits in dreams and visions. And the following afternoon, always at five o'clock, he would meet the old man again, first to give him an account of what he had seen overnight, and maybe ask for expla-nations of the things that he had not understood, before continu-ing with the rest of the rituals and teachings on schedule.

The revelations would often come to Amanoofwom in the form of visions or dreams while sleeping, or in the form of thoughts while languishing or meditating in his spiritual retreat. Some other times he would be visited by very strange animals and birds, or human faces appearing stealthily in the air in front of him. The faces would say a few words while flickering or fading away. On other occasions, Amanoofwom would feel strange vibrations across his body accom-panied by curious sounds perceived as ringing in his own head. And the experiences would be so frightening at times that he would run out, shrieking with terror.

There are things that no man can look at without quivering, whatever his degree of bravery, serenity and wisdom. If you are wise enough, you can face death with derision. You will not even wobble on your way to it. You will walk towards it straightaway and merrily, so as to prove how wise you are; hence the old saying goes "The ulti-mate challenge of a man of wisdom is to be not surprised by his own death. Yet, only by killing yourself, or at least causing your own death, can you get there." A great many people have done this across history, and we know them. Socrates, for example, openly laughed on his way to the lethal hemlock ladle. That was heroic enough to prove how wise he was. But there exist some spiritual experiences that have no challenger among the exalted human beings. And yet, they are not as fatal as death; but facing them remains harder than facing death.

Imagine that you are half asleep in the morning around seven o'clock, and you feel somebody touching you gently to wake you up, as if to tell you that your breakfast is ready. Now, as you wipe up your slimy encrusted eyes to scrutinise who the woman whose voice is so soft is, you find that it is an all-white human skeleton that is caressing you smilingly.

Or else you have been deeply asleep and you feel a bit annoyed by some kind of strange tickling in your throat. And, as you come around and wake up, you find that a snake has been sneaking itself into your oesophagus, confusing your mouth with a rat hole. And, as you get up suddenly and horrified, the snake keeps hanging low from your mouth.

Or else you wake up in the morning and get your toilet case to wash your face. Then you turn to the mirror. But you see instead the face of your grandmum, who died years earlier, and the face seems to come off the mirror to kiss you.

Or else you are taking a soft gentle walk alone in the garden, and suddenly you notice that you have just trampled on and crushed the skull of a baby corpse. And as you jump, terrified, the head breaks off and the skull remains stuck under you foot.

Or else some kind of one-eyed and one-footed creatures just land in front of you from space and start licking your body with their sticky tongues, while you feel completely paralysed; and once their gluey saliva ties you up immobile, they start speaking to you to teach you something.

Those were the kind of manifestations that Amanoofwom would face in his spiritual retreat. And, at a very acute level, some spirits would come quite smartly. They would just appear in front of him and start speaking to him. That was the way in which the strange spirit named *Aduma-the-elect* came to Amanoofwom one day, while he was sitting in the old man's garden talking with people. *Aduma-the-elect* just appeared to him during the sunlit daytime.

The vision of Aduma was so shocking to Amanoofwom that he did not even give the account of it to the old Meyaba in the following session, because he did not want anybody to know about it. He wanted to veil it and never teach it. He did not agree with it, in fact.

The revelation of Aduma came to Amanoofwom in the daylight, at three o'clock. It was on a Friday, in the fifth year of his sojourn in the old Meyaba's temple. Amanoofwom was then eighteen years old. He was sitting in the garden behind the vestry talking with one of his teacher's several wives: the first one. She was the one regarded as 'the mother'. Everybody called her Nahn'Nkom, which means 'Mother Founder of Everything'. Even Meyaba himself and his other wives called her 'mother'. This must have been borrowed from the famous way in which the Fanghish call God. They say *Nzam-Nkom*, which means 'God Creator of Everything'. But the word *nkom* itself means maker, organiser or repairer. No wonder if *Akoma-Mba* is regarded as the founder, the organiser and/or the leader of Engông, the spiritual picture of Odzab. This is not very hard to understand. The Fanghish believe that all things that exist, even inanimate and artificial beings, have a spiritual picture through which they were conceived in order to be created. This picture is their spirit. So, Odzab, as a nation, was created through a spiritual picture that was conceived by the Creator in order to create it. Engông is the name by which the Fanghish call the spiritual picture of their nation. But Amanoofwom never knew what that old woman had created or founded to deserve such an attribute. It was true that she was very wise, caring and helpful towards the needy students. But that had nothing to do with the concept of the creation or foundation of something. Anyway, understanding the tortuous meanings of spiritual people's language is never guaranteed.

Two explanations were possible, however. First of all, it is known among the Fanghish that spiritual revelations always come through women. Therefore, maybe the knowledge and the secrets that

Meyaba possessed and used had come to him through that woman, in the same way the knowledge of good and evil came to Adam through his wife in the parallel case of the Middle East version. Women are very sensitive, intuitive and vulnerable. That is why spirits find it easier to penetrate them than to enter man's world. Secondly, apart from the metaphorical meaning that is used in the spiritual field, the verb *ákom* from which the active adjective *nkom* is derived means make, organise, repair or fix. Maybe Nahn'Nkom was the hidden organiser of Meyaba's activities. In the spiritual world, women do not deserve public position, even though they can play very important roles in the shadow within systems. The Old Covenant of the Middle East version of God's revelations certainly banned women from preaching the word of God in public.

Amanoofwom was feeling quite bad that afternoon, as he had spent a very tormented night. He was feeling tired and frustrated, and he was very worried about the possibly negative meaning of the visions he had had the night before. He started a mitigated conversation about them with the old woman.

In the centre of the garden was the big mango tree with its branches widely spread all over the garden to make a secure shelter. Amanoofwom had noticed that there was a tiny opening through the leaves of the mango tree just over his head, making the sky visible to him.

But, about an hour later, while speaking with the old woman, Amanoofwom realised that the opening over his head seemed to be widening little by little. He did not really see it widening. But he took notice that, each time he glanced at it, it seemed a bit wider than it had been the last time he looked at it. He did not make it a big issue, however. He just kept sitting there talking and looking at the sky from time to time through the opening. But, as the minutes strode past, it became so clear that the opening had really become gaping and it was now occupying more than a quarter of the whole shelter over Amanoofwom's head.

There was a relaxing wind blowing through the vegetation. And

Amanoofwom, quite rational, thought that the wind might have been strong enough to blow a branch apart for a while, leaving the opening that widely agape for a few seconds. And he kept looking up there expecting the wind to slacken and release the branch back to its normal place. Unfortunately, this did not happen. The opening remained steadily wide.

Amanoofwom became quite curious about the opening. Then, as he had his head down looking thoughtfully at the ground and trying to find out what was going on, and at the same time as he was conversing with the old woman, he felt as if somebody was holding his head in order to force it up, saying to him close to his right ear: "Look! Look up! Can you see this?"

It took a few seconds for Amanoofwom to obey, as he wanted first to settle the question about the opening. He then thought that it was the old woman who had approached him to hold his head and ask him to look up. What did she want him to see that could be more important than the problem of the opening?

Amanoofwom remained so preoccupied that he was tempted to ask the old woman to hold on a moment, and maybe tell her what was annoying him. But once he straightened up to start saying something to the old woman, he was hit by two surprises. First, the old woman was still sitting about two metres away and was not holding his head; nor was she asking him to look up. And, as Amanoofwom turned around to see who was there, he saw nobody; but there was somebody close to him holding his head and talking to him. "Look up!" the voice said again, while the hands were exercising a light pressure on his temples. He touched his right temple with his hand and felt no other hand on it. He then decided to look up and see what was going on up there. And, once he looked up, what he saw was indescribable. The opening was even wider, and, through it, he saw Aduma's face. It was there all bright, suspended in the air and looking at him serenely in a form that was not very different from what he had often seen on some 'popular posters' of Aduma displayed at some sacred places.

Amanoofwom panicked for a few seconds, but then he kept quiet, almost numbed, on his bench, looking at Aduma. His torpor lasted no less than 30 seconds before he came around and began to wonder what was going on. Was it real that Aduma could be seen so genuinely and so truly?

Tata Mba, the old Meyaba's assistant practitioner, walked into the garden just at that very time to have a short chat with the student. He had not seen him the night before.

Mba did not live with the old Meyaba. He lived about a mile away from the holy place. And not only that; even at times of intensive practice, when he would come to spend two or three days in the temple, he would spend three quarters of his time out, always sent around for something by Meyaba.

Once he had walked into the garden and looked at Amanoofwom, he was straightway warned by the sixth sense that the student was experiencing something grave, and refrained from talking to him. There is always a sign that tells that practitioners that a student is in connection with the spirits. They often say: "He is on the trip. So do not disturb."

Amanoofwom kept looking at Aduma in amazement. And while he was realising how real and true his experience was, he heard the pounding words of Aduma strike his heart with an incredible power.

Thus spoke Aduma: "Son, you have knocked at my door and it has been opened to you. Will you still doubt that my door can be opened to men?

"You have sought me and you have found me just as I am. Will you still doubt that I am alive and that men like you can see me?

"You have asked for my grace and it has been given to you. Will you still doubt that my grace can be given to men?

"I will give men the things they want if they ask for them.

"But a man may still feel unfilled if he ignores what he has already received.

"Your worries have come to me and I will stand you by in your strife.

"I will show you the way to truth. But, behold, if on a mango tree one single mango springs up and turns ripe out of the right tide, it will be eaten by one single man or very few. But, just the way five loaves and three fish fed 5,000, so one single mango can feed a whole world, for nothing is impossible to me.

"It is true that, if you light your torch to see your way ahead, only five people following you will follow the beam; but the rest will follow the line. But, in a world in which all men seem to be fond of the torch, whereas they are not all among the first five following you, you will tend to have a torch for every five people on the line. And the line will tend to break into several lines of five people following their own torches. Will they all follow the same way?

"There is just one way, however. And I will show you that way. But, remember, if the single mango does not feed the whole world, who will survive then?"

Amanoofwom heard all these things from a source that he could not locate. Aduma was suspended aloft in the air in front of him. But the words he heard did not come straight from the figure. He heard them wafting from all parts of the space, and especially from his own heart. Amanoofwom also noted that the people he was sitting with, and especially the old woman, did not seem to partake. He seemed to be the only one to see Aduma and the only one to hear the words.

Then Amanoofwom wanted to speak to Aduma, and in particular to ask him some questions about certain things that annoyed him. But he felt very embarrassed. Firstly, because, if he spoke, this would make him a fool insofar as his interlocutor was neither seen nor heard by the people around him. Whom would he then be speaking to? Secondly, he was so surprised and shocked by the vision itself that he nearly lost his ability to formulate relevant questions and pronounce them soundly.

In fact, Amanoofwom did not really find anything to blame in Aduma's words. But the problem was Aduma himself. Why should Amanoofwom meet him? What could really be the relationship, or simply the link, between them? Amanoofwom was a Fanghish following a Fanghish spiritual rite; and Aduma was a *Yudi* having done the things of the *Yudi.* They had nothing in common.

Besides, in the Fanghish society, Aduma's word was said to have been brought by the invaders. And some local dissident and rebel groups that stood against the invaders would think that Aduma's word had nothing to do with the truths of the Fanghish god. They would accuse the invaders of having brought them a message from their own god for the purposes of deceiving them. And Amanoofwom seemed to be sympathetic enough to these groups to be critical of the revelation of Aduma.

He grew very eager to speak to Aduma to really discover what Aduma was up to. Why should he interfere in a Fanghish traditional rite? What were his rights to do so? What were his powers to penetrate a foreign spiritual system? Moreover, Amanoofwom did not remember trying to find Aduma. Why did Aduma tell him "you have sought me and you have found me"? It was like the stigmata of the agnostic.

While Amanoofwom was fighting with all these questions in his mind and heart, Aduma's face began to fade away; and it went off leaving but the white clouds, which also hid themselves behind the leaves of the mango tree as the wide opening closed up a few seconds later. Amanoofwom prayed in his heart, begging Aduma to come back and make things clear between them. Unfortunately, Aduma never came again. Thus, exasperated and rebelled, Amanoofwom decided not to talk about Aduma to anybody, not even to the old Meyaba. So he kept Aduma hushed up for the two years that followed the vision. In the meantime, he learnt many other things.

But, one day, by the seventh year of Amanoofwom's sojourn in the temple, as the time had come to talk about Aduma in the old man's teaching programme, Meyaba tackled the question while he was in a study session with Amanoofwom.

Thus spoke Meyaba: "Aduma was a good man. Aduma came to

teach truth to man, and he did it very courageously. The things he said are very important for our existence now and afterwards."

But, after saying this, Meyaba kept staring at Amanoofwom with a meaningful expression, as if he suspected some kind of reluctance in the way Amanoofwom had somatically received these words. The new world from which Amanoofwom had come was indeed, surprisingly, suffering from a strong spiritual schism. While the invaders had brought up the majority of young people in their scheme of conceptions and beliefs, a few who had a traditional background remained sceptical as they grew suspicious of the sincerity and truthfulness of the invaders. They perceived the death of something precious in the building of such a new world. And, as it has been said above, Amanoofwom was sympathetic to them. And, to Amanoofwom, it was so bizarre that the old Meyaba, as a local spiritual teacher and practitioner, seemed to have a particular interest for Aduma in his teachings. That was not logical! It was not understandable. Was the old Meyaba spiritually corrupt, or what?

The old Meyaba went on, saying: "Aduma wanted to create a perfect world of love in which there would be no evil. He wanted to create a world of beauty and greatness; a world of prosperity and happiness; a world of respect and safety; a world of enlightenment and wisdom; a world in which men would share the marvels of the universe and be exalted as high as the children of the Very High. But the world did not listen to him. His contemporaries even prosecuted him and punished him severely for his visions; and some of those who followed him were also prosecuted after him."

"How could he think that such an order could be established on the earth? Was he a lunatic? Were there no psychologists or psychiatrists to examine him and declare him ill so that he would not be prosecuted as a normal person?"

"No," answered the old man. "Aduma was not a lunatic. He said things that were true and possible in our world; but these things were shocking in the sense that the world was divided between masters and captives. And masters took great advantage of their captives, so much so that setting them free would certainly make them go bankrupt. So they condemned Aduma in order not to lose slaves. "

"Are all masters against Aduma's words?" asked Amanoofwom.

"There exists not a single master in this world who can agree with Aduma. Aduma's words were, are, and will always be a threat to any master," responded Meyaba.

"But, if that is true, how can you be justified if you know that Aduma's words were brought to us by our masters? I rather find that Aduma's words are meant to serve the masters, since they keep them and make captives through them. Besides, the book in which Aduma's words are written encourages captivity, commanding a slave to be obedient to his master. Why should we, then, keep such words if we want to restore our nation?"

The old Meyaba knew that the points were relevant, and that this was the occasion to tell the truth to the young student. He approached Amanoofwom unexpectedly, looking at him fixedly with the big rings under his blinking eyes.

And thus spoke Meyaba: "Son, there are no abominations in the words that were brought to us. If there is something positive that has come to us from those years of invasion, it is the words of Aduma. But the people of our nation, instead of reading the words, they would rather listen to the corrupt and deceitful among Aduma's ambassadors, who always read them the other way round to make more slaves. What you should note is that slaves are always ignorant and gullible. For example, Aduma had taught that a good citizen should serve his king and be faithful to him. But they turned 'good citizen' into 'good slave', 'faithful' into 'obedient', and 'king' into 'master'. So they deceived their slaves with such a tricky transposition.

"I tell you, my son, the only thing you can blame the power of the Very High for is that it works even for evil purposes. If you know how to use it, no matter if your intention is to do evil, it will work for you even though you might not succeed to the full, but it will work to a certain extent. And, if there is somebody to suffer from the effects of your evil deeds, he will suffer even though he might not be destroyed totally, but he will still have suffered to a certain extent.

"Those who brought the word to us brought it for their own purposes, and they have been successful to a certain extent, and we have been destroyed to a certain extent. But the question today should no longer be centred on their partial success or our partial decay. The question is: will we now start reading the words ourselves instead of listening to the traitors of the words?"

The discussion on the contradictions around Aduma's word lasted for months before Amanoofwom and the old Meyaba came to some preliminary agreements. Amanoofwom was meticulous in seeking the truth about Aduma and his word. But many doubts were assuaged through these talks with the old man, and equally through some additional revelations that came to the young student over his last two years in the temple.

Amanoofwom lived under the old Meyaba's stewardship and custody for nine years, during which he got trained to understand the rules of knowledge, the laws of justice, the principles of wisdom, and the order of the unseen. And he was prepared to meet Mefan as the ultimate experience of a good student of mysteries among the Fanghish. He had to go for a seven-day fasting stay in Minsisim Forest, where he would meet some invisible masters, and especially Mefan, the symbol of the Fanghish spiritual inheritance.

CHAPTER 9

FACING MEFAN

Minsisim Forest, or the forest of the spirits, was very famous for being the host of the spirits of the nation. It was to Minsisim Forest that you would go if you wanted to meet special spiritual figures, to which you could pose the most intriguing quandaries of your life. And they would answer you thoroughly, with exact precision. But, before you could go to Minsisim Forest, you needed a spiritual visa issued by an accredited spiritual teacher and practitioner; otherwise, you would not come back from Minsisim.

When Amanoofwom left for Minsisim Forest, he had only some matting, a calabash, a spear and a knife. Out of the four elements, he was allowed to use three. But he had to choose which one he would never use during his stay in Minsisim Forest. And he did it cleverly. But nobody can tell the one that he chose not to use.

Amanoofwom set out for the mysterious forest at five in the morning that last Thursday of his ninth year in the temple. It was a long way to go. It took him ten hours' walking to get to the depths of Minsisim Forest, where he was to settle in for a seven-day period of fasting. It was down a thickly wooded valley in the middle of the forest. The ground was covered with dead leaves and dry twigs, and it was a bit swampy as the sedimentation was thick and moist.

Amanoofwom walked up a hill looking for some drier ground where he could sit and rest. But once up the hill he discovered a downward slope ahead, from the bottom of which he seemed to perceive sounds of water gurgling. He then decided to walk down the slope instead of sitting at the top of the hill. He got down the slope, tiptoeing to avoid the noise of the leaves under his feet as he walked. It was a smooth valley with a brook flowing along. Amanoofwom discovered amazing sand beds and flat rocks all along the two banks. He got near the brook after sneaking his way down through the massive trees, and stood there for a while to mull over the wonderful outlook.

A series of vague quandaries came across his mind. How was he going to survive the seven days in such a strangeness and desolation, however beautiful and relaxing the environment was? How did God create such a beautiful place in the middle of the forest? How could sand banks and rocks be so ordered – as if fitted out by some kind of marshalling service in charge of developing special and exotic places? He sat on a bank near the brook to observe the water gurgling through several little reefs along the stream. It was a little sandy embankment. He remained seated there, motionless, for about two hours, meditating and praying.

A locust made a sudden shrill yell by his side. Amanoofwom was severely startled, jumping on his numbed buttocks like a crippled dancer. A band of birds that were pecking at the pistils of a heavily flowering tree flew off, terrified by Amanoofwom's bewildered leap. It was already around five in the afternoon. Darkness was approaching, and the young student was a bit worried and frightened. He was already used to the terrors of the temple, where he could scream, pour out his feelings, and be hugged by somebody who would warmly comfort him. But here, in Minsisim, nobody was near. Who could save his life in case of any kindred attacks?

Amanoofwom spent five monotonous days lost in the wilderness of Minsisim Forest, without meeting any special figures. He started feeling a bit disappointed. It was true that he was frightened and very afraid of meeting horribly petrifying beings. But meeting nothing would be worse than facing the horrors, for the reason why he had gone to Minsisim was precisely to brave its horrors. Eventually, on the sixth day, Mefan ended up revealing himself to Amanoofwom. It was by half past two in the afternoon.

The announcement of Mefan's arrival was a ravaging storm in the middle of the forest. A large part of the forest was violently shaken about. But, ironically, only the riverside on which Amanoofwom was settled was shaken by the storm. The other riverside was miraculously quiet. Amanoofwom started running around bent over, trying to dodge the enormous branches that were falling as they were broken from high by the violent hurricane blowing the trees around.

Amanoofwom ran down to the river with a determined intention of crossing it to save his life. But he remembered the advice that the old Meyaba gave him. He had said to him: "When going to Minsisim, if you ever come across a river you should stop at the river-side you have arrived at and remain there. Don't you ever try to cross the river!"

Amanoofwom was stuck, and his heart was throbbing so hard, trying to work out what would happen should he cross the river. He would certainly be lost; lost forever!

Soon afterwards, strangely, the storm calmed down. And, as Amanoofwom turned back to take a look at the natural damage the storm had caused, what he saw was indescribable. Mefan was just behind him. Amanoofwom started wildly and fell back into the river, quivering like a fever-stricken namby pamby in the water. Amanoofwom was terrified at the sight of Mefan. But he gathered his strength to stand up, all shivering and shaking, to face the thing.

Mefan appeared to Amanoofwom in the form of a big black snake. It was true that Mefan would often visit special babies as they crawled by themselves and played in a yard. Mefan would appear to them in the form of a little python, and the baby would look at it as a self-moving toy, and then start playing with it. But the toy would always disappear once it sensed an elderly person approaching. Amanoofwom might have met Mefan in that form when he was a baby. But nobody could know about it, since nobody could have seen it. Only Amanoofwom himself could know; but he never made any pronouncement about the matter.

And then, in Minsisim Forest, at the final stage of a student's exploration of mysteries, he would rather reveal himself in other forms, depending on the message symbolism. To some, he would come as an eagle; to others as a lion; to others as a huge lizard, to others as an owl, etc.

But, to Amanoofwom, he came in his original form. Why?

Perhaps Amanoofwom was to be a great liberator. Because, as it was known, the god of each people takes the shape of a serpent if the message to be delivered is to free them from any kind of captivity or a plague. In the Fanghish symbolism, the serpent stands for conquest, awareness and salvation. Was Amanoofwom going to be a conqueror, a sensitiser, or a saviour?

Mefan was enormous; but Amanoofwom could not evaluate his length since he never saw him crawl. He just appeared as he was, coiled around himself, forming a huge heap on the ground with his head at the top. Amanoofwom had neither seen nor heard of the existence of such big snakes anywhere in the world. It was extremely frightening. But Amanoofwom was prepared to keep quiet in front of anything he saw. And he stood there, lost in the depths of Minsisim Forest, facing a full-size Mefan; just as he had never imagined he would be.

That was the highest vision of Mefan ever achieved. Even those who had seen Mefan in other forms were said to have achieved the highest level of spiritual vision. They were said to have nothing left to see. They could die just after that vision and would not regret dying, for there was nothing to meet in life as beautiful and great as Mefan.

To start with, Mefan was bizarre! He was a black snake, but seemed to look like a spectrum at the same time. He was all colours. It was an overwhelming wonder and terrific amazement to see such a dazzling variegation on a monstrous beast. The whole forest was vibrating and gleaming with Mefan's colour reflection. Mefan seemed to be everywhere. It was scary. Amanoofwom did not know what to do and, above all, where to go. It was as if he was caught between Scylla and Charybdis.

Not only that, Mefan was a single snake, but – at times – he seemed to become two snakes that looked as if braided along, plaited together, and at other times he was perceived as just one snake, but double-headed.

Moreover, once Amanoofwom tried to courageously look into

Mefan's eyes, he found that they were rather like the piercing gaze of a human being.

And, more amazingly, the black spectrum of bipartite coil that was heaped in front of Amanoofwom was not really lying on the ground. Mefan was floating a few inches above the ground, while giving the impression of lying on it.

Another thing was that Mefan was really dangerous. His fangs were like a wolf's curved teeth. He could, therefore, hack you to shreds.

And more astonishing was the fact that Amanoofwom could see through Mefan. Therefore, Mefan was not completely opaque. He was somewhat translucent.

Amanoofwom took notice of all these wonders in a few seconds, just before beginning to wonder where such a phenomenal creature could really have come from. Was he dreaming? Was it a hallucination? What was going on?

The vision of Mefan was very different from the visions he had had in the temple, and different from the vision of Aduma. The visions at the temple were like flashing sparks, showing stealthy figures accompanied by faint voices. As for Aduma, he was suspended quite far away in the space, though his voice sounded near. But Mefan was just about three steps away in front of him.

While Amanoofwom continued his internal questioning, Mefan surprised him. He addressed him straightaway. And, once Mefan began to speak, Amanoofwom seemed to rather start perceiving some kind of blurred human face, with no neat traits that could be described, and his eyes became like lights, or nearly burning fires.

And thus spoke Mefan: "Young man, I saw your glory among the people of Odzab a long time ago, and I saw your evaporation from Nkole'e Engông. That is something you could not ward off."

Here, Mefan had just revealed to Amanoofwom that he was the reincarnation of one of the four brothers who had died in a calamity in Nkole'e Engông about 1,000 years earlier. Nkole'e Engông was the presidential palace of Odzab, the earlier name of the Fanghish nation, and it had been ruled over by four brothers who were said to have inherited incredible powers from the Spirit. They died in a miraculous whirlwind that wrapped the palace for fourteen days and reduced it to bits. The story was still told by the elders, but in fact nobody really took it seriously any longer in a modern world in which real stories of amazing facts from the remote past were deemed mythical. Anyway, the truth was there and Mefan went on speaking.

"The accident that destroyed your brothers and you could not be avoided in any way. Destiny is the most tragic thing in our cosmic system. It comes when it has to come. Nothing can stop its march. It destroys what it has to destroy and builds what it has to build. Nothing can avoid it. But, to him [Destiny], everything is Construction. Destruction and Construction are both constructive. And man has to make them both constructive within destiny, unless he voluntarily chooses otherwise.

"It is true that, if you lose a limb in an accident, you cannot get it back. You have lost forever the additional help that the lost limb could have provided. That is a pity. But watch out! The lost limb can, rather, stimulate you to create something much more powerful to replace it. You will not have your limb back; which is a tragedy, but you will have a more powerful replacement.

"The event that destroyed your bothers and you has proved to be calamitous. But that time has gone past; and, today, you have been chosen to come back into this world, and I have seen your birth.

"You have grown up in my presence, and I have seen your march up to Minsisim. I have been with you all this time; and, now, you have seen me. You are the elect among the Fanghish and I give you my blessings.

"You have been chosen to teach truth to your people. This is the hardest task that may be given to a man. Sometimes you will be unseen by the blind, unheard by the deaf, reproved by the fearful, and insulted by the arrogant. In a word, you will be rejected. You will be challenged by the all-knowing people of your world. But you will have to be wise to carry out your task. Wisdom is therefore the key to your mission. But, if you want to be wise, do not listen to the people of the world, for their conception of wisdom is deceitful.

"A wise man is not an emotional subject. An emotional chap is a fool. A fool always ends up delighting in things he had abhorred in the beginning. A fool is like your wife. The first day you meet her, she says 'no'. But she ends up bearing your name, cooking your meals, and suckling your children. Do not forget that a depraved man has no friends; not even from his peers; but he will have a wife. Do you know why?"

Amanoofwom did not answer the question, and Mefan continued: "A fool is also like a child. A child is an unconscious being. A newborn child is very wise in the sense that it can hear and see everything, but it will understand neither what is heard nor what is seen. A child is sound in the sense that it makes a noise, but it does not say a word; for 'a child that cries, there you have a child'. Do not follow the fool!

"A wise man is not an intellectual, for intellect wanders. An intellectual is the one to whom everything is right and wrong at the same time. An intellectual has no notion of truth. He is trained to make everything debatable. He practises sophism. Yet sophism is ignorance, for knowledge is a way out. Do not follow the intellectual!

"A wise man is not an intelligent bloke, for intelligence is like beauty: you do not labour to get it. A wise man, on the other hand, requires much effort to be wise. Do not follow the intelligent!

"A wise man is not an experienced worker, for experience is like a literary review. It is a compilation of stories in different contexts, but not an efficient formula set up for practical use. In your nation, you will find that elderly people are automatically deemed wise because of their long experience of life. But I tell you: not all those who have lived long are wise. Some of them are but dustbins into which only rubbish has been cast over several decades. But your people call them wise on account of the grey beard. Do not follow the experienced!

"A wise man is not a taster. A wise man does not try things and see what happens before veering around. A wise man chooses his way and adheres to it. Do not follow the tasters!

"Do not follow any of these specimens, but be wise!"

None of these words really came to Amanoofwom the way you hear somebody speaking to you face to face or on the phone. He perceived them, rather, in the form of images visible in his mind or in the space. For example, in the first counter-definition of wisdom, Amanoofwom would see a man approaching a woman as to ask her out, but the woman would spit in his face. And then afterwards he would see them again in the following picture, living in the same house as husband and wife, and the woman would be cooking and serving meals and suckling a child. Then there came something like a big cross covering the picture, so as to show that this is not wisdom. Then there came a lapse before the next series of images start rolling.

After this, there reigned a deadly *silence* between Amanoofwom and Mefan. Amanoofwom ceased to shiver. Mefan had become somehow familiar to him. He could now look at him straight in his eyes. Amanoofwom wanted to ask a question. But, to be honest, that was not the kind of being you could try to speak to. You can speak to something strange but only if it, at least, *looks* human to a certain extent. Mefan had nothing human, except the background perceptions that made his face turn into something close to a manly, hazy zombie. But that was not enough to make you trustful about his human nature.

While Amanoofwom was standing in silence, observing the legendary snake, he heard something like a voice from inside saying: "Now that you are wise and anointed, I give you my blessings and order you to go to your nation and teach them the truths of life. Close your eyes."

Amanoofwom first thought that the words he heard were springing out of his own consciousness, and that he was certainly making up self-imagined speeches in his mind. Anyway, Amanoofwom's mind had become very prolific in formulating and expressing questions, explanations, declarations, requests, evocative statements, etc. Besides, some of the spirits that he had met had equally used internal communication with him. But Amanoofwom would sometimes be very confused about differentiating between his own thoughts and the messages of the interlocutors. Here, he was experiencing the same confusion. He could not really tell whether it was Mefan, another spirit or himself who was speaking. But the voice burst out again: "I say, close your eyes now."

This time, overcome by fear, Amanoofwom obeyed unconditionally. He closed his eyes in front of Mefan. His main fear was that of becoming a sacrifice rather than a messenger. The idea that Mefan could just swallow him while his eyes were closed was consuming him terribly. And, above all, a few seconds after he closed his eyes, he started feeling something cold and gluey touching the top of his head. Amanoofwom stiffened up with fear. The idea of running away came across his mind for a tenth of a second, but he rejected it, not because he could not run, but because it would not be worth running to escape something that had occupied the whole forest. There was no place where Mefan was not omnipresent. He was everywhere. Why, then, run? Run to go where? Amanoofwom just kept quiet, waiting to find himself deep inside the beast.

Gradually, the moist and sticky thing became heavier and heavier on Amanoofwom's head. He felt preoccupied by the idea of knowing what was on his head. But there was no way he could cheat on Mefan. He could neither open his eyes nor send his hand to feel what the soggy thing on his head actually was. Amanoofwom waited for more than an hour with his eyes closed, and did not get swallowed by Mefan. But he started feeling very uncomfortable. He was getting very cold, as he could not get out of the freezing river waters; and his feet were now hurting. But there was nothing he could do about it.

Fortunately, a couple of hours later, the heavy, clammy burden suddenly began to lighten until Amanoofwom could not feel it any more. He did not really feel it getting off his head, however. He then thought that his head had certainly got so used to the thing that he could not feel it any more even though it was still there. But there was no possibility of verifying such a hypothesis. And Amanoofwom kept standing painfully.

Another hour passed, and Amanoofwom became so uncomfortable and exasperated that he decided to open his eyes and see what was going on whatever the consequences. And, once he opened his eyes, he saw no trace of Mefan. It was now about six o'clock in the afternoon. Amanoofwom was terrified by the dubious absence of Mefan. Anyway, Mefan could reappear instantly if need be.

Amanoofwom felt like going back home straightaway to escape any further mutilation. But he remembered that he had to complete seven days in Minsisim even though Mefan had come on the sixth day. God! One more night in such an anxiety!

Amanoofwom set out for Edwangane the following morning at nine o'clock, and got to the old man's village by one o'clock in the afternoon. And, according to Meyaba, Amanoofwom had nothing more to do in the temple. He could go back to Messanza, immediately if he wanted. But Amanoofwom was so tired that he postponed his journey to Messanza until the following day.

CHAPTER 10

THE RETURN

Back in Messanza, Amanoofwom was to meet his friends again, and especially Ebongué, the dearest. Ebongué had kept in touch with Amanoofwom's mother over the years. He acted like the missing son. He would pay regular visits to her, and sometimes spend a whole Sunday in Mbeng's house, along with his wife and children. Other times Mbeng would be invited to his house and Ebongué's wife would serve her a good meal and plait her hair. Ebongué was extraordinarily sympathetic.

So, now that Amanoofwom was back, the first person his mother talked to him about was Ebongué. Upon that recognition, Amanoofwom decided to meet Ebongué the same day he arrived in Messanza, at four in the afternoon on a tropical sunny Friday. Ebongué was therefore the first person that Amanoofwom visited after his mother. Mbeng suggested to Amanoofwom to call Ebongué to break the news to him on the phone. But Amanoofwom refused that idea.

"I just want to surprise him in his house."

"But, Aman!"

"Yes."

"Aman!"

"What is the matter, Mum?"

"Aman, I have to tell you something important first."

"What is it?"

"Your father is back. He came back just a year after you went away."

"What? Listen, Mum…Just forget about that story. Let me see Ebongué first, please!"

Amanoofwom slammed the door behind him with a little bit of nervousness, and he soon jumped into a taxi to Oveng district, where he met Ebongué in the most exciting way. The old friend was now married, and father of two boys, and was holding a job as a director of something in the tourism office. He was also a part-time lecturer at university. Ebongué felt very embarrassed as he introduced his family to his friend and talked to him about his job with considerable reservations. He thought that this would be shocking to his friend. Amanoofwom would certainly have the feeling, as we say, that "he was late in life" – or, bluntly, that he had definitely missed it. But Amanoofwom was already a different person. He had already lost sensitivity for social values and objectives, especially in such a decadent world. Amanoofwom even greeted his friend's wife and children with a remarkable indifference, which could be interpreted in various ways.

Ebongué was sure that Amanoofwom's lack of enthusiasm was an expression of jealousy. It was true that such a friend, and especially Amanoofwom, could never be jealous, however, whatever the volume of his friend's fortune compared to his own indigence. Moreover, Amanoofwom was not needy as a result of being unfit or anything like that. Amanoofwom was an enlightened boy – not to say super-intelligent. Nonetheless, the two friends shared good food and a little bit of wine. Amanoofwom then went back to his mother's house in the evening, at half past six. He was very preoccupied, however, by the story of his father, who had disappeared while he was but a baby and who had come back a year after Amanoofwom went to Mikolongo. The boy went to the old man's village when he was thirteen, which meant that his father came back fourteen years after his disappearance. Where was he? Why did he go there, wherever he was? What had he been doing there? Why did he come back then? Amanoofwom travelled all the way from Ebongué's house back to his mother's trying to figure out what was going on. And, as he was approaching the house, he saw a little boy who entered the front door of his mother's house just a few steps ahead of him. The boy dumped his rucksack on the dining table while Amanoofwom was stepping up to the doorway.

"Good evening." Amanoofwom greeted the boy.

"Hi," muttered the little boy, looking dubiously at the young man.

Mbeng recognised Amanoofwom's voice while doing the washing up in the kitchen. She didn't know that the little boy was in the lounge as well, and thought that Amanoofwom was rather greeting her.

"Are you back?" She started a kind conversation so as to seek softer ways of tackling the unfinished story.

"Yes, I'm back."

"How was it?"

"Very exciting, Mum. Ebongué has become a father of two so quickly. People do not really sleep in this Messanza."

"Did you say 'Mum'?" asked the little boy frenetically.

"Yes. What is the matter?"

"Are you Aman, my elder brother?"

"Are you my brother?" Amanoofwom replied, asking the same question of the little boy.

The little boy had always known about Amanoofwom, his elder brother, who had gone on a trip to Edwangane, in Mikolongo, and who would come back sooner or later. His mother always told him that his brother was the most intelligent child she had ever seen in her life. And she would make it relevant by saying to the little boy: "I do not say this because he is my son. Anyway, you are my son too, but I have never said that you are that clever!"

Now, as Mbeng heard the conversation between the two brothers, she rushed into the lounge:

"Oh, my God! I just didn't know you were here too, Atôm. When did you come in?"

"Just right now."

"Did you then come together?"

"No. I was just walking behind him."

"Oh God! Atôm, this is Amanoofwom."

She did not need to complete the sentence with the phrase "your elder brother". The little boy jumped with joy, hooking himself around his elder brother's neck.

"Where were you when I came this afternoon?" asked Amanoofwom, stifled by Atôm's grip around his neck.

"And you, where did you go like that, just after coming back?"

"I had to see Ebongué."

"Oh yes! Ebongué is fantastic. Look! He bought me a bike last month. Come and see! Here it is," Atôm said, grabbing Amanoofwom's hand and dragging him back into the garage.

Amanoofwom and his brother kept playing outside because of the excitement of the little boy. But 'Big Bra', in the deepest recesses of his heart, was more excited by the prospect of discovering what had happened for his father to leave and come back fourteen years later. What a wazzock! Was it an accident? Did he want to get away from something? What really happened? What a weird coincidence! He went after Amanoofwom's birth, and came back after Amanoofwom's departure for Mikolongo. Was he going to disappear again as Amanoofwom was back? Was Amanoofwom the problem, or was it just a coincidence?

"Hey, boys, will you stop playing now; the dinner is ready!"

"No, Mum. I ate too much with Ebongué. I really can't add anything into my stomach now."

The little boy might have been hungry, but he was too excited to give up playing with his brother for food.

"Go and eat. You have been at school for the whole day. You must be hungry. Besides, it is dark now. We will bike again tomorrow."

Amanoofwom and his younger brother came in and carried on an interminable conversation, which was eventually cut short by the advent of a visitor.

At eight in the evening, a man came in through the front door without even knocking. The man arrived while the mother and the two sons were seated in the lounge chatting, and Amanoofwom was eagerly expecting his mother to kick off the story. Perhaps it was too embarrassing to start such a talk in the presence of the little boy. The little boy had never known that his father had vanished after his elder brother's birth, and that he just came back nearly a year before his own birth. Nobody knows why the parents concealed the story from the little boy. Perhaps they did not want the child to have a negative perception of his family's history as he grew older. He would certainly think that his father was an irresponsible man, a delinquent. He would certainly think of his mother going with another man, or even different men, in fourteen years to fill in the void. He would probably regard his elder brother as having grown up as a bastard. Anyway, he was aware of nothing.

Now the visitor walked into the lounge, where he found Mbeng, Atôm and a third person chatting. Who was that young man? At first he thought it was Ebongué. He was the only young male whom he would expect to find there at any time, talking with Mbeng and Atôm. But, as he got nearer and nearer, just before calling Ebongué mechanically, he saw somebody else.

"Mbólán." (This was to say: "Good evening to everybody.")

"Hà," the three responded.

Mbeng didn't know how to start introducing people to one another. But things started to look quite bizarre to the little boy. If it was true that young people changed a lot as they grew up, and certainly that Atôm's elder brother had changed too much in nine years, this was not the case for his father. He had not changed at all. How could it be explained that his elder brother seemed not to recognise his father? The young boy expected to see his brother hug their father hard once he saw him. He didn't even need to think about it. It was natural to him. Moreover, for the young boy, the nine years were not really nine years. He had started having the ability to really recognise people maybe five or six years earlier. And, since he had known his father, he had not changed at all. He was always the same, and Amanoofwom should have known him like that too. Anyway, children do not really know that people change as they grow older. They even think that their parents were born exactly as they are, or that they have always been like that eternally. But now, something was going on.

"Hey! What is wrong, Aman? Don't you recognise Daddy?"

Mbeng was shaking with fright. The secret was out! What a misfortune! What a curse! But, suddenly, Amanoofwom stood up wisely and hugged his father.

"Aman! I don't know what to say…I am desperately sorry…"

"No, no, no, Daddy. I don't need your apologies. Sit down."

Amanoofwom was impressively wise. "Where have you been?" he asked, looking into his father's eyes. But this question was difficult to answer. Ongongora didn't know how to start the explanation about his disappearance 22 years earlier, when his newborn son was but a few days old. It was certain that, whatever the excuses, nobody would forgive such a horrendous act. The family was on the brink of total disarray. This was not what Amanoofwom was asking for, however. The question was clearer once he resumed saying, "I mean, do you work?"

"Oh, yes! But I can't really take a real job now. I am still hiding."

"Hiding from what?" Amanoofwom asked, surprised.

"You know, son, I do not really know why God destined certain things to be the way they are…" Ongongora started an emotional discourse to explain a hard situation to his son.

In the meantime, Mbeng asked the little boy to follow her into the bedroom for some reading exercises. "Listen, Atôm, you'd better show me what you did at school this afternoon and leave your father and you brother to chat for a while," she shouted, to divert the boy's attention from the conversation, and straightaway she dragged her younger son into his room.

In fact, Ongongora had been abducted by a group of police officers after being suspected of plotting a coup, with some of his friends, to overthrow the fiendish political system of his country. He was then held in secret detention for about two months. But, as he sensed that death would be his only fate after that imprisonment, he sought ways and means to get out, like a commando. And, after escaping detention, he fled straightaway to a foreign nation as a political refugee. And, since then, he had not had a chance to contact his family until he courageously set out to return fourteen years later. Who would not understand and sympathise with such as case?

The following morning, Amanoofwom went for a walk around Messanza with Atôm, his younger brother, to take a look at all that might have altered over nine years. But the outlook was rather bleak. Instead of visiting what had evolved, he rather met everything that had decayed. Messanza was a small town of about 400,000 people, though, in the subcontinent, this is enough to be a city. The whole town was on low-lying land on the Atlantic coast, in the middle of what is called the Gulf of Guinea. It was naturally protected by a mountain chain that formed a natural semi-circular fence around the town, from Mikolongo in the north to Bissibang in the south, through the Nkole'e Engông Hills that were part of the chain at the back of the town. The inner town was, therefore, a vast plain extending down to the seafront, where there was a long stretch of sandy beach, reclined and sprawled with hazardous rubble covering almost the whole sandy surface and filling the wavy coastal sea waters.

That is one of the things that shocked Amanoofwom. Such a beautiful site was in such a dilapidated state; and no public amenity could be found nearby; no rescue teams; and no safety equipment. The site and its lovers were abandoned to themselves, and providence alone would decide about those who had to go and those who had to remain alive. It seemed that there existed no public order, no local authorities in charge of anything. Or else, if such institutions existed, they just did not give a hoot about anything. Yet people's lives were at stake.

The second thing that Amanoofwom noticed concerned the street pavements. The gutters were but traps. They were open all along the pavements. Suffice it that you tripped, you would find yourself swimming in the toxic and stinky mess at the bottom of an open culvert. You would have your teeth broken; you head cracked; your spine damaged; your ankle sprained; your arm fractured, and you could end up joining your ancestors. The pavements themselves were covered all over with rotten waste material from households and companies. It seemed that there were no refuse collectors. The only one that existed there was the tide of heavy rains. Nature is very good at performing tasks that people should provide for themselves.

The third thing was the condition of the roads themselves. They were all rough and bumpy. The tar was damaged everywhere, leaving deep wells of muck all along the roads. Only four-wheel drives could go in the town centre.

The fourth thing was the town planning. A lot of districts in the heart of the town centre were just enclaves. Even if you had a car you would still have to walk, for the nearest road to your house could be about half a mile away. You had to park your car that far away, and leave it to the mercy of night technicians. And, if a member of your family fell sick, you had to carry him on your shoulders and walk half a mile before you got to your car.

The fifth thing concerned the popular markets. They were nothing more than squalid jumbles. Food was displayed on sticky and mucky surfaces in the open air and covered with thousands of infected flies. The merchants would say that nobody could die of filthy and infected food because, according to them, dark-skinned people were born with special protective blood cells against microbes of all kinds. They called this 'kimbarranko immunity'. The word 'kimbarranko' was borrowed from the Bamiliké language and it meant 'superior' or 'strong'. But none of those who praised this kimbarranko immunity of the dark-skinned people of the subcontinent could have taken notice of the fact that the 50-year life expectancy of the subcontinent was a sufficient evidence of the premature decay of bodies that had been excessively attacked and gnawed up by microbes of all types. This is something that has nothing to do with your belief in God. You cannot pray for it. God Himself does not fight against bacteriological laws. If you are damaged, you are damaged.

The sixth thing was the dilapidated state of the schools. Amanoofwom had an elder brother called Essône-Nkombot.

Essône-Nkombot was the son of Nkombot-Evung, who was the brother of Taht'Ndong-Evung and Ongongor'Evung, Amanoofwom's own father. The three brothers were born of Evung-Mendang, the throat-chopper. In fact, Evung-Mendang had been a gladiator in the Fanghish way about 70 years earlier. That is another story.

Actually, Essône-Nkombot was Amanoofwom's cousin. But he was regarded as his brother because, in the Fanghish family conception, the notion of uncle does not exist. Your uncle is your father, for he is the brother of your father. That is why they call him *ndzihm'a éssa*, which means 'father by blood extension', or – when literally translated, it means – 'parallel father'. The son of your parallel father is, therefore, your parallel brother. The term 'parallel' disappears at the level of the children, however, for they never say *ndzihm'a mohn-ñangh*, or *ndzihm'a ndôm*, or *ndzihm'a kál*. They just say *mohn-ñangh* [brother of male or sister of female], or *ndôm* [brother of female], or *kál* [sister of male]. Thus, Essône-Nkombot, being Amanoofwom's brother by blood extension, was simply regarded as his brother.

Essône-Nkombot was a teacher in a military primary school. He was himself a serviceman. He invited Amanoofwom to share a meal with him during his lunch break in a restaurant no far from the school. Amanoofwom got there a few minutes before lunchtime to have a good look around the school. The school was a little clutter of kind of slums at the back of a yard covered with untrimmed shrubland. The most visible rubbish that littered the grassy yard were pieces of rafter, sharp stones, and metallic parts of broken cars and motorbikes. Only some paths snaked through the little bushy area. That was quite risky on a site designed for vulnerable children.

Getting near the school, Amanoofwom perceived a man in the posture of a vigilante standing on the other side of the little bush but it looked likelier that the man was a teacher. Amanoofwom shouted to him, asking for his brother. The man vaguely pointed at a corner by the slums, shouting back to Amanoofwom "C2A", while his facial expression indicated a pretty bad mood. The man was holding a wooden cane. He might have just flogged a very annoying subject, and he was still feeling furious.

Once Amanoofwom got to the door that was marked C2A, he found his brother teaching in a room of 150 children, half of whom were sitting on the dusty and filthy floor. Shame!

"Essône! What is this?"

"Aman, just don't talk about it."

"How do you manage?"

"I just do my best. The genii who can understand what I say are blessed by their ancestors. As for the dolt who cannot get anything from my yells, well, magic is for the witch and the prophets."

"How did you agree to work in such conditions?"

"Can you say 'no'?"

"Of course, you should!"

"Brother, the 'no' option is something that we do not try here; I mean, it does not exist."

"In this case, you have to make it out."

"You know the consequences."

"What about the future of these children? Is this not the biggest consequence?"

"Aman, we do not think very much about the future here. What tells you that all these children are not going to die in an impending civil war? Why put your life at stake for something that might not survive instead of keeping safe your daily bread until you die yourself?"

"Essône, this is not human."

"Yes, it is. This is our humanity in the sub-world. You know, little brother, each hemisphere has got its own type of humanity. This is our type, and you have to stick to it. The things that you might have learned about other hemispheres turn out to be wrong when it comes to our case."

"Essône, you are poisonous. You cannot just surrender like this and conclude that you have got some kind of special humanity in which the future does not exist. Who created such a humanity, yourselves or the Creator?"

"We have created nothing, Aman. This is just what was given to us. We could be better if we had been given something better. But the donor, your Creator, found us so low that he gave us what we deserve – I mean, life with no future. What do you want us to do? Do you want us to fall on our knees and beg for whatever to your Creator? Listen! We did not kill the Creator's mother; we did not rape his wife; and we have no links with those who prosecuted his son. We have never done anything against Him to deserve such a miraculous muddle in our world. Just look for yourself. The political behaviour in our world is simply amazing. You cannot understand that the people who seem to be so normal and so well-intentioned in their speeches are the ones who cause such hideous and devious conditions. This is miraculous. You cannot justify it. Even your Creator cannot justify it. He just likes to see us suffering; and we say, well, we are going to help him make us suffer; maybe this will please Him.

"Let me teach you something very important, Aman: 'if a man is meant to be destroyed, he will complicate his fate if he does not indulge in destroying himself to make things easier'. This is what we are doing. Your Creator has shown that He does not care about us, and we are trying our best to show Him that we also do not care about ourselves.

"You know, Aman, if a woman does not like you, just go your way. Do not humiliate yourself trying to beg for something. Your Creator is just like a woman. He is so tantalising that He can just say 'no' for no good reasons; just for selfishness. And, now, what does he want us to do? Beseech? No way! This is too capricious and ridiculous."

"No, Essône. I do not really approve of your picture of the Creator. The Creator is not like a woman. They are very different from one another. A woman says 'no' if you have nothing to offer her. But the Creator says 'no' if you have nothing to offer yourself. A woman steps away from you if you cannot fill her up, whereas the

Creator keeps aloof from you if you cannot fill yourself up."

"No, Aman. This can't be true. What do you think we do not offer ourselves?"

"I don't know. We have to find out what is wrong with us. But we cannot just accuse the Creator like that. The Creator is not illogical, He is not unfair; I mean, He cannot just play you up like that. The Creator's ambition is the well-being of every one of us. But He does not interfere in our choices. The Creator is tolerant and sympathetic to our needs and choices."

"Aman, the god that you are trying to teach me sounds really bizarre. Who taught you about that kind of god? How can God be sympathetic to man's choices if these choices do not satisfy His own initiatives?"

"That is, unfortunately, the way it works. God is like a very wealthy and high-ranking aristocrat whose son is determined to marry a proletarian girl. The moral principles of social class separatism do not allow such marriages, but that man is so sympathetic to his son's choice that he will try to understand it. He will certainly say to his him: 'Son, you know that it would be a great honour for me to see you with a girl of you own class. But, as you have chosen to go so low and pick that filthy uneducated thing, well, I respect your choice, and I give you a quarter of my fortune so that you can settle with her in your own home.' What I mean is that man is free to take the options he prefers, and his god is in him to assist him in his own choices. For example, you have chosen to destroy yourselves, and your God is just going to help you do it."

"The picture of the wealthy aristocrat sounds very real, but I just have the feeling that you are being quite heretical by comparing such a man with God; I mean, God cannot assist a man to do evil unless He is Himself the initiator of that evil."

"This is even more heretical to think that God would be the initiator of evil in man's life. God has no personal willingness to initiate anything in our lives. It is man himself who drags God to the way he wants his life to take, and his God simply assists him in that way."

"Listen to yourself! Are you really aware of what this implies?"

"What does it imply?"

"It implies that all men who do evil things are assisted by God. Can you measure the consequences of such a statement?"

"Of course. God assists them in their evil deeds. How powerful do you think that man is to achieve something if God is not by his side, and especially if God is against it?"

"They are simply assisted by Satan."

"How powerful do you then think Satan is to assist a man if God does not give His consent? Is Satan more powerful than God to succeed in assisting a man to achieve something against God's Will?"

"This question is quite hard, but the answer is not very difficult to find. You know, according to the Holy Word, that God handed over this world to Satan to run it in his guise."

"Rightly. That is what I am trying to show you. God gave the authority to Satan to help evil deeds to be performed; which means that, if Satan assists an evil man, it is God himself who assists him indirectly, for you would not give permission to somebody to act upon your property if you do not consent. Moreover, God is not like you and me. He is fully aware of everything that Satan does, but does not stop him because He Himself gave him permission to act to assist those who choose evil. Do not forget that, every time the children of God gather together to plan their assistance to humanity, Satan is in the very middle of them to equally get permission to implement his plans upon humanity, and God gives him carte blanche. But the point is that Satan himself will never assist you — of course, with God's permission — if you do not ask for his assistance. He will never force you to say 'yes' to him. He only comes to you when you call him to you. You have the choice."

"Aman, are you trying to hold us responsible for our own destruction?"

"That is exactly what I am saying."

"Be serious, Aman. Why would a man choose to destroy himself?"

"To find the answer to that question, start asking yourself why you have chosen to destroy the future of these children."

"I do it because the political leaders of this country have chosen to destroy the whole thing. I am responsible for nothing. I am just reacting against the situation."

"No. You are not reacting against. You are, rather, acting in favour of the situation, and your god is helping all of you to achieve your evil dream; and, if you are not willing to stop your destructive dream, your god will not force you to do it."

"How can we stop a dream that has so fully penetrated the mind of the whole country?"

"It is not too difficult, Essône. You just have to start saying 'no' to the destruction of these children at your level. Just look at them! They are miserable, lost, massacred."

"No, Aman. This is not my responsibility. I do not want to have my throat cut. These children are sacrificed, not by me, but by the leaders. I am just seeking my daily bread while waiting for my own death – my natural death, not my martyrdom. I am not a prophet to be a martyr."

Amanoofwom was totally intrigued by the shocking words of his brother. Nevertheless, the two brothers had lunch together in the restaurant, and Amanoofwom went home soon afterwards, thoughtful and worried.

The seventh thing that astounded Amanoofwom was the condition of the medical centres. Amanoofwom visited the main public hospitals of the town, and found that not even a single tablet was available. The work of the practitioners consisted of telling the sick the kind of medicines that could have treated their diseases. The doctor would then give them a list of the medicines and recommend them to order the medicines from a Western nation if they could, or try the costly VIP clinics and chemist's shops, where the supposed normal prices of medicines were multiplied by five. This was a ridiculous practice. Maybe the practitioners also thought like Essône-Nkombot. Maybe the people, instead of dying in an impending war, would be better off if they died sooner of their diseases.

There was a lot more that Amanoofwom discovered within about two weeks, with the greatest indignation. His burning ambition to teach truth to his people was, from then on, his singular motivation; to hold memorable chats on every occasion, from the day Bekale Be'Nguema discovered him in a pub in Pope's Avenue to the day he handed in his resignation at President's University.

But now Amanoofwom had gone missing and nobody knew where he was. He was, in fact, in Ekot'e Beyem, a savannah on a sandy plain near the Nkole'e Engông Hills, to the north-east of Messanza, not only to escape impending arrest but also to get prepared for something he had in his mind. For him, Ekot'e Beyem seemed to be an appropriate place where he could make a successful spiritual preparation for what he had in mind.

CHAPTER 11

THE ENCOUNTER WITH BIBUBUA

Ekot'e Beyem was a small sandy desert. Well, it wasn't really sandy; clay, sand and quartz were blended together to make a variegated and multi-textured ground. Vegetation was meagre. It was like the whole region lacked oxygen. The outlook was not very different from the pictures that Armstrong brought back from the moon.

Some dry shrubs were scattered all over the parched plain. The grass looked as though it had been burnt or asphyxiated, either by the ruthless solar rays or by intoxicating engine oils. It looked as if a big company had carried out massive agricultural operations there years earlier and that the soil was either recuperating or simply desiccated forever. It looked like a land left fallow.

There were no traces of animal life, except for the presence of locusts, cockroaches and ants. It was true that Amanoofwom saw there a viper, which he nearly trampled on, but this was not convincing enough to conclude that there was life. Snakes are very mysterious beasts. You cannot trust their presence alone to deduce that there is life somewhere.

Life in Ekot'e Beyem was wild and harsh. Food and drinking water were a big problem. Fortunately, however, Amanoofwom found a little brook far away in the bush, although the water was filthy, full of horrible little amphibians that pervaded and infested the waters with their dung. But this was the only place around to get some water. Anyway, it is not what goes into man's mouth that will sully him, but what comes out of it.

Amanoofwom also found some fruit-bearing trees around. Some of them, fully abloom and heavily loaded with edible fruits, were on the other side of the brook. But he could not get there as he kept the old precept: he never crossed the river. Amanoofwom therefore spent his time in Ekot'e Beyem eating some meagre fruits and drinking polluted water, while meditating and praying.

The most critical moments were night-times, during which he would be mercilessly exposed to dangerous reptiles and insects while getting some sleep. He would be very disturbed in his sleep. He would be repeatedly awakened and have to fight hard against the insects that would be trying to sneak themselves into his nostrils and ears. At times he would also be chilled to the marrow by the noise of a serpent's crawling close to him. Some would even crawl across him and pass on. These are the conditions in which Amanoofwom lived in Ekot'e Beyem. But the most important event was Amanoofwom's encounter with Bibubua, or the spirit of stupidity, at the end of his sojourn in Ekot'e Beyem. Bibubua was well known as the demonic spirit that would corrupt the souls of young people in their process of self-destruction. He was therefore referred to as a representation of evil. If a young man became a thief or a criminal of any category, he would be said to be assisted by the spirit called Bibubua in his crimes. But nobody knew that Bibubua was a real spiritual manifestation; not even Amanoofwom himself knew about it.

It was on day 40 of Amanoofwom's sojourn in Ekot'e Beyem that Bibubua appeared to him. A very heavy rainstorm started showering the site the third hour of the day. Amanoofwom had nowhere to find shelter. It was strange. It had not rained for about two months, almost the whole time Amanoofwom had been living in Ekot'e Beyem. The rain was accompanied by such a fog that Amanoofwom could not see anything around him. The strange foggy rain made him tempted to leave the site straightaway. But he had to wait for the sunset before starting his way back.

Amanoofwom was soaked and blinded. The pleasure was that he had not had a proper shower for 40 days. It was, therefore, a good occasion to cleanse himself before getting back. He then got undressed and started to enjoy himself exuberantly in the water. While delighting in his shower, one single thing worried him: his clothes. How was he going to manage with wet clothes? Would he have to stay one more night for them to dry out?

Fortunately, the shower eased off after about two hours, though the fog remained heavy. The last thunderclaps provided some helpful lightning for Amanoofwom to locate his clothes. He took them and spread them over a leafless shrub nearby. A drizzle from the fog continued to wet the clothes, however, and Amanoofwom kept waiting, totally naked.

By the sixth hour, a shiny sun appeared at the zenith, and it became suddenlyboiling hot over Amanoofwom's head, while the heavy drizzle was petering out little by little, chased by the powerful rays of the sweltering star. Amanoofwom was happy at having had such a good shower and starting a pleasant sun-bathe soon afterwards, and he was especially happy for his clothes. His body began to gleam, with the sun's rays reflecting off his sweaty chocolate skin. But one last thing annoyed him: he was very hungry. He had not really eaten anything substantial for about twelve days. He was feeling very uncomfortable. His stomach was churning very noisily, and that was painful.

Amanoofwom took his underwear and spread it out on the ground. He sat on it to avoid getting dust on his buttocks, and was still sitting there waiting for his clothes to dry out when, suddenly, he perceived a stealthy and swift human silhouette a few metres away in front of him. This made him frightened for two reasons. First of all, he thought that he was running the risk of losing consciousness because of hunger and starting to have deadly hallucinations, even though he had managed to keep himself physically strong thus far. And, secondly, he was afraid of being discovered naked by a real someone lurking in the undergrowth, or anybody who might have got lost or was just hunting game or looking for something.

Amanoofwom rubbed his eyes to make sure that he really had seen a living being, and at the same time got ready to put his clothes on in case his vision turned out to be not a hallucination. He was just getting up when he saw the same swift silhouette again flash before him, this time in a bit more distinguishable appearance. He then forgot about his clothes in his desire to find out who it could be. Was it a spirit or a witch? A whole host of recollections of his visions in the temple and in Minsisim came into his mind. He had already been separated from the spirits since he left Minsisim Forest. And Ekot'e Beyem was not a spiritual site. He was not expecting to make any spiritual encounter there, even though he had gone there for a spiritual preparation.

A very strong wind began to sweep out over the dusty soil. And Amanoofwom's trousers were lifted up and taken away by the wind. He began to follow the trousers to catch them. This happens mostly when the wind takes your hat off while you are trotting about; you follow it as it keeps rocking on and veering to and fro. That was how Amanoofwom came to be running about the plain, stark naked, trying to get hold of his trousers. It was miraculously ridiculous and incredible that Amanoofwom kept running after his trousers, for about 50 seconds, in vain. Maybe it was because he was feeling tired and uncomfortable due to hunger. This made him angrily desperate. What was that thaumaturgic wind that could pull Amanoofwom's trousers around rhythmically and, coincidentally, just as his hand approached them move them just out of reach?

Hungry and angry, Amanoofwom stopped running and just stood upright, overcome by exhaustion, showing his flat tummy and bony limbs. Suddenly, a peal of laughter burst out behind him. And, once he turned round to see who it was, he saw a man dressed like a clown laughing till he cried. Amanoofwom had nothing to say. He was so ashamed and weakened at having been watched galloping around completely naked by a bloody clown.

The clown laughed and laughed and laughed. Amanoofwom was tempted to laugh too, once he looked at himself and tried to imagine the way the clown must have seen him dangling between. It was amusing, but very embarrassing. Then, tired, Amanoofwom sat down on the ground, face to face with the clown, and kept observing the nasty buffoon suspiciously.

The clown approached Amanoofwom, still laughing and dancing

acrobatically with his strange costume on. And, once he got near him, he started a ghastly but evocative song:

"Oh, young man!
I see you gloomy in this sand.
And I see it; it is so clear,
As you are sitting over here,
That you have been sold
To face the scold.
What do you want to do with this?
Where do you want to go with this?
You are so plucky, so intrepid!
But, do not be stupid.
Too lion-hearted you are!
And you have forgotten to follow your star.
What a booby!
It is really a pity!
You have been given a suicidal mission;
Which is a faulty passion.
That is beautiful for the putrid, sloppy, lost subjects
Who have nothing to gain in life, and who can be
used as objects.
They can go.
It is even far better for them to go.
But you, brilliant young man!
What are you doing in this Stygian sand?"

Intrigued, Amanoofwom suddenly turned and asked: "O ne nzà?" – "Who are you?"

"Are you serious?" the clown started to reply maliciously. "Are you being serious that you do not know me? You should know me, young man. You have already heard of me several times in your life. You are just pretending that you do not know me."

"Do you think that I am not sincere enough to say that I know you if the truth is that I do know you? I ask: who are you?"

"Oh, young man, it is a pity that you do not know me. Just think again. You will find it."

"How can you be so stupid? I ask: who are you?

"Oh, mongh'a mot! Engongol abuiñ à wha ná o adzime mha. Me ne djuiñ ná Bibubua, nkore'e bot. – My name is Bibubua, the saviour. I have come to rescue you from your fatal fall. I have come to save your life. I am your saviour. I am the saviour of the lost."

Bububua got closer and closer to Amanoofwom, still dancing. But Amanoofwom kept quiet, looking at him with indifference, albeit a bit inquisitive. And, once he got very close to him, he stretched his hand as to invite Amanoofwom to dance with him.

"Young man, do not be indifferent to me!
For, if you do not listen to me,
It will be too late
To get you out of your fate.
Just see for yourself
How you are displayed on a shelf
To be sold and cast into the delf sea.
Just look and see!"

Bibubua was a very skilful tempter, who possessed some kind of magic with which to project scenic pictures in the air showing Amanoofwom a very dreadful dichotomy. On one side Amanoofwom saw himself as a very wealthy and comfortable man possessing a big house, a beautiful wife, four nice children and over-loaded bank accounts; and, on the other side, he saw how he was detained and living in extreme dejection in a tiny prison cell. Bibubua then said to Amanoofwom:

"Young man, if you listen to me, this is how you are going to flourish.
But if you do not listen to me, here is how you are going to finish.

You see, life is beautiful;
But your mission is painful.
Just see for yourself, and tell me, little dor:
Is this what you came to the world for?
Is this the honour to those who gave you life?
Is this the best aftermath of your strife?
Is this the aim of your stance on the earth?
Is this the price your father paid at your birth?
Were you so well hatched
To end up so badly dispatched?

The pictures in which Amanoofwom saw himself wealthy and comfortable were very tempting. And those in which he was in extreme dejection were very frightening. Besides, it was quite logical and real to Amanoofwom that, on the one hand, due to the admiration that people had for him, he would become a mogul in the future if he agreed to integrate into the system; and, on the other hand, it was obvious that, considering the political furies that were running after him, he would finish oppressed should he never collaborate. But this was no news to Amanoofwom. He had been aware of the whole thing well before Bibubua displayed the pictures to him. And he was conscious of what he was after. So, he was not really impressed.

"What do you choose, young man?"

"Let me get dressed first and I will answer you."

"What do you need to get dressed for?"

"I say, let me get dressed. I do not feel well like this."

"Listen, young man, you do not need your clothes on for this. Just say 'yes' to me, and I will save your life straightaway." Bibubua kept rushing on trying to get an immediate answer from Amanoofwom.

That is what is terrible with demonic contracts. You are so pressurised that you do not have time to think twice. And that was the last straw that broke Amanoofwom's back. The man suddenly reddened before the tempter:

"Woe is you, miserable tempter
And foolish distracter.
You, who use your silly dance
To kill my people's conscience,
I order you to get away!
Away from me, I say!"

Terrified by wrathful Amanoofwom, Bibubua immediately faded away, laughing mockingly. "Ha ha ha, ha ha ha, ha ha ha; I told you!"

As he gathered his clothes up to put them on, Amanoofwom felt so anxious about his experience with Bibubua that he instantly decided to set out for Messanza, after having spent 40 days and 40 nights in Ekot'e Beyem.

Back in Messanza, Amanoofwom found that his mother and his father had been seriously molested by the forces of public order trying to find where he was. Although six months had gone with no news of Amanoofwom, however, the forces of public order were still awaiting the man. And now Amanoofwom was back to meet the people again. And, on one of these Thursday mornings, flyers appeared unexpectedly all over the town announcing that the teacher was going to speak in public the following morning. Nobody knew who had distributed the leaflets, and at what time of the night. And, according to the message on the flyers, the meeting would be kicked off on the Mekie-Me-Kwule playgrounds late in the morning on Friday, lasting, if possible, until the masses were satisfied.

Now, as every single household opened its doors to let its inhabitants out on Thursday morning, the big surprise was there. The flyers told the story. The following day was going to be a great day. The teacher was back! But where was he back from? Nobody could tell, anyway.

CHAPTER 12

MY DESPERATE BATTLE FOR THE SUBCONTINENT'S FALLEN IDs

The commotion in every single household that Friday morning was great. Ten o'clock was too late. Some people got ready at five in the morning, so excited were they about attending the meeting and listening to the teacher: listening to fresh revelations. Some people could not sleep at all over that night. Thinking about what was going to happen the next morning was so stirring and rousing that they couldn't drop off at all. Those who could sleep would have spent the whole night dreaming of the encounter. Their minds were so strongly latched onto the thought that the following morning was going to be very hot that they made exaggerated mental projections about it.

It was reported that a teenager sleeping with his girlfriend suddenly started shouting in the night. He recounted that he had seen the sky opening a massive double-panelled door and, out of that door, he had seen the teacher descending from on high, surrounded by angels, while the rabble was acclaiming his triumphal arrival on the Mekie-Me-Kwule playgrounds.

Somebody else was said to have seen him coming on a huge, winged black horse, followed by freaky figures from another world, to wage war on the people. Another man dreamt of him attired in a black cassock and reading the scriptures to people in a temple.

A great many people dreamt of the event that night. And, what happened was, once somebody had dreamt of something, he then woke up all the other members of the household to tell them what he had seen. And they kept on talking and sharing views. Many families held the same kind of conversations that Thursday night.

Now, on that Friday morning, the solemn encounter on the Mekie-Me-Kwule playgrounds was now a reality. People flowed down to Mckic-Me-Kwule from seven in the morning in order to occupy the best places. The atmosphere was hot and exciting. A continuous symphony was being played all over the place. The various conversations of groups of people in the crowd sounded like an indistinct, loud buzzing.

Nobody was 100% sure that the teacher would come, for he had not been seen for quite a long time. How could he have been absent and suddenly reappear without giving any indication of where he had been?

Amanoofwom arrived at ten sharp, driven in by a taxi. He stepped down carrying a smart black suitcase while waving warm greetings to the people with his left hand. He was looking very different. He was skinny, hairy and swarthy. He was totally transfigured. His escape from the forces of public order about seven weeks earlier, the adverse conditions that he had undergone in Ekot'e Beyem, and – above all – his encounter with Bibubua had completely changed him. Amanoofwom was even now dreadful. This was not very far from expressing the saying according to which horrible experiences make one wonder whether he who has experienced them is not himself something horrible. Hence, smiling is the magic of fawns, for a prey that cannot smile, by the very fact of its experiences, looks horrid. The teacher was looking horrible, though very high.

Some local paparazzi began to fire off their flashguns from all parts of the crowd while a few journalists approached him to snatch his first words. A very strong young man popped up to escort Amanoofwom as the crowd had blocked the way to the stage. The young man kept pushing people away with a powerful backhand until the teacher reached and stepped on the stage.

A bloke, probably in his late 20's, instantly approached the stage with a microphone in hand to try and ask the teacher a question. But, suddenly, the crowd broke into a loud and embarrassing hue and cry as the young man tried to step onto the stage, with his microphone in hand, to put the question to Amanoofwom.

"No. Get off here. Get off. Get away. No. No…"

Amanoofwom raised his fleshless right hand to calm the crowd down, and then asked: "What is the matter?"

To that question, somebody from the crowd retorted angrily: "What is this guy doing here? What do you think he can really be doing here? Look at him, and look at us, then tell me what you see! What is his place here in the midst of your people?"

The young man was, in fact, of the same skin colour as the invaders. We commonly say that he was white. The crowd was made up of local people. And, generally, they were sympathetic to the trend that stood against the invaders. And, as they were sure that Amanoofwom belonged to the same trend as a local and spiritual leader, they could not accept an invading gene among them or, at worst, see him go forward and pose a question to somebody who was regarded as an anti-invasion leader.

The young man was said to be a blend of 'French-Arabic' origin. His paternal grandparents had come from Lebanon, and his father, a very successful and well-known retailer in the town, married a French girl, who had gone there on an adventure about 50 years earlier. The young man was born of that 'French-Arabic' or 'French-Lebanese' couple, and he had himself become a very brilliant journalist, working for a local television channel. So he was well-known too. But he was very much resented for his skin colour, and he had sometimes been a victim of aggression on the streets of Messanza.

And while the young journalist remained standing there in front of the teacher, hoping for an opportunity to ask his question, the sulky voice from the crowd went on: "Honestly speaking, I have never seen people so stubborn as these strange genes of the West. When they want to get something, they will still go for it even though they see death around the corner! What do you think you are doing here? What are your plans? Have you been paid to spoil our meeting? Do you want to die? Do you want to have your throat cut? Do you want to make us guilty of murder and alter the course of this meeting? Please, just go away. You have a nation, do you not?

Go to your nation and leave us alone. Leave our teacher alone and go and put questions to the teachers of your nation."

Some people began to wildly decry and rebuke the man in the crowd for his lack of respect at such a noble encounter in raising such embarrassing points. But he continued: "You will understand my reaction when you go to these people's kingdoms just for a while. I have been there and, I tell you, they don't like people of your colour. They look at you as an animal or whatever – inferior. They are unimaginably disdainful, swaggering, uppity. The are racist. Why do you have to serve them your delicious meals in your nation while they make you chew caterpillars in their kingdoms?

"I pity us who bless where we are cursed.

I pity us who enrich where we are impoverished.

I pity us who respect where we are humiliated.

I pity us who host where we are rejected.

I really pity us."

The crowd was so moved by the man's revelations that people instantly began to throw stones and empty cans at the journalist in response. But Amanoofwom raised his hand again. He had also been hung on the words of that man, but he had no intention of stoning the journalist, down as the crowd did. Rather, he turned to the man, to whom he suddenly began a powerful reply.

"Brother," he started, "your remarks are real and your worries are legitimate. But you did not have enough time to look into our world to understand the way it works. In the history of our nation, for example, it is said that the *Bekwèñ* – also known as the *Ndong* in some regions of Odzab – used to scoff at the *Essa-Bekang* and may other clans around them because they knew the secret to heal fractures. Nobody knew where these people had discovered their surgical methods. If you had a leg crushed in an accident, the *Bekwèñ* would get you walking in a matter of days. And, as nobody else could do it, they became so boastful about their surgical genius that they would look at other people as inferiors.

"Even in your society today, the most fulfilled and richest men often deride and neglect the dumbest and the poorest ones because they feel superior to them by the very fact of being more fulfilled and richer.

"Now, what do you think the difference is between them *Bekwèñ*, the fulfilled and the rich on the one side, and the *Essa-Bekang*, the dumb and the poor on the other side? The difference is that some do something better than the others; or some have something more beautiful and useful than the others, and they feel more powerful, and can make light of it for that very reason.

"You will find this principle at work everywhere. Any man will always feel very superior from the very day he achieves something greater than someone else. And he will deride all those unable to reach the same level of achievement for that very reason. And that has nothing to do with racism. If you are married and have children, you may happen to regard a single person as irresponsible, and you can be swaggering towards him for that very reason. If you have been very successful in business, somebody who has gone bankrupt may appear unintelligent to you, and you can neglect him if you want. If you invent a complex device system that proves to be of an impressively higher order, why not boast about it if you want to?

"When a superiority complex affects the spirit of a meliorist thinker-tinker for that very reason of thinking and tinking better than someone else, he will appear very embarrassing to the incompetent. And the victim will call him by all sorts of names. If you say that the Westerners are racist, will you say that the *Bekwèñ* were also racist? And, yet, their behaviour towards the *Essa-Bekang* was not very different from that of the Westerners towards us.

"Brothers, the problem of this young journalist that you are rejecting so fiercely does not hinge on his colour but, rather, on the fact that you are unable to integrate him into your nation and make him one of yours. What do you think he is? Is he Arab? Is he Lebanese? Is he French? Or is he Fanghish, or whatever local group you prefer? If a man is born in a nation, where else do you want him to be from? Truly, I tell you, if you reject a son of your nation on the basis of complexion, you will make a brother of yours an outsider in your society, and for that his passion for self-realisation in life will be crippled. Thereby, you will have created an ignoramus in your society. Can you see how wrong you are by doing this?"

"Teacher, what you are saying is right. But how can we justify the persistent racism of these people even towards those of colour who were born in their nations of the West?" the man asked insistently.

"Brother, you have to be very careful about the concept of racism." Amanoofwom started a complicated explanation to give an answer to the man. "By definition, racism is the theory that all members of each race possess the same characteristics, abilities, qualities, etc., which are seen as different from those of another or other races. Now, behaviourally speaking, racism is the rejection of other people on the basis of colour differences. But the main objective of such a rejection is biological. A racist is a naturalist. A racist is a man who believes that God did not make a mistake in creating racial differences between men; and that, if we want to honour God, we have to fight for the preservation of each race as God created it. A true racist fights against the procreation of mulattos the way in which an ecologist fights against the destruction and alteration of natural fauna because, for him, a mixed-race child is not very different from a genetically manipulated plant. It is like mixing genes and cells the wrong way to create something fake. All believers and moralists are in accord that such practices should be banned. That is why you will undoubtedly find that religions are the places in which you will find the most radical conservatives and, in consequence, the most unsuspected racists because, for them, we should not create an artificial race between the real God-made races; and this is not wrong. A mulatto belongs to no real race! A mulatto is like an artificial creature. He is just like GM food. Some religious tendencies, such as the Jehovah's Witnesses, have stood against blood transfusion for the same reasons; and some other creeds and organisations are fighting against the building of human beings by cloning on the same basis.

"I understand that it would certainly be irrelevant for man to build human beings in the sense that we already have a more natural and virtuous way of doing it: I mean, natural procreation. But this is vastly less irrelevant than homosexuality for instance, since we already have a more natural and virtuous way of mating, which, in addition, helps us to perpetuate our species. Why, then, contrive another way of mating that, obviously, is of no importance for sustainability? The potential question at this point is: why legitimise one irrelevance while casting a ban on another? Only our legislators and politicians can give the right answer to such a question.

"Brothers, real racism is not obnoxious. A man who fights against what he considers to be an awkward manipulation of nature should not be charged with criminal offences. Incriminating a racist is like incriminating an ecologist. And, likewise, a man who fights against cloning cannot justify giving his support for mixed marriages and the subsequent fake creatures that come out of them. However – I have to repeat it once again – those who are so engaged in the fight to keep their colours are simply not aware that colour is but a mistake, an error of creation. Colour will take us nowhere. Some people still spend time bragging such absurdities as 'black is beautiful'. Others vaunt that 'white is pretty', or that 'Indian is stunning'. But they are simply not aware that all these looks are but errors of creation.

"Of course, errors can be very attractive at times. But this is just a question of perception. For example, one day, a friend of mine made a glass of shandy for one of his guests; and after drawing a few gulps of the brew the guest went, 'Oh! This is tastier than real lemonade.' And, yet, a shandy is nothing more than an error of lemonade.

"Some people find that mixed-race kids are more gorgeous than pure-race kids. But this has no major consequence in life. Keeping our racial errors as they are, trying to correct them, or making more errors do not matter, because race is of no importance. I am not trying to vulgarise a dogma that satisfies my personal visions. Anybody can see that the 'cult of colours' has no end and that the fight for racial conservation is neither consistent nor harmful. It is just the expression of human capricious feelings. What I mean, in a word, is that racism is not criminal. It is just a feeling.

"Maybe we should try to look into something else, such as, say, supremacism – as the belief that one racial or social group is superior to another and that it can bully and exploit it at will because of its supposed superiority. Here, we may regard supremacism as criminal. But this is not because regarding oneself as superior is criminal, but rather because all supremacists tend to bully and exploit other men for being inferior to them. Yet, oppression and exploitation of man by man is evil. A supremacist is very different from a racist. A man can be a racist without being a supremacist. For example, good believers in God are racist in their fight against wrongful mixtures, but they have revealed themselves to be the best associates of the most horrendous imperial powers and colonialists throughout history in the framework of the exploitation of the 'uncivilised' worlds. And, conversely, a man can be a supremacist without being a racist. That is the case of the Anglo-Saxons in North America, who bullied and exploited Negroes in slavery while they had children with black women. They did not find any problem in mating with them. I even wonder whether the first white men who mated with she-negroes had any idea of what such babies were going to look like – or if it were to be possible to produce babies from such an anti-natural and, perhaps too, anti-biological coupling. Did they ever imagine that the babies would probably fail to be white? Notwithstanding this, they mated with them even though they believed that, because of their civilisational superiority, they could bully and exploit them. They were not racist, but supremacist.

"Brothers, those of colour who were born in the white man's hemisphere but who still suffer rejection today are not rejected by the racists, for the racist will need them at least for the purpose of exploiting them; nor are they rejected by the supremacists, for the supremacists may need to use them sexually. They are rather the victims of the third category of these patrons: the phobic. A man who suffers phobia is not a supremacist. He might certainly be classified next to the racist. But, unlike the phobic, the racist is not repulsive. A racist can have very good friends of different colours, but will never mix up with them biologically, whereas a phobic is an aggressively repelling rebel.

"I have nothing against man's freedom to like and dislike. Some people like meat more than eggs. Others prefer cats to dogs. But, if this is normal to us, why should it not be normal too for a man to prefer Indian to Chinese? Why not feel free to like white and dislike black? Fundamental individual freedoms should not be repressed by trying to get people to consume products to which they are allergic. However, the problem of the phobic is that they tend to sabotage everything they don't like. The phobic wish all that they detest had not existed at all. That is why they are always tempted to destroy it. But, if you don't like something, why not just step aside and leave it alone to those who might like it? If you fail to understand this, then you are in severe need of assistance.

"Brothers, you have to be very careful. We have to understand life before engaging in fights. We have no problems with the racists, for the racists are fighting for a good cause; and this will harm nobody. We shall not waste our time with the phobic either, for the phobic are ill. The phobic are not very different from the demented. If you have a sick child, you simply need to take it to the hospital.

"Our real problem is with the supremacists. But we have to understand the underpinnings of supremacism in the first place. I have already referred to the opposition between the *Bekwèñ* and the *Essa-Bekang* on the very matter of fixing fractured limbs. It is no longer too hard to understand that 'supremacism lies in competition'. If somebody achieves something great, he may be tempted to proclaim his superiority to you on that very achievement if you fail to compete with him. We do not really need to go too far into lengthy explanations on this point. Just take a look at the world today. You will find that, on the one hand, ex-President Clinton of the United States was banned from presenting himself as a candidate in the AD 2000 presidential elections for having already served his two mandates according to constitutional disposals, while ex-Vice-President Gore failed to be the winner despite winning most votes, giving way to the victorious Bush. In the opposite camp to this we have President Bongo of Gabon, who has spent his entire premiership multiplying mandate extensions through fraudulent elections, legislative manipulation and even killings, since 1967. Equally we have the president-elect Bédié of Ivory Coast, who was ousted from power in the wake of a military coup and was banned from setting a foot in his so-called country. We can also take the case of President Kabila of I-don't-know-if-it-is-Zaire-or-something-else, who was shot point-blank by one of his nearest army generals, etc., etc.

"Behold these manners, brothers! What do you think colour is doing here in comparing the ways of doing things between different civilisations? The point is simply that one way looks smart while the other looks lousy; one way sounds intelligent while the other sounds stupid; one way goes smoothly while the other is rough; one way appears advanced while the other appears backward; one way is regarded as civilised while the other is regarded as barbarous. In a word, one way is human while the other is bestial."

"What about President Kennedy? Was he not shot too?" a man shouted somewhere behind Amanoofwom.

"Of course he was. And the truth is that those who could not shoot their presidents at the time Kennedy was shot were feeling more civilised than the Americans, and they must have expressed some kind of contempt against them for that very reason. I am not creating a nefarious dissimilarity between human beings upon artificial mindsets. The thing is simply that if a man 'A' transcends the creative and organisational abilities of another man 'B' and becomes so powerful as to be capable of subjugating him, he will necessarily feel superior in that very matter. And he may end up subduing him in one of the many forms of slavery. And my point hinges on the question as to whether there exists any form of logic in human reasoning on the basis of which it can be claimed that 'a slave equals his master'."

"No, teacher. This is not the logic of God. God says that all men are born equal!" a man shouted in the crowd.

"Yes, brother. I don't even need you to quote the Scriptures in which you read it. Let's just suppose that this is true. But all men are born equal just the way all living beings are equal at birth. But, as highly conscious beings, human beings, rather, pave an intelligent way after birth to become the masters of the plants, the fish, the birds, and the animals. That is why you are not equal to your dog. And, likewise, if a man or a group of men goes higher than another in some activities and becomes more capable, they will cease to be equal, just the way you are not equal to your dog for being able to achieve things that your dog cannot achieve. That is why the stronger can conquer the weaker, tame them, and subdue them just the way you can conquer, tame and subdue a dog. This is a social fact that has nothing to do with God. You cannot pray for it. We were born equal, of course. But our activities in our societies result in great differences. And this is what makes us different and unequal to a certain extent. And this has nothing to do with skin colour. Competence is something mental and it is at the centre of the gaps between different individuals or groups of individuals. There was a time when the members of the same society and race could not share the same leisure sites because some were from the aristocracy and others from the plebs. They were not equal; and you cannot say the opposite unless you want to be very polite. Now, if you look at that class separatism, will you tell me that this is very different from racial segregation wherever it exists? We can take, as an example, the very interesting picture of North America to understand this. Between the 18th and the 19th centuries, the most capable Negroes, such as Moses Dickson or Frederick Douglass, then called 'Exceptional Negroes', were automatically integrated into white affairs and would even be accepted by some of the most outstanding white conservatives of their communities – who, yet, would be regarded as extremely racist towards the 'Ordinary Negroes'. They would say to their Exceptional Negro friends: 'You are not a Negro like those Negroes.' You who are telling me that you had been living in the West, did you not notice that the very people who would insult you for being a Negro while walking down the street were the same ones who would like to ask for Denzel Washington's autograph? And yet, you are both Negroes.

"Truly, I tell you, the very day you achieve something more beautiful, richer and stronger than someone else you will start feeling very superior to him. And if you are tempted to disdain him for that very reason, this is just human. That is what racism is all about. Those that you call 'racists' are simply 'meliorists'. And, as a rule, any victim of someone else's 'meliorism' will have to face some form of disrespect as long as he remains in his 'peiorist' position; and that has nothing to do with 'colourism'. The fact is that some peoples have explored their potential to the full and their struggle has borne fruit. Some nations have achieved such a thorough political and social organisation that they have become boastful about it. Some cultures have engaged to such an explosive advancement that they have transcended other cultures, subduing them under their supremacy; and the vanquished ones have accused their conqueros of being uppity; and they call them 'racists' by mistake.

"You who want to fight racism, I tell you, fight uncivilisation instead, and you will defeat racism as a consequence of your victory on primitivism, ignorance and backwardness. However, you won't fight uncivilisation through the method you are so massively applying in these present times. I see millions of the subcontinent's men and women now crossing the river in search for of a better life. But this will take us nowhere, because if you cross the river you will just get lost, and the world behind you will not be saved. The only fight we have to engage is to turn our culture into a powerful instrument of improvement. Brothers, this is the only way out."

"What does he mean by such a pompous phrase? How can we turn our culture into a powerful instrument of improvement?"

somebody muttered at the back of the crowd as he put his mouth to a friend's temple.

But Amanoofwom heard it. "Who heard that question?" he asked in full voice.

"Which question?" Almost everybody in the crowd was surprised. Indeed, nobody heard anything, except for the one to whom the question was asked in a whisper near his ear.

Amanoofwom pointed at a man standing far away in the crowd: "Brother, can you speak up and ask your question?"

The man was terrified. Even his friend to whom he was speaking had asked him to repeat the question because he did not hear him clearly. How could Amanoofwom have heard him? The man apologised in order to escape having to put the question, which he eventually asked indirectly: "Sorry, teacher; I was just trying to figure out what we could do to turn our culture into an instrument of improvement."

"Brother," Amanoofwom started to answer, "do you know the story of 'the Four Brothers'?"

"Er...yes, I have met some elders who know about it."

"Can you tell us about it, then?"

"Er...OK."

"Go on, then."

"I know, according to what the elders say, that there were four special Fanghish brothers in the ancient times who had very astonishing powers. The four brothers are said to have been a phenomenal quadruplet born of a rare woman. They were miraculously witty from babyhood, and yielded remarkable signs of singular intelligence from childhood. The tale says that it was obvious that they would achieve something impressive in life; and it was so. Indeed, at the age of twelve, the four brothers were submitted to the tricky crucible of Akoma, an old witch fellow who had the secret of a rare intellectual quotient test among the Fanghish. The crucible was like a cultish riddle that was generally part of young people's mystical initiation into intellect and spirituality in the Fanghish culture.

Through general knowledge questions, guessing, temptation and startling encounters, the children were expected to uncover four treasures, and there were five possible outcomes. The entrants would come out empty-handed if unsuccessful in the tests. Or they would walk out carrying a huge bronze peccary if they had got just one single treasure; a silver horse if they had got two; a golden lion if they had got three; or a serpent in diamonds if they had got the four treasures. The peccary signified that the entrants would be excellent land and sea workers. The horse represented the future of great soldiers. The lion was the sign of sovereign rulers. And the serpent indicated that the winners would be greatly enlightened teachers. The four brothers got three treasures out of four upon completion of Akoma's tricky crucible, and appeared from the entrance of the big maze with a beaming golden lion as thousands people clapped and cheered. It was the first time in the history of Akoma's riddle that three treasures out of four had been won. For that reason, the four brothers were crowned in the public place as the most phenomenal masterminds that had ever existed in the history of the Fanghish, and they were appointed by the Spirit to be the leading body of their nation.

"The success of the four brothers in losing one treasure and getting three was said to be a perfect representation of the story of God's own life, as it was known that God Himself had lost his oneness to become a threesome. Indeed, according to the teachings of some Fanghish masters of mysteries, God was, of course, the fourth person who had been lost, and left behind our present cosmological space-time system to bring into being the three persons that we know today. He is henceforth the fourth, but the lost. I think that we all know about Mebegue-Me-Nkpaa, the lost, who begot Nzam-Ye-Mebegue, Ñiengon-Mebegue and Onohn-Mebegue. The success of the four brothers was, therefore, a perfect representation of the story of God's own life. That is why they were crowned to govern. And, from then on, the elective system ceased among the Fanghish, and the four brothers became sovereign rulers for as long as they remained in life. The tale also says that the four brothers ruled over Odzab with respect to its intrinsic credence, philosophy and vision.

"They ruled over it as it had been handed over to them by the Spirit, and they ran it through twelve offices shared out amongst the four according to their abilities. *Bingongom*, or 'the master of trouble', had a special gift for matters of defence, security, and law enforcement, and he took charge of these three offices. *Mfule*, or 'the providing slot', was in charge of nutrition and public health according to his skills. *Ozugle*, or 'the restless toiler', was said to have received from the Spirit the power of moulding and reshaping nature and environment; hence his nomination as the officer of buildings and ways. And, finally, *Nhyemmam*, the 'heir of knowledge', was the one revealed by the truths of the Spirit, and he was given carte blanche to run three offices: education, arts, and spiritual improvement. He was also the spokesman in direct connection with the citizens and in relations with friendly nations. The savings office was the only one jointly run by the four.

"Equally, the tale says that, among the four, *Nhyemmam* was the most popular. His popularity was held from his position as an educator and spokesman. Every young person had met him at least thrice. Each year, *Nhyemmam* had no more than 40 days' rest in Nkole'e Engông Palace. He would spend the rest of time lecturing all over Odzab, region by region, county by county, town by town and village by village.

"The four brothers, according to the tale, ruled over their nation for 700 years, at the end of which they disappeared in the wake of an unfortunate event. They were cleared out from Nkole'e Engông Palace after a violent thunderstorm had spat a powerful bolt of lightning straight onto the palace. The violent whirlwind that started then wrapped the palace in a twirling cloud that made it invisible and inaccessible to the people. The whirlwind remained active for fourteen days, during which nobody could access the palace and nor could anybody come out of it. It ravaged the palace to such an extent that, once it calmed down, the people found nothing left on the site. The palace had been destroyed and swept away. And the four brothers and their sentry and the servants had also disappeared. Comments on the event say that it was incredible. Some people even came to think that the four brothers might have been a dream. The whole nation might have been hijacked by some crafty medium into a communal dream for as long as 700 years, over generations and generations.

"Besides, the elders say that the perfect governance that the four brothers had applied on their nation was too beautiful to be true. Such a perfect government for so few people had never existed in the history of human civilisations; and the most horrid thing about it was that the whole of it had been swept away in just fourteen days with no substantial reasons; just a natural calamity. Who could believe in such a joke? Anyway, the four brothers and their glory evaporated, eclipsed into nothingness behind the wall of the unseen. Some people tried to think of further miracles that would bring the four brothers back to life and the palace back into existence. But nothing happened until today.

"That is what I know about 'the Four Fanghish Brothers'. But what is the link between this tale and what we have to do in order to turn our culture into an instrument of improvement?"

"I have to start by congratulating you for giving us such a brilliant feedback on the *true story* of our culture, and then tell you what the link is between this story and our civilisational duties today."

"No, teacher. I do not think that you have got it right. This is not a *true story*. This is mythology."

"That is exactly the reason why I referred to that story. I know that you have been brought up to believe that this is not a true story. But why do you think that it is not a true story?"

"Teacher, this cannot simply be true."

"Why?"

"It is not possible at all."

"I am asking you why."

"Teacher, let us be serious. I have just said that, according to the tale, the four brothers are said to have live for as long as 700 years. This alone is enough to understand that, here, we are dealing with sheer fiction."

"Young man, it is true that 700 years is too long in comparison with the average life expectancy average of a few decades among the Fanghish. But, are you not taught that Noah was 930 years old when he died? And yet you all believe in that story. Now, if you look with attention into the story of Noah, you will easily understand that 700 years of age is nothing and cannot constitute the foundation of an argument denying the existence of the four brothers, for this will simply imply that Noah had never existed. But nobody is foolish enough to believe that Noah is a fictitious character. Can you now see why the age of the four brothers cannot be a conclusive argument to deny their existence?"

"What about their powers?" somebody shouted from the crowd.

"What do you mean?" Amanoofwom queried.

"The four brothers are said to have been fabulous. They had incredible powers. For example, they would not use weapons or dogs to hunt game. They would use their very hands to catch any kind of beast. Fawns, lions and tigers were even torn apart by their powerful hands. The four brothers also seem to have used a special fish to act as a submarine to travel underwater between the Bibulu islands and the Odzab mainland. Can this be real?"

"Brother," Amanoofwom said as he turned to him; "if catching fawns with their very hands and travelling in the belly of a fish sounds unreal to you, what did Samson and Jonah do? Do you not believe in these stories? I tell you, brother, the lazy will always think that successful people use magic but not efforts. Your disbelief in the story of the four brothers has nothing to do with their powers, since you believe in the stories of Samson and Jonah, who performed exactly the same wonders."

"No, teacher. There is a very big difference between Samson and Jonah on the one hand and the four brothers on the other hand."

"What is it?"

"The difference is that God is almighty whereas man is 'little-mighty'. Samson and Jonah were chosen by God. It was, therefore, the power of God that they used to be so powerful. But the four brothers – if they existed at all – are not said to have been chosen by God, but by the spirits of their nation. So, they could not have been as powerful as Samson and Jonah."

"How do you know that Samson and Jonah were chosen by God?"

"It is written."

"Where is it written?"

"In the Bible."

"Who wrote the Bible?"

"The prophets."

"Are they God?"

"No, but they were inspired by God."

"Who said that they were inspired by God?"

"God Himself."

"When did God say this to you?"

"No, not to me, but to…to…Moses, for example. You know that Moses met God."

"Were you there with him when he met God?"

"No."

"Who brought you the news about Moses meeting God?"

"Moses himself. He spoke to his people."

"How do you know this?"

"Listen, teacher, it is clearly written in the Bible that Moses spoke to his people after meeting God."

"But, though written, by whoever wrote it, how sure can you be about what Moses said he had experienced, if you were not there with him?"

"Teacher, Moses would never had become powerful if he had not met God."

"How do you know that Moses had become powerful?"

"Because he achieved wonders."

"How do you know that Moses achieved wonders?"

"Teacher, you are not going to deny things that happened in the daylight."

"Who saw these things in the daylight?"

"The Hebrews and the Egyptians."

"How do you know that the Hebrews and the Egyptians saw these things?"

"My God! All this is written, teacher!"

"Calm down, young man. This is the third time you have given me the same answer, and you will be tempted to give it to me several times more, because it is the only answer to the question, and this is exactly what I wanted you to discover. There are only two ways by which you could can get people to believe in the story of the four brothers: either you just tell them that they were chosen by God, or their story should have been written."

"No, teacher. It cannot work like that. You do not just need to tell people that a man is chosen by God or to have the story written down to get them to believe blindly. The conditions in which that man operated must meet the actual functioning of God's principles."

"That is true, young man, but I have just shown that everything that the four brothers did meets the same conditions as the conditions of those in whom you believe as God's messengers; and that is what confirms that the four brothers were God's elects."

"I understand this, teacher. But there is one crucial thing that you seem to omit about the story of the four brothers that does not meet God's principles."

"What is it?"

"We all know, according to the addenda of the tale, that the four brothers were the reincarnations of *Ndong-E'Nzam*, *Ohula-Nzam*, *Akure-Nzam* and *Elám-Nzam*, all born of *Nzam-Elo'o*, a hunter who had lived about a millennium earlier. Nobody knows why his father, Elo'o-Nkwule, chose to name his son after God. Never mind! The problem here is, as you know, that reincarnation and supernatural appearances are the practices of the evil spirits. How can you expect people to believe that the four brothers were chosen by God with such a record?"

"Brother, the fact that evil spirits practise reincarnation and supernatural appearances does not imply that these practices are opposed to God's own functioning. For example, you believe that Yésuh was from God, and yet he practised supernatural appearances and disappearances, especially after his mission. You may also be aware that Elíah came back as Yans the christener."

"Oh, yes, that is true!" somebody shouted in the crowd and he continued, "I read it in the 'Transfiguration'. Not only Yésuh himself was strange – almost ghostly – but he also clearly asserted that Elíah was fully present in the person of the christener of the desert."

"Thank you, brother," Amanoofwom yelled in appreciation of the man's precision, even though the passage was not quoted the way in which it should have been. But that was enough for a spiritual communication. Highly spiritual teachers never point things out straightaway. They always circle around them through enigmatic parables. Let those who have ears hear and those who do not have ears go astray. This is the unfortunate but authoritative maxim that has always made true spirituality hard to grasp. Indeed, what Amanoofwom was trying to make clear was that it would be very clumsy for one to take the four brothers for shamans or demons if one believed that Yésuh's transfigurations and supernatural appearances, as well as Elíah's reincarnation into Yans, the christener of the desert, were manifestations of God's power.

"I tell you, brothers, there exists no parallel or independent source of power that would be different from or opposed to God in our universe. I have already warned you not to give Satan the chance to think that he is powerful. God is the only source of power, and He gives his power to the ones He wants according to his own criteria. Any man who has achieved anything great in our world has inevitably been touched by the power of God. The powers of the four brothers were from God; that is something that our great magi, Tsira-Ndong and Mvom-Eko, had taught. The only trouble is our precarious system of communication. The message of Tsira-Ndong and Mvom-Eko was highly spiritual and very few people could understand it, chiefly because they used very enigmatic utterances to express themselves. For example, they used the word *djôb* which means, 'on high', instead of using the word 'God' straightaway.

"The first problem here lies at the lexical level. The Fanghish use the same word, *djôb*, to translate 'sky' and 'heaven'. The question is: what kind of 'on high' were they talking about? If 'on high' is used to designate 'heaven', then what comes from 'on high' would be viewed as being from God. But if it designates 'sky', in this case one would consider it as coming from a realm lower than God's realm, because the heaven is considered to be higher than the sky. And yet the magi never referred to the sky, since they clearly said that 'the powers of the four brothers came from an invisible source on high', whereas the sky is visible. Secondly, the medium of communication is another important factor as to how credible a message will be to its receiver. A young Fanghish scholar said one day that 'An information is true; but you will not believe in it because it is true, but because the medium through which it comes to you is true.' For example, if you tell somebody that you are a member of an organisation, he will not receive that information with the same degree of acceptance as if you showed him straightaway your membership card. But what does a membership card represent to be so credible?

"A membership card is simply a board bearing symbols that say the same words that you said when introducing yourself as a member of that organisation. But your mouth is not as truthful as the board of symbols. And, lo, human beings have become less reliable than the objects that they themselves have created. This is the rule of civilised humanity: the Scripture Rule. And it is that rule that turns cultures into powerful instruments of improvement. Imagine a Koranic surah or a biblical chapter, inserted wherever appropriate, telling you a similar story to that of the four brothers, or even the very story of the four brothers, but with characters and places bearing Arab or Jewish names. Will you still doubt the story?

"If you are a Christian, you will reject it just as you reject the entire Koran. And, if you are a Muslim, you will ignore it just the way you ignore the Bible as a whole. But you will not question it as a particular piece of information. The debates on some Koranic and biblical aspects are intellectually and archaeologically relevant. But the believers believe in everything because, not only is it about an almighty being, but also and essentially because it is scriptural. It is formal. This means that the medium through which a message is conveyed plays a considerable part in the way the receiver will accept it. In a word, written messages make a special impact on the reader while spoken ones are somewhat plain to the listener. That was the real reason why the four brothers were neglected. Their story is not written. Hence the disbelief concerning the story of the four brothers was simply aggravated by the introduction of the Scripture Rule among the Fanghish. That is why, when I asked you to tell me how you knew that the Hebrews and the Egyptians had seen the wonders of Moses, you exclaimed: 'My God! All this is written!' That is what will help you discover what we need in order to turn our culture into a powerful instrument of improvement. We have to apply the Scripture Rule to our culture so that people will not cast any doubt on our truths. You will find that the students who write dissertations are wont to quote the sentences of literary authorities, not because these sentences are truthful, but because they are academically authoritative from the simple fact that they are written. Millions of publications tell us lies. But because they are written and published, we consume them without asking questions. Do you now understand why our culture needs to be a powerful instrument of improvement?"

After Amanoofwom posed this question, a young man in a very desperate mood started shouting in the crowd, saying: "Anyway, you are not the only one to point out the cultural backwardness of the subcontinent. But things have never changed. Maybe God did not create the Negro for such things. I just find that, if a poor man yearns for improvement, he just has to go away, because there is no way in which the sub-world can be improved. We are just not up to it."

"Where do you think the a poor man should go, then?"

"Anywhere else, in search of a culture that works."

"Is this what you want to do?"

"I am really tempted to do it."

"Be careful, brother. No self-conscious human being should yield to the temptation of giving up his fight."

"What does it change, teacher? Our elders have fought – or shall I say that they have *pretended* to fight – and here we go, still captives and backward."

"Exactly! You said it right. Our elders *pretended* to fight. But they did not fight at all, because they did not see where the problem was, and, for that, they could not follow the right procedure. That is why I am here. I want you to discover the truth and get hold of the right – not deceptive – formula that has always exalted man high."

"I am not being pessimistic, teacher. But, to be honest, nothing has been so painful as being eager to have an anthem that works but finding that yours does not work at all. My deepest regret today is only that an anthem is not like a dead wife; because, if it were, I would start thinking about marrying another woman."

"Everything is possible, brother. But it would be a pity if you chose the remarriage option in the framework of anthems."

"No, teacher; if only this were possible, I would do it shamelessly and remorselessly."

"Of course, it is possible. But it would really be shameful."

"I don't care."

"Young man, I am not a dogmatic teacher. I am a man of wisdom. That is why my name is Amanoofwom, which means 'the *four* brothers who lost *one* treasure out of *four,* in the image of the Very High'. While my duty is to show the way to *Good,* I will also show the way to *Evil;* for he who possesses the knowledge of *Good* shall also possess the knowledge of *Evil,* and then choose freely. However, son, be very careful should you choose *Evil.*

"Indeed, you can cross the river in search of a living and working anthem if yours is dead. Again, be very careful should you choose that option, for you know, by principle, that *you should never cross the river.* However, if you remain determined to cross the river, behold, my son, you will first need to build a bridge across it. Yet, as you know, the two riversides are steeply uneven. One disappears into the clouds, while the other is only a few feet high. Now, tell me, can you build such a bridge? For, I tell you, there is nothing so thwarting as to build a bridge between uneven riversides. And even crossing such a bridge, when it is built, is another problem. You will constantly slip and fall back onto the rocks and pebbles of your previous anthem, upon which your bridge is planted. And this can last a lifetime. Is this what you want?"

"Has nobody ever crossed such a bridge?" the young man insistently asked.

"Yes. Some have, at last. But, once they got to the other side of the river, they got totally lost in the midst of the unknown. That is exactly what will happen to you should you eventually get there . I tell you, my son, this is not a joke. It is the hardest thing a man may ever face in life. You will start feeling dumb and wobbly weak. Your feet will quiver, your hands will shake, your eyes will blink, your lips will stammer and your tongue will become heavy. You will become a professional in the performing arts because you will use very much of your body to speak as your mouth will be wordlessly shut. You will repeatedly jump off the boat in your conversations. I mean, you will be kind of deaf, and begging people's pardon all the time will be embarrassing. You will be sick with no bodily anomalies, no mental defects. You will be somehow disabled. Your intelligence will be dubious, not because you have no intelligence, but because yours will be different. And everything about you will look and sound bizarre. You will even be ashamed to be called by your own name, but changing it will leave you nameless. Let me just say that you will be worth less than you really are. That is when you will start understanding that renaissance before death is the worst enemy of excellence and dignity; and that a deported man is better off dying, and maybe dying again and again, to start and restart a worthier life in his new anthem. This is hard, brother. But, if this is what you want, then go ahead."

"But have there never been any successful bridge-crossers at all?" the young man asked.

"Yes, of course, there is always an exception in every rule. There are some successful ones, who are very fascinating figures today. I love, for example, Sir Trevor McDonald of Britain. I think that he stands as one of the most outstanding cases of cultural integration in such a conservative world. And I think that we have to acknowledge the part he plays in the British pride today. Arnold Schwarzenegger is another such specimen. But can you try and figure out the price paid by such successful bridge-crossers? Some have paid with several deaths and rebirths over the centuries before their accommodation in the new anthem has been made complete; and others have been exceptionally lucky, or gifted with some kind of uncanny knack, to deserve a rightful place up there. But the question is, will the whole subcontinent's population have to cross the steepish bridge and pay the same prices? Is everybody disposed to die several times over the centuries? Is everybody a chosen someone? Or do we just need to cross the bridge for the sole sake of crossing it, and then live sloppy lives once settled on the other side of the river? For, I tell you, brothers, mediocrity is something that must be incidental, but not a choice."

Amanoofwom stopped for a while, and resumed soon afterwards: "I am very worried about the way we have fallen apart and given up with our anthems, which are withering, and, instead, chosen to cross the bridge in massive numbers. Some time ago, our forefathers crossed that bridge as physical captives towards North America. And we have acerbically blamed their weakness. And yet, today, we are voluntarily crossing the same bridge rather as though we are mentally disorientated. Is this blameless?

"Go, then! But don't forget that one day the light will turn red.

The bridge will become as fragile as a mere strand of rope while the number of bridge-crossers will have increased in exponential terms. Yet, down there, in the still waters, hundreds of hungry alligators are awaiting the event. Can you visualise the holocaust!"

A man hidden right at the back of the crowd did not like these words for he wrathfully yelled out to Amanoofwom: "That is your problem, you who cross the bridge. Anyway, you can see that we are not all crossing your bloody bridge!"

"Brother…" Amanoofwom started a timid response. "I know that we are not all crossing the bridge. But, if you look carefully into the reality of that bridge, you will see that even those who are not crossing it must have pondered, at least once in their lives, about crossing the bridge; or they have used a return ticket in search for of something beautiful and useful; for they know that only from the other riverside can we get something beautiful and useful. That is the reality, brother. Today, all your fellow citizens that you respect for their intellectual brilliance have had to cross the bridge in search of what you respect them for, because they knew that they could not get it here at home. Coming back or not is not important. The real disease resides in our tendency to consider that if a man does not cross the bridge he will be regarded as a lesser man even in his own world. I am wrong?

"Let me translate this point into real words. Why is it that, in our society, we tend to give priority in job opportunities to somebody who produces a less valuable Canadian qualification than to somebody who's got a higher diploma from a local institution? How do you explain the fact that almost all cabinet appointees in our government have a Western academic profile, apart for some cases of presidential nepotism? Do you still not understand why crossing the bridge is not something frivolous? However, the question is: how long will we believe that there is nothing beautiful and useful that can come out of our local genius? How long will you contribute to the death of your own genius and identities like that? How long!"

While the teacher was pausing after uttering this interrogative exclaimation, somebody in the crowd suddenly shouted: "No, teacher! Our identities will never die. They won't die like that!"

"Who said this?" Amanoofwom instantly queried.

"Me, teacher." A young man put his hand up assertively and boastfully, quite far away in the tumult. Amanoofwom got off the stage and took a few steps forward so as to approach him. The teacher made a sign with his hand as to asking him to go forward.

"Come on here; yes, here; come on, brother."

The young man approached, splitting the crowd with one of his shoulders.

"Where are you from?" Amanoofwom asked once the bloke got next to him.

"I am from Alen Nkoma."

"Right. What is your nationality?"

"Er…what do you mean?" The young man seemed to suspect a trap in the teacher's question.

"What is this question? I am asking you what your nationality is."

"Euh…je ne sais pas ce que tu veux que je te dise; de toutes façons, je…je suis Fangh…I mean…I am Fanghish…I am Fanghish, anyway."

"No, brother. Don't totter about it. Tell me truly if you are Fanghish or something else."

"No, I am not tottering. I am Fanghish – positive!"

"OK. Can you show me your national ID card, please."

The young man tapped on his pockets to find his national ID card. But, "Sorry," he muttered, "I don't have it on me."

"Who's got his national ID card on him?" Amanoofwom asked the whole crowd, beggingly.

"Here is mine!" A man approached with his card in hand.

"Where are you from?"

"Kumameyong."

"Your nationality?"

"You don t need to ask me such a question. I am 100% Fanghish, whatever happens."

"OK. Let me see your ID! Listen here! Amanoofwom shouted, holding the card in front of his eyes. "Listen, brothers! It reads:

Nom: Minko Mi'Obiang
Prénoms: Justin Antoine
Nationalité: gabonaise
Coutume: fangh

"Listen carefully, brothers, it reads: 'Nationalité: gabonaise; coutume: fangh.'

"Thank you, brother," Amanoofwom said, stretching out his hand to give the ID card back to him.

"Be serious, brother," he began, with a severe warning. "Be very serious. You told me that your nationality was Fanghish, while I have just discovered, as it is written on your ID, that your nationality is Gabonese. Now, can you really tell me what your nationality is?"

"Teacher, this is what the white man wrote, but this is not my business."

"Be very careful. If this is not your business, why do you then carry this in your pocket as your ID card?"

"Teacher, when I was a little boy, my grandfather told me that he wasn't born Gabonese; he was Fanghish. Gabon was artificially invented in his eyes by the white man. That is why he had always refused to be registered as a Gabonese citizen. But he was a villager. He used his common sense to understand life; he fed by fishing and hunting; he used wood and straw to build a shelter; he used raffia to hide his nudity. He didn't need to register. But what about me living in this modern city? Did I not need to go to school? Do I not need to find a job? How much can I not help keeping this ID card, however fake I know it is?"

"Be careful, brother. That is exactly what I was saying. Nobody can neglect the imperative necessity of making a living. But, if you were a normal human being, you would rather fight to make a living with your real identity rather than give up your intrinsic values because you want to make a living. What does making such a living stand for? When you agree to put in your wallet a piece of paper in which your Fanghish cultural and national identity is called 'coutume', what do you think you are? Tell me what the word 'coutume' means. What does it mean?"

The teacher abruptly paused, covering his mouth with his right hand. It seemed that he had coughed at the very end of the question "what does it mean?" as his throat had surely gone dry. A young woman sneaked herself swiftly through the crowd, holding a bottle of filtered water from which she had already drunk three-quarters in that tropical heat. Frenetically she groped with the cap to turn it open as she got close to the teacher. She stretched out her hand to offer him the open bottle. Amanoofwom took a few gulps of it. "Thank you, young woman," he politely muttered as he returned the bottle. While Amanoofwom's neck pivoted to let him take a cautious look around the invading crowd, the young woman kept standing by his side – perhaps to offer the bottle whenever the teacher needed water again. Or maybe it was for another reason. Maybe she was just so amazed and mesmerised by the wonders that she forgot to go back. In the meantime, some people were tempted to answer the question, but they did not know exactly which formal definition to give. 'Coutume' was a polysemic lexeme, and its immediate lexical equivalents were numerous, so were their extensive dictionary definitions and encyclopaedic explanations. Where was anyone going to start? Anyway, this did not really matter, for what was important in the teacher's question was not to get the compilation of lengthy academic output on the word 'coutume'. The most important thing was its contextual reference in the exclusive framework of that man's national ID card.

And Amanoofwom resumed: "Brothers, we have to be very careful. *Nnam'e Fangh* is our mother. Our duty in the mainstream of human civilisations today is to revive her in all her glory because *nnam'e Fangh ó se foghe fe áku nal. Nnam'e Fangh ó se ki áku, ngaa?*" the teacher intoned in full voice.

"*Kah! Nnam'e Fangh ó se ki áku,*" the rabble responded in concert.

There was a young man hidden somewhere in the crowd, who got such a courage as to say: "My goodness! This is really bizarre. Does this guy not know that the time of promoting his Fanghish shit has gone? Does he not know that we are now all Gabonese, whether Fanghish, Ipunu or Myènè, and that it is high time we started thinking about what we can do for Gabon, all together?"

But, to this, Amanoofwom instantly turned to ask: "Where are you from, young man?"

"Lékoni."

"Just like the president."

"100%."

"Oh! I understand your problem. You, the Bakongo people, are too blind; but I cannot blame you for being blind, because I know that you are still too far behind human intelligence. But I have to teach you that we are not all Gabonese."

"What!"

"Young man, none of us is Gabonese."

"My God! What are we now? Do we not have a nationality?"

"Of course you may have a nationality. But it will be anything but Gabonese. Gabonese is not a nationality. Gabonese is a colonial territoriality that was delineated by the conquerors for their own purposes. That has nothing to do with what you are and what I am."

"This is bullshit! Don't make up stupid reasons to hide your pain. Just be honest and make it clear that you are jealous because the president is an Itéké, period!"

"Young man, I have nothing against your president. What you cannot understand is that we are not human creations. We are divine creations. If we suppose that our identity is Gabon, we therefore recognise that we are the creations of the creators of Gabon, which is foolish; and that is what the retarded mind of an Itéké like you cannot see. Because, if you are an Itéké, your nationality is Itéké; and it is right that the president be your president since he is an Itéké just like yourself; and he should remain your president, even eternally if need be. That is not my business. But he should only be the president of the Batéké in your Itéké country. And, as for us, we also need to solemnly elect our Fanghish president in our Fanghish country. This is what I am saying. And I know you won't get it until you understand the problem of the subcontinent."

"What is this problem that you are trying to develop for your sub-continent?"

"I am not developing a problem for my subcontinent. The sub-continent is going down in front of your very eyes due to the funny names that have been made up by the Western conquerors to des-ignate pieces of land delineated for the purposes of economic and political preemption. And these are what you now mistakenly call 'countries' and regard as 'nationalities', to the detriment of your real *national identity*, which you now tend to call 'a custom' or 'a tribe'. You think that your Itéké identity is a tribe rather that a nationality, and this is what all of you people of the subcontinent have been taught by your conquerors. Today, a typical Igbo has been brought up to say that his nationality is *Nigerian*. A Shona has been nurtured to think that his nationality is *Rhodesian,* or whatever – *Zimbabwean*. A real and authentic Fanghishman is now forced to say that *Gabonese* is his nationality.

This is the problem of the subcontinent. But this problem is pri-marily historical and philosophical. At the historical level, I think that I need to tell you a little bit about what really happened for you to understand what it is to be Gabonese today. When the Westerners decided to explore the subcontinent between the 18th and 19th centuries, they did not plan to take up the mission with a view of cre-ating political alliances with the people to be discovered with the discovery of the subcontinent. They did so in search of exploitable resources to enrich their own worlds. And once they got there, the business they engaged in was to delineate lots intended for exploita-tion. Thus, because their objectives were more economic than polit-ical, the most pressing interest was for every Western exploiter to delineate lots comprising regions that had the type of natural resources that he needed rather than collating the kind of men whom he could communicate and work with. Here the human aspect is not a big deal to the colonial exploiter, as the objectives for which he engages in delineating these pieces of land are primarily economic. Moreover, he is very lucky in the sense that the kind of men that he has just met do not really seem to have any human values. Hence it is easy to manipulate them, impose onto them a condition that does not even frame with their own aspirations — if they could even have any aspirations. In fact it is a kind of man that is pretty rare: always ready to submit to conditions that are imposed onto him as he's got no aspirations. It is even for this reason that he is sometimes denied true human consciousness.

"This is the way the Europeans expropriated themselves the right to delineate this map on that virgin land for the sole purpose of designating economically preempted lots. It is, indeed, an economic map. Here the concept of nationality as the description of such or such a nation does not exist. All you have here is a series of 'nomenclatures' that are but appellations invented just to designate pieces of land to be exploited: some kind of European extra-territorialities. No wonder if they are sometimes called 'overseas territories', where the sorts of men discovered on such territories are mostly viewed as riches discovered together with the discovery of the territories themselves and exploitable together with the exploitation of the territories, like some sort of special fauna. I don't think I'm exaggerating anything here. If a being has neither the knowledge nor the power, nor even the right to delineate its own territory and name it according to its own cultural substance — if it even has one —, such a being is not very different from a gazelle that finds itself in a forest by the grace of Mother Nature alone , who would have cast it there by chance, but there would not be a purpose designed and planned by that gazelle itself. And, if, now, there is another being from a different level of consciousness having the knowledge and power to delineate such a forest, who engages in doing so, it would not do it to the profit of those gazelles that he would have discovered there. It is in this sense that, one day, a friend of mine even stated that the South African Negro is not very different from the South African elephant. And I did agree with him. Let me tell you why.

"Imagine a vast forest in which you happen to find different animal species, each of them having a specific territory. I mean, in a forest where you have, for example, elephants and gazelles, these two species do not often live together. The gazelles often live in their own territory without intruding into the elephants', their neighbours. However, if a man discovers that forest, he will have no idea of where the virtual border passes between the two territories that host these two animal communities; and, most importantly, he has nothing to gain in holding them separate. All he will do is delineate that forest for the sole sake of making it his own property in the prospect of exploiting it in any way, maybe to build a domain in there, an industry or just to exploit its natural resources; and he will tend to believe that all animal species that live in there, however different, are but animal; and he will exploit them the very same way he will exploit the forest itself in its entirety as discovered with these different animal species. He will not see a particular interest in erecting additional barriers between these animal species to give the chance to the elephants to live in their elephant community without causing any trouble to the gazelles that, for sure, have a different way of living that would derange the elephants in a certain way. We may already be aware that some people believe that there is no substantial difference between one animal an another: they are all but animals. This is the way in which the Western exploiters could not perceive any substantial difference between Negroes: they were all but Negroes; they were all alike in their eyes. How could they then perceive a difference between, for instance, a Nguni, a Zulu, a Sotho and a Venda if they were all but Negroes opening their mouths to push exactly the same kind of meaningless yells that they would themselves regard as a means for communicating.

"This picture may somewhat horrify many of you spirits of the 21st century. But this is the real perception that the Westerners had of those they discovered when they discovered the subcontinent. Albert Schwetzer himself had confessed having had the impression that all the peoples that he met in the Komo region all and along River Ogooué seemed to 'speak' the same way. That impression had preceded Schwetzer, and it lasted until the first anthropologists and ethno-linguists of the 20th century introduced their famous classification tables on Negro languages. Thus, in the eyes of these Western exploiters, all Negroes were the same and spoke the same sort of way. Therefore, why would they have taken pains to distinguish them culturally? Did they even have cultures?

"Let us look at the problem in a pretty technical fashion. If you meet a group or groups of people speaking a language you have no knowledge of, whether civilised or primitive, there will be two possibilities: either your ears are deadened like Schwetzer's, and you will have the impression that everybody speaks the same way as you cannot perceive the differences; or your ears are too fine, and you will begin to distinguish the speakers just for having different tones of voice though speaking exactly the same language. You can experience this with any language, whether primitive or civilised, provided you know absolutely nothing about the language. A friend of mine already remarked that what he had found very bizarre with the English language was the fact that if you had a conversation with five English people, each of them would seem to speak a different kind of personal English. 'Why is that?' he asked me. But the problem of that friend of mine was that he did not know that any language, whether primitive or civilised, comprises accents and dialects as its regions go. Some people that I have met to discuss the matter even told me, according to their convictions, that the notion of dialect does not exist in Western languages as they are civilised. But no language was born civilised. The reason why these people to believe this is that Western languages are taught to non-Westerners in a formally uniform version. Even myself, before I undertook to travel around the Western world, I could not imagine that the French language was spoken in different ways between different regions of France. My own conviction was that the French language was spoken in exactly the same way everywhere in France simply because the French that I was taught at school in the subcontinent was exactly the same in every single book that I had read. The only possible variation could be but diachronic, I mean, a book written by Jean Baptiste Pocquelin should, obviously display a different kind of grammatical structure and lexical paradigm from the one written by Jean Paul Sartre. But, from a purely synchronic point of view, all French people should speak exactly the same way. I tell you, this was my own belief, however funny or even stupid it may sound.

"Now, imagine that you know nothing about the French language, but you are an intellectual and ethno-linguist in another language, say, in the Itéké language. The reality is that you may happen, when investigating the French language, to believe that a native of Marseilles speaks a different language from the one spoken by a native of Paris. And you will begin to categorise them in different groups if your objective is to classify them. And yet they all speak the same language but with different accents. As far as my own personal experience is concerned in this, the first time I travelled to Britain, some Northern natives very often gave me the impression of rather speaking some form of German, although I knew nothing about the German language. And yet, they were speaking English, but with a different accent.

"This is the phenomenon that could not be grasped by Western ethno-linguists at their arrival in the subcontinent, but also, and above all, those who engaged to designing the map of the subcontinent. They had no knowledge nor even the ability to listen carefully to the Negroes so as to determine accurately who spoke what; who could communicate with whom. And, as a consequence, they designed a territorial map that entrapped people who did not speak the same language for them to be able to work together and found a legitimate nation. And this is the problem of the subcontinent, even though it is also true that these maps had equally sundered these different peoples in different territories making each people to have extensions of itself in different neighbouring territories. This is why, today, you find the Nguni in South Africa and in Rhodesia at the same time, as the Nguni were sundered by the faulty border that was erected in the middle of them by those who designed these two territories. But this is not the most important side of the problem.

"I would like you to follow me quite carefully at this point. I am not pointing at one of the problems subjectively to endorse a certain tone on the subject. I am not choosing insidiously one single side of the problem probably more vulnerable than the other in order to aggravate the problem. Dividing a nation into different regions, provinces counties, sub-counties, divisions, municipalities or federal states is something pretty common in modern and even medieval or classical state structure. Thus the problem of the sub-continent would not lie in the fact that its nations have been divided into different states. The biggest problem resides in the fact of having states in which you find different nations entangled together and being held to sharing common political institutions: some sort of political convergence that is trying desperately to defy their cultural divergence. This is what has fabricated the *socio-fiction* that I am underlining in this talk.

"First of all, since communication is impossible between the citizens of such territories, due to the very fact that they belong to different cultural substances and, thus, speaking different languages, the colonising powers have had to lend them an external language, because no one is prepared to abandon his own language to the profit of that of his neighbour. You, as an Itéké, could you agree to abandon you Itéké language and rather make the Myènè language your official language in your country? I do not even need you to answer this question as you would view this as an insult. That is, mainly, why you have to speak French today.

"However, if you speak French, this does not mean that this is the best language for you to transcend in your history as a young Itéké scientist or politician, for instance. The evidence is that, listening to you, your French is but a gibberish full of mistakes. I am just trying my best to understand you just like this because I know you cannot do any better. But what do you think you can achieve with such a precarious use of the French language or this compromised use of your own Itéké language for the well-being of your nation?

"Young man, if you did not know this, I have to teach you that you and all the people of the subsontinent are all meant to achieve nothing in history, as you are held to make use of a language that is not yours and, consequently, that you will have no mastery of in order to help you surpass in science, politics and whatever else a man needs a language to achieve. Because you should not lose sight of the fact that linguistic abilities are the foremost factor in IQ measurement. This is the debate that had opposed Stephen Gould to Robert Sternberg when the former published, in his book entitled *Mismeasurement of Man,* the argument according to which the IQ of an adult Negro was 'naturally' low and equal to that of a white baby. This is a position that Robert Sternberg opposed by rather establishing, as he put it in *Metaphors of Mind,* that if the Negro has a low IQ this was essentially because his intelligence was measured unfairly. Upon this, he posed the question as to the way it was possible for a Negro child to 'naturally' have a high IQ if his IQ was measured by his ability to express himself in a language that was not 'natural' to him.

"Nevertheless, you have to speak the language of your French masters, since this is the only way in which communication is possible between you and me as citizens of this country – even though it is so obvious that this is exactly what is killing your Itéké genius in you – most surely because you still look at the French language as the language of God: something that would be a blasphemy to stand against or to give away."

"You're talking nonsense again. Who told you that we look at the French language as the language of God?"

"Young man, I know that I cannot point at anybody in particular to answer your question. But do not forget that between the 18th and the 19th centuries, when Christianity engaged in escorting Western explorers – the very ones that designed your country as it is today – it recommended that you humiliate yourself and totally abandon your values before your God, your sovereign. It is true that this argument may not appear politically relevant in this subject, but it is a psychological prerequisite for preparing the minds of those like you who were meant to humiliate themselves and abandon their values before the personal representatives of the Almighty Lord that was brought to them: give your lives to your Lord. That is why, even though you seem to reject the Myènè language for being a foreign language to you, you have not rejected the language of those to whom you were meant to give your life: your French Lords. And yet, your condition is exactly the same in either case. A foreign language is a foreign language, whether French or Myènè. But why should you yield yourself to one but not to the other?

"Now, watch out! As it turns out that each of these territories is inhabited by different peoples having different identities, it is not possible to name the territory after either of the associated identities. That is where apocryphal names had to be contrived to designate the territories. We are no longer at the stage of economically preempted pieces of land (we are now dealing with sorts of countries in the wake of their independence proclamations). So, once again, as an Itéké would not like his country to be named after the Myènè identity, a funny name such as Gabon had, thus, to be fabricated instead to name your country. But what does Gabon mean? What does it mean to you, as an Itéké? What does it tell you about your real identification, as an Itéké?

"Young man, this is the problem of the subcontinent, which you thought I was trying to make up. But I have never made it up. It has always been there, made up by someone else, even before I was born in this present form. I am just trying to help you see it. The names of the subcontinent's countries are but funny descriptions of rivers, fish, animals, geological incidents etc.etc.

"If you take Cameroon, for instance, you will see that it was a Portuguese explorer came down the subcontinent and, as he approached a coast in the very middle of the Gulf of Guinea, he saw there in abundance some species of prawns, called 'camerues' in his language. Much later, he decided authoritatively to baptise the whole land by the name of these prawns that overwhelmed him at his arrival in that land. And what he did then was to identify all that existed in the land in relation to these prawns. And, in the end, even men became identifiable by the prawns. When a man tells you that his nationality is Cameroonian, I don't know if he even notices that what he is telling you is that he is a 'prawns national'.

"Now, if you take your own case as a Gabonese, you will see that it was a Portuguese explorer too, who, as he arrived here, stated that the day he first took a look at our coast down Messanza seafront, the outlook of River Nkoma was rather like a 'hooded cloak', which, in his language was better expressed by the word 'gabaõ'. And this is the funny word that was then taken on to designate the piece of land that he had discovered, as there was no way in which this territory could be named after any one identity amongst the different peoples that he discovered in the land. And now, you are telling me that your nationality is Gabon, and you are even defending it with you heart, spirit, body and soul. Are you a hooded cloak? Look at the way in which you are ridiculing and belittling your human identity and status by calling yourself a hooded cloak! I pity you, witless Negroes!"

Amanoofwom stopped to breathe while the young Itéké seemed wordless, and the teacher resumed:

"Brothers, this is the historical side of the problem of the subcontinent as well as its implications. As far as the philosophical side of it is concerned, It simply lies in the world's erroneous belief that Negro African identities are only tribal. But this is wrong. If some African peoples look at themselves this way, this is not the case of the Fanghish; because we are not a tribe. We are not an ethnic group. We are not a restricted kind of indigenous society in the purely

Negro African, Amazonian and aboriginal sense that has been developed by our modern anthropologists to bestialise the people of the subcontinent. We are a nation, a great nation, just like the Portuguese, the Russians or the Chinese.

"The world thinks that all niggers are the same and that you can just entrap them in whatever the hell, wherever and whenever you want. But this is wrong in principle. The cultural differences that exist within other races to make them distinctive nations exist equally within the niggers. The niggers are just like the god-like genes of the West. Each nigger has got a culture that can, surprisingly, be the diametrical opposite of that of another nigger but the problem resides, indeed, in the fact that this map had entrapped different peoples together, which tends to deaden their real identities to the profit of these funny names that we know today. "Of course this may be quite hard to understand because it is about the subcontinent. But, imagine the Spaniards and the French becoming more powerful than the British and deciding on impulse or in a premeditated way to invade the British main island. The armada battalion will probably conquer the South of England and Wales, and then expand their land expropriation up to the Midlands; and the cuirassiers regiment will take up position in the northern part of the island from Midlands (where the border will pass through), including Scotland. The armada soldiers will certainly call their territory 'Santa Fe', while the cuirassiers may name theirs 'Sainte Merci'. What comes next is that the native English people and the native Welsh people, who will be living in 'Santa Fe' and they will, in addition, be forced to swallow the Spanish language and culture, will be regarded as 'Santafean citizens'. And the Spanish crown will even make up some kind of 'Santafean' passport, and the rest of administrative paperwork that follows will be 'Santafean' as well. The French political power, too, will follow the same process in the case of 'Sainte Merci'. And lo, here you will have two men: one Southern English and one Welsh, both 'slaves' of Spain, who will start pitifully calling themselves 'Santafean' citizens. On the other side, you will also have two other typical men: a Northern English and a Scottish, both 'slaves' of France, who will pathetically regard themselves as 'Saintmercian' citizens. Now, if you meet such people in a social event, the ones from Cardiff and London will introduce themselves to you in Spanish saying: "Nosotros somos de Santa Fe" while the others certainly from Newcastle and Glasgow will say in French: "Nous sommes de la Sainte Merci".

"Brothers, this is exactly what happened in the subcontinent when our so-called countries were created by their creators. And the thing here is that the Englishman from London is going to tell you that Santafean is his nationality and that his English identity is rather his tribe. Will you acknowledge true human self-consciousness in such a man? I guess no. And yet, this is exactly what you do. You tell people that Gabonese is your nationality and that your Itéké identity is your tribe within Gabon. Are you a human being? Look at the way in which you are ridiculing and belittling your true and unshakeable Itéké genius by deeming it a mere tribe! I pity you, witless Negroes!

"Believe me, brothers, we won't get nowhere in human history in such an inhuman condition. If we don't systematically revise the map of the subcontinent, to give every single people the chance to work as a real identity that they can defend and develop, we won't get anywhere! We have to wipe out our present faulty borders and design genuine ones between our peoples if we want to stop clumsy coexistences and awkward separations. The way the other world dissolved the Soviet Union to give to the Lithuanians the chance to recover their real country, which is different from that of the Russians, is exactly the same way the Zulu need to part with the Nguni. The way they broke the Ottoman Empire so that the Hungarians, the Rumanians, the Yugoslavians, the Czechs and the Slovaks could regain their real national identities, is exactly the same way the Swahili need to be demarcated from the Moungala. The way they cracked down the Berlin Wall so that all Germans could get back to national harmony and grow together in peace, is exactly the same way the Fanghish need to crack down the faulty walls that sundered them in five pieces forcing some to call themselves Gabonese, and others Cameroonians, and others Congolese, and others Spanish Guineans, and others Central-African-Republicanese, in order for us to recover our real national identity and work in harmony in our true Síefangh.

"The peoples of the West are so human and efficient in correcting wrongful maps around them. But when its comes to the Negro cases, they rather prefer the contrary and continue to support faulty unions and awkward separations, because in their percept, the niggers are but a kind of fauna that you can rear wherever you want by delineating animal reservations into which you are at liberty to fling different species. But beware, brothers. Cultural diversity is the very opposite of biological diversity, and it can shake the world.

"Our cultural differences need to be political if we want to have a human stance in human history. The world should understand that each subcontinent people needs to recover its genuine identity that it can defend and develop. When, for example, the Scots and the Welsh demand independent parliaments different from the English parliament so that they can run their societies with respect to their cultures and traditions, which are different from those of the English, nobody talks about tribalism. But if the Yoruba and the Igbo demand a Yoruba and an Igbo parliament different from the Hausa parliament in what you call Nigeria so that they can run their social affairs with respect to their cultures and traditions, you will start accusing them of being patently and intolerably tribalist. They will even be charged for crime against democracy in Nigeria. And yet, the principle is exactly the same. The Scottish National Party is not an obstacle to democracy in Britain as a federation of nations each of which is yet devoted to defending its own identity.

"Moreover, we should not forget that the United Kingdom, though viewed as a federation of different nations, holds its successful union from the fact – very mistakenly overlooked – that, practically all of Britain is English. I am not an Anglo-maniac. But the sociocultural reality of the United Kingdom is that it has been entirely anglicised. What this implies is that if the United Kingdom comes to political separation today, a country like Scotland will be but an English colony, just like Australia, New Zealand or English Canada, as it will be bound to the use of the English language in its social, academic and political life. But this is the kind of cultural assimilation that doesn't exist in Black Africa. There are no cultures that have dominated any other in the way the wonderful association between the Angles and the Saxons (English) has so well succeeded in dominating all of the Celtic cultures around (Scots, Manx, Welsh and Cornish); or the way the French have tamed the Corsicans, the Bretons and the Occitans; or the way the Spaniards have overcome the Euskarians and the Basques. In the subcontinent, on the other hand, all cultures remain sharply distinctive, and can't just put up together. The only cultural assimilation that exists here is Western colonisation. This is why most Africans tend to recognise themselves through Western cultures by the very fact of being bound to the use of Western languages in their social, academic and political lives. But this will take you nowhere, for you will never end up becoming French, the way the Corsicans, for instance, have become French. You will rather be left with no proper human identity to be defended and improved in human history. Thus, you have no future, as there is no way in which you can build a country with several cultural identities. You cannot build a nation of several nations. This is what I am talking about."

"But, if you say so, what about the United States of America, which stands today as the most developed country, and yet, as you know, that country is multicultural?" The woman that asked that question, Ms Felicity Foster, was personally known to Amanoofwom. She lectured at President's University in American Civilisation. And thus spoke the teacher to reply:

"Sister Fête," that was the nickname by which her colleagues of the university use to call her, and Amanoofwom had, obviously, been one of them, "you who teach American history to our children, don't you tell them that the Americans themselves had to kill all the thousands of American Indians who had refused to become Anglo-Saxons, and bullied all the Negroes and Hispanics who had tried to reject the use of the English language, as their objective was to build a typically Anglo-Saxon civilisation in North America?

"Let me remind you, just in a few words, what really happened in North America. To begin with, you should not forget that when Anglo-Saxons engaged in building what we know today as the United States of America, they did everything they could to erect there an Anglo-Saxon nation, which they imposed on the whole territory. This is, obviously, what created the sociopolitical controversies that mark the history of the USA today. Indeed, at the time the Anglo-Saxons set out to establish some sort of New England in North America in the 17th century, they found themselves confronted with people who were very hard to deal with: the American Indians. First of all, the Indian refused to submit to slavery labour into which the Anglo-Saxons tried to force them. To do so, they started practising the method of hunger strikes. Many died in these strikes and others died of cruel whipping and scolding. That is the situation that pushed Bartolomé de Las Casas – a Spanish clergyman who took part in 17th century transatlantic expeditions –to fabricate his astounding syllogism, by saying, as he put it in one of his chronicles (a text reproduced by Ali Mazrui in *The African Condition*), that "Since the Indians died so easily in slavery, God did not intend them to be slaves. But since the Negroes did not die, they must be natural slaves"

"But Bishop de Las Casas' syllogism loses its consistency insofar as the death or the survival of a being facing a condition that surpasses his organic immunity has got nothing to do with slavery. It is like saying that since child death is higher in baby boys than in baby girls, the girls must be natural slaves, which is not relevant. So, if there was only a small number of Negro deaths compared to a massive number of Indian deaths in slavery, this would not mean that God created the Negro for slavery, but simply that the Negro's body is more resistant to an intense physical activity, compared to the Indian body, just the way a baby girl's body is more resistant to bacterial attacks compared to a baby boy's body. That's got nothing to do with submission to slavery. Submission to slavery is not a matter of physical strength, but rather of mental strength. Moreover, if the Indians died, this was not essentially because they were too weak, but because that was the only moral way to show the Anglo-Saxons that they had no intention to submit. For example, if the Asian Indians were beaten to death by the English without fighting back, this was not because they were too weak to fight, but because Gandhi had asked them not to. Mahatma's non-cooperation philosophy was, thus, so ubiquitous that it would not even let you join with somebody who would be smattering you.

"So, after the Indians rejected slave labour and, above all, the learning of the English language, the Anglo-Saxons found themselves in an uncomfortable position. If the Indians rejected slave labour and were so hard to tame to become Anglo-Saxons, then there were only two solutions left: kill them and expel the survivors into remote reservations to avoid the erection of a parallel culture within a nation meant to be Anglo-Saxon. And that is what they did. And that is when they finally had to totally turn their expectation to the Negroes, mainly in view of using them for slave labour, as they were in need of cheap, and even unpaid manpower quite badly. But what eventually happened – which many of you do not know – was that the deal with the Negroes turned out to be more complex than the one with the Indians insofar as it fell on two types of resistance. While some lucky Negroes felt that they could claim their freedom and their Anglo-American citizenship, a vast majority of their community rather chose to tread in the Indians' footsteps. They rejected the Anglo-Saxon culture, probably because of their hatred against white people in general as they had so cruelly ill-treated them in slavery and in their social lives. Such was their position that the American culture was a 'white culture'. It was the culture of these very white people who were hitting them, jailing them, killing them, raping their women and holding them in slave labour. Therefore, they found that it would be better for them to try and develop some sort of black culture instead, as opposed to that white culture that they hated, not necessarily because it was a bad culture, but essentially because they hated anything related to white people. But there rose another controversy at another level. While many of them planned to create some kind of 'New Black American Culture', a good number of them rather fought to perpetuate their African identity instead. This is what is depicted in Alex Haley's *Roots* through the story of Kunta Kinte, that Mandingué slave who tried to preserve his Malinké culture on a North American territory.

"But the problem of the Anglo-Saxons in the face of such a complex issue was that, if they killed the Negroes the way they had killed the Indians, and expelled them back to Africa the way they had expelled the Indians into remote reservations, they would be short of agricultural machinery. This is even why the Liberia project failed soon after a few shipments, not only because a lot of businessmen feared going bankrupt, but equally because an overwhelming number of Negroes preferred to continue building their black American culture instead of going back to Africa. Therefore, it seemed wiser, to keep them alive in America, mainly for economic reasons – unless they resolved to become Anglo-Saxons.

"Let us look at this quite carefully. The objective of the Anglo-Saxons, here, is to built a purely Anglo-Saxon nation whose citizens are all Anglo-Saxons. Otherwise, interaction, coexistence and equality would not be envisageable (it is only an Anglo-Saxon that deserves to be a citizen in an Anglo-Saxon nation).

"It is that Anglo-Saxon culture that imposed itself all over what you know as the United States of America, first through the muscular presence of the English language; then by the kind of philosophy, aspirations and expectations that the traditions that were enforced there had eventually moulded. Even the states that were French or Spanish such as Florida, California, Texas, Louisiana, etc., were finally subsumed into that Anglo-Saxon culture that, expressed in the English language, all citizens of the country were going to identify themselves .

"Moreover, we have to recognise that the Americans are very clever people. They knew perfectly what they were doing when creating a country called New England, and later dubbed the USA. Because, although it was an Anglo-Saxon culture expressing itself in the English language, in order not to simply be confused with the English of England, I mean not to be simply 'English of America' like the 'English of South Africa, or the 'English of New Zealand, etc., these people, subsequently, encouraged the practice of some form of English that would be typically American and that we now call – unconsciously – American English or, simply American, which now differs from the English of England in many aspects, spoken and written.

"It was the forceful integration to this unique Anglo-American culture, mainly by its language, that makes a man an authentic American citizen. That is why, at the time when black people were still vastly illiterate and were still looking at themselves rather as Africans (many of them even still call themselves African Americans as though a man could have two identities at a time; because, in this case, their white fellows should be calling themselves European-Americans, which they don't), it was then quite difficult for them to justify their American stance. Booker Washington himself had already been acerbically criticised for stating that it would be silly of the Americans to allot the right to vote to people who could not even understand the language spoken by their local representative congressmen. On which basis would such people choose their representatives? (I know Dr Washington had been attacked quite badly for saying this as many people perceived his statement as insulting to black people. But how could a man be insulting himself?)

"So there was no way in which you could envisage cohesion and equality between these people if the 'Anglo-American condition' was not met. And this is where I totally agreed with Malcolm Little when he said, as he attacked Martin Luther on the grounds of his 'Love bids', that 'nobody should ask black people to love white people, nor ask white people to love black people, because if the conditions do not allow them to love one another they will not'. However, the point at which Brother Malcolm didn't quite get it right was to think that if the blacks and whites of America couldn't love one another, this was because some were black whereas the others were white, or simply because white people were cruel. But the real condition that was needed for the blacks and whites of America to stand together as one was cultural: it was 'Anglo-Saxonism for all' that was needed. That is where you will probably understand that America is not a multicultural country. It is more likely that you are confusing two compound adjectives that have a similar resonance but that do not have the same meaning. The diversity between Americans is not cultural, but racial. America is not multicultural, but multiracial. I know that many of you still believe that race and culture are synonymous. But they are not. For example, Collin Powell was not appointed Secretary of State in America because he had turned white, but because he has become a typical Anglo-American, capable of defending Anglo-American cultural and political colours as a 'true American', not merely as painted on the American flag, but as implanted in the souls of the American people through their education, their visions, their convictions and their expectations.

"I have to note that the concept of a 'true American' also poses some controversies that I would equally like to address quickly. There are many people who still adhere to the opinion that the American Indians are, in fact, the 'true' citizens of American, but not the invading Anglo-Saxons. But this just cannot be true, because, when we speak of human civilisations we do not speak any longer of the chanceful acts of nature alone in casting living beings in such or such an environment, but, rather, of the willingness and ability of man to establish himself in a determined place to set out for his development there. It is the culture that founds such or such a country on such or such a territory that is its unshakeable guarantor, and its builders and developers its true citizens.

"Again, we fall back on the same kind of case as that of the elephants of South Africa. Because, if it is the Anglo-Saxons who founded, built and developed what we know today as the United States of America, and it is their culture that works there, as expressed in their language, how can we justify that the Maya be the 'true' citizens of such a country simply because Mother Nature had cast them in there the way She had also cast the Hyenas in that environment?

"I have always reminded you that a civilisation is like a machine. It is something you invent, design, build and develop through some appropriate source of inspiration. But you will not claim any authorship rights or copyright entitlements for a machine of which you are not the manufacturer. Things don't just work like that.

"So, even though the Americans seem to be the foremost democratic people on the earth today, things didn't really start there. Anglo-America, to be what it is today, had, obviously, needed to kill anything non-Anglo-American around for it to stand firm as such. And this rule is not just an Anglo-American rule. It is no 'cowboyism'. It is universal. I have just spoken too of the English themselves ,who have forced the Cornish to look at themselves as English by killing their Celtic language and culture, as well as the the Basques and the Corsicans in the cases of Spain and France, or even the Cantons and the Chechens in China and Russia...

"In fact, there is no great nation in our world that was founded on a democratic basis. Democracy often comes much later whence some sort of fundamentalist fascism has done the job for such or such a nation to impose itself on such or such a territory. Democracy is but a retarded son of worldwide fundamentalism in the building of great civilisations.

"However, I have to note that this is not chronological. You don't need to be a fundamentalist to become a democrat afterwards. The problem is just that it is not very easy to act democratically or politically fairly towards strangers. Again, I have to remind you that here, I'm not talking race. I'm talking culture. I'm not saying, for example, that white people cannot act politically fairly towards black people. What I'm saying is that an Anglo-Saxon, for example, will not be fair on his fellows in an Anglo-Saxon nation as long as those ones are not typically Anglo-Saxons, whatever their colours. And I'm not trying to dismiss the existence of the phobic. But I don't care too much about them, for they are just sick.

"My point here is, thus, that, if you have the chance to have a uni-cultural nation, you won't need to be a fascist for the sole sake of political rejection, as there will be nobody to reject, nobody to be unfair to, though you may still suffer biological phobia.

"Therefore, I am not asking you to grow fundamentalist, but rather to erect legitimate nations and build your true countries as your genuine identities go; because, there is no way in which you can have peaceful societies, developed countries and civilised nations out of the multicultural structures that characterise your territories in these present times."

"But, brother Aman," it was Ms Foster again intervening to remark something. "I understand that your argument over uni-cultural fundamentalism in the building of great nations proves quite relevant not only on logical grounds, but also historically. But, in this case, what is the place of Belgium, which is yet, developed and civilised, though multicultural?"

"Sister, I know that you may have an exception in every rule. But you shall not have a continental exception. All the countries of the subcontinent are not going to be exceptional cases. Moreover, it is not really practical to compare the subcontinent's countries with Belgium, or Switzerland, or Canada, where you find different cultures expressed in different languages coexisting in one single country that yet seems to be developed. The reason why this comparison falls short is quite simple. Each of the cultures that coexist in these countries evolve separately. Each one of them has developed its own inspirational instruments for its own development deriving from its own mode of vision and expression. This is why they have different academies expressing themselves in different languages as their cultures go. I believe that you can see my point. The academy of the French people of Belgium reads and writes in French; which is not the case when it comes to the subcontinent. The academy of the Itéké part of Gabon, for example, doesn't read and write in Itéké, which is of such a consequence that it inhibits the Batéké people of Gabon from developing themselves the way the French people of Belgium do. How can you compare the two?

"And not only that. I do not really need to challenge your belief that Belgium is a developed country, or even that it is a country in the first place. I just wonder how many languages, cultures and traditions the king of Belgium needs to master at the same time to have a proper and intimate communication with his 'nation' region by region. Is this feasible?

"I shall warn you to be very careful with such deceptive cases. Even civilised people make mistakes; and we can't legitimise a mistake because it is made by a civilised individual or individuals. Belgium is a civilisational mistake, just like Gabon. A mistake is a mistake, whoever makes it, a civilised man or a primitive man, this doesn't matter. For example, some people will tell you that anger is a capital sin, but they will then say that if God gets angry this is not a sin because it is God that 'sins'. Such a position sounds like the one maintained by some uncivilised societies in which it is believed that a father can never be wrong if involved in an argument with his son, which is absolutely senseless. But these people hold onto such a stupid position simply because they are not socially civilised yet, for a wrongdoer is a wrongdoer whoever it is, father or son. A father may have a richer life experience than his son's. But such a father can still get a lot of things wrong before his son. And, likewise, the believers who keep holding onto the position that God can't sin don't hold onto it because it is true but simply because they are not spiritually civilised yet, for a sin is a sin whoever commits it, man or God. And, in the same way, those who tell you that the problem of the subcontinent does not lie in the heterocultural structure of its states do not say this because it is true but simply because they are not politically civilised yet. They think that, if the civilised world makes a mistake, this is no longer a mistake. This is the case of some of my friends from President's University, to whom I have often pointed out certain things that need to be rectified in our society. They often go: 'No, Aman; this is not wrong, since this is what is done in France too.' But who told them that the French can't get anything wrong?

"It is true that the Western world is politically far ahead of us, just the same way that God is spiritually far ahead of man. But this is not to say that they can't make any mistakes. A mistake is a mistake. Political fellowship can't be achieved between people observing different traditions revealed in different cultures and expressed in different languages. Such people cannot build a civilisation together. They will not have a civilisation at all. That is why you can talk about French civilisation, Chinese civilisation, English civilisation, Russian civilisation, etc., and even Anglo - American civilisation; but you can't talk about Belgian civilisation, because it is just not feasible. For the pragmatic question here is: from which one among the associated cultures could such a civilisation take its inspiration? From the French, the Dutch, the Flemish, or the Walloons?

"Brothers, we can't succeed with mistakes. All niggers are not the same; and all Africans are not alike. We are culturally distinct, and, for that, we need to build different civilisations as our cultures go. But we still have to be very careful about the definition of the notion of culture. One day, a friend of mine told me that 'Chinese food' has become part of the English culture, because the English have such a liking for Chinese restaurants. But this is not culture. Culture is what defines your identity. And yet a dish can't say who you are; and it would be far harder for a Chinese dish to tell you if a man who eats it is English or anything else. Other people will talk about 'black culture' or 'white culture'. But a culture is not a colour. If you met a man somewhere in the street, his complexion would not help you tell whether he is was French or German. The definition of the notion of culture is no way near any of these things, and it is not as complex as some of you are seeking to make it to mislead the masses. Your identity is not the food you eat; it is not the colour you are; it is not the dance you practise; it is not even a passport script. Your *name* and your *language* are the simple and prime criteria that determine your identity in the world. Your name and your language are the two simple things that establish the values that you are meant to defend and the nation that you are destined to labour, fight and die for, with dignity, in your human existence. It is not by looking at a man's complexion or into his plate that you will know who he is; but, rather, and only by getting his name and the language he speaks that you have an idea of where he comes from. And that is what identity, nation and nationality are all about. That is where people like Cassius Clay got it totally wrong. Mr Clay was an Anglo-American citizen, meant to defend his nation. But if your name is Ali while your language is American English, can you then tell me who you are? Mr Clay needed to apply for Saudi Arabian nationality if he were to be consistent in his choice. Alas!

"Another case is that of Malcolm Little, a dark-skinned Anglo-American in rebellion against his bright-skinned fellows, who once resolved to go to Egypt in search for his Negro Egyptian identity. Not only did Mr Little fail to notice that his skin colour couldn't make him an African or – more precisely – an Egyptian, but, most ironically, what the famous panther brought back from his trip was Islam. I believe that you can see how anachronistically ridiculous this is. Did our Egyptians ancestors believed in Muhammad? Very obviously, Mr Little simply missed his mission because, while looking forward to meeting his Negro Egyptian ancestors, he met the Arabs instead. And, as a consequence, he was taught by the Arabs and ridiculously became a Muslim, which has nothing to do with the ancient Egyptians' credo; and he ended up calling himself 'El Malik'. But Mr Little did not take notice that, by calling himself by such a name, he had just undergone an individual colonisation by the Arabs in their mitigated imperialism via Islam, just the way the West itself had made use of the Christian Bible to conquer the uncivilised people of the subcontinent.

"In fact, what I find aberrant with democratic modernity is its keenness on multiplying opportunities and free choices, to such an extent that dogs are allowed to call themselves cats, as dictated by their hysterical inclinations. But nobody takes notice of the noxious consequences of such a mischievous freedom. Because, behold, brothers; some doggy nations will see themselves ripped off by their own nationals, who would be supporting a catty nation at war with them, by the simple fact that these dogs will have been allowed to call themselves cats at will. They will explode bombs to destroy their home cities and kill their fellows just because they were permitted to change their names a few months or years earlier.

"I tell you, brothers, the political parties that stand to be as keen advocates of multiculturalism in their nation have to be very careful. They don't know the game they are playing. They seek the electoral support of millions of so-called nationals who call themselves by foreign names, and cherish foreign traditions, and worship foreign gods. Such politicians label themselves 'tolerant democrats', and they expect the world to praise them for being so humane. But they have no idea of where such constituencies can lead them. They will be invaded and defeated. They will fall in ruins one day or another under the double-edged sword of their own fellow citizens.

"The concept of 'identity' – 'nation' and 'nationality' – is one of the easiest things to define. But it is not a joke. It is a matter of survival and collapse, of dignity and shame, of triumph and defeat. It is a matter of human self-predication. Thus, if you know that you are Fanghish today, I have one a single command to you: set about the formal institutionalisation of your Síefangh in all her glory, and leave the Batéké and the others alone. Build your nation with your genius. Leave the French language and German names alone, and you will be developed, civilised and sovereign. Do this with love, passion and courage, and you will be saved.

"Those who sing love songs to you to appease your strong desire for the building of Síefangh are the enemies of your liberation from mental captivity. They are the enemies of your realisation in human history, because there is no civilisation that will reach its topmost inspirational level until its bookshops suffer the fiction disease. But, be careful. Poetry is not fiction. Poetry is a cruel mockery. A poet can tell you that a beggar is richer than his donor; that a delinquent should be more respected than a noble; or that a slave is superior to his master. This is poetry! Do not follow the poets. They are drunk. Let the poets sing their triumph in their defeat. Let them eulogise about their greatness in their belittlement. Let them express their joy in their sorrow. Let their despair be their hope! I tell you: do not follow the poets. They are drunk. You have to watch out, brothers. There exists nothing called 'the Gospel of Success'. Man is simply at the fringe of life if he is not successful. That is why, if a friend of yours gets stripped to expose his beauty, don't be tempted to follow him until you make sure you have no blemishes. Thus, those who tell you that they enjoyed visiting and helping the famine-stricken regions of eastern Mboga will make you wonder whether it would not be a pleasure to go to hell for a short journey if there were no fire. But, I tell you, if a man suffers famine, he shall kneel down before the birds and call them lords. Those who have ears, let them hear."

Amanoofwom stopped for a while. There were two Spaniards who had come as tourists to visit some regions of the Mboga subcontinent that were very reputed for their falls, and, coincidentally they were there at Mekie-Me-Kwule while the teacher was enlightening his people. The two Spaniards were escorted by a young local boy, who was a student in the department of Iberian and Latino-American studies at President's University. The Spaniards asked the student what on earth a slovenly man like that could possibly be saying to attract such a massive crowd.

"That man is a prophet; the greatest Fanghish prophet of all time who came to teach liberation to his people." The young student said this in Spanish, and he continued: "He has already given a series of very eccentric lectures in the town, in which he tried to revive the Fanghish spiritual beliefs and intellectual convictions. And now his recommendations are becoming very political. His vision is that the Fanghish, as a nation, have to demarcate themselves from neighbouring nations and erect their Fanghish country, in which they shall explore their culture and turn it into a great civilisation. For this, he has demonstrated that the map of Black Africa is wrong, and that it needs to be immediately revised so that every single Negro culture can be developed as a nation on its own on the basis of its language."

This was the concise explanation that the young student gave to the two Spanish tourists, after which one of them frowned to his friend and said: "Seriamente hablando, la particularidad de los fangheses respecto a otras naciones morenas es que el fanghés actual parece reconocerse como tal, en todos los sentidos."

But, unexpectedly, Amanoofwom instantly turned in the direction of the two white men, who were standing on a little mound:

"¿Dónde está la diferencia en realidad, si tu fanghés actual todavía vive como un mono en un campo de reserva de bestias bajo su maestro? Those of you in the West who want to show admiration for a Fanghishman who talks about Síefangh to his people must understand that the best way to praise me is to lever off the yoke of colonialism that they put onto my people and let my nation flourish in peace."

It was now about one o'clock in the afternoon, the hour of the *Lunchtime News Bulletin* on TV. The news said that Amanoofwom, the evil Fanghish teacher who had insulted the leaders of the country by calling them 'animals' months earlier at St Michael's Church, was back after a two-month absence. And, now that he was holding a popular talk at Mekie-Me-Kwule, he had just created a subversive movement among the Fanghish advocating the rejection of the president on the ground that he was not Fanghish. Not only was this an instigation to tribalism and an incitement to national division, it was also, and above all, a direct political attack on the president as a personality and his team as an institution. The presidential press correspondent who reported the events on live from Mekie-Me-Kwule added that the rabble was getting so agitated about what the the teacher was imparting that the meeting could possibly get out of hand and result in a violent riot. And it seemed that the government might have already held a hasty cabinet meeting in the meantime to establish ways of pursuing that evil Fanghish teacher, who had, apparently, begun to form some kind of ethnic rebel faction to undermine and perhaps even attempt to overthrow the established political power.

At that time, Ebongué was in a European private clinic – the type that local people call VIP clinics – where he watched the news while sitting in a waiting room with a TV provided. He felt that he had to pop down to Mekie-Me-Kwule and warn Amanoofwom, if he was not yet aware of the news, of the possible consequences in the near future. But he could not leave the hospital as his son was still in a surgical ward. He then tried to ring up his dear friend, but the teacher's portable telephone was switched off.

Amanoofwom seemed to have worsened his case, according to the points that were underlined in the news. The charges were now so obviously serious that the teacher would face criminal prosecution, if not fiendish persecution. Nonetheless, the teacher went on enlightening the people on the Mekie-Me-Kwule playgrounds, where the saga just grew more and more captivating. Thus spoke Amanoofwom: "Brothers, our future is not in the French language, nor in this ill-designed and ill-named lot that you mistakenly regard as your country. The real future for the beautiful Fanghish race like you and me is in the exploration of our own cultural expression, in a country geographically delineated in such a way that our sons can *all* be united in a state in which their Fanghish language will be the instrument of social communication, academic instruction, spiritual worship and political governance. The Fanghishman needs to learn French just the way the English learn Chinese for the sole purpose of international exchanges, but not to make it his only operational language. And our country itself has to be geographically designed in such a way that each Fanghishman ought to go to the ballot to choose only among those capable of promoting his intrinsic cultural values that he can defend and develop. This is a task that an Itéké or an Ipunu, whichever, cannot fulfil. You don't need to think twice to understand it. A head of state is democratically chosen by his people on the basis of his ability to promote their well-being and development; he is chosen on the basis of his ability to guide and conduct his people towards their destiny. Yet no man can conduct a people whose history he doesn't know; a people whose traditions he can't grasp; a people whose philosophy he doesn't have any mastery; a people whose social realities are strange to him; a people whose visions are different from his own. Nobody in this world will be up to conducting strangers to their destiny in life. Things don't work like that.

"Thus, we have to let the Batéké build their Itéké country; let the Bapunu build their Ipunu country; let the Hausa build their Hausa country; let the Myènè build their Myènè country; let the Bami build their Bami country; let the Douala build their Douala country; let the Ubangui build their Ubangui country; let the Bakongo build their Bakongo country; let them go their different ways, and let us go our own. We are not meant to go the same way. You don't need to be a fascist to understand this. Even those who fought the Nazis know how to defend their cultural identities. I even know some of them who have introduced some laws to require a minimum knowledge of their language, culture and traditions to immigrants who want to apply for naturalisation. They are not foolish, though claiming to be the foremost fighters of fascism. They are unconsciously bound to abide by the rule; and this is the universal rule that the Nazis themselves had simply expressed in a crude way. And we can't escape from that universal mainstream, even though we shall never grow fascist."

Amanoofwom paused for a minute after these words, and while

he was still running his eye over the crowd to find the best route to resume his progress, four men clad in police uniform suddenly appeared from nowhere and began to push their way into the crowd towards the teacher, shoving the people aside pretty violently. It was now two o'clock in the afternoon.

"Pouvez-vous venir avec nous, monsieur?" the one who got closest to Amanoofwom said, with authority.

"Pour aller où?" Amanoofwom asked.

"Vous êtes convoqué au ministère de l'intérieur demain matin."

"Mais, nous ne sommes pas encore à demain matin," the teacher retorted.

"Non, le fait est que la gendarmerie nationale a quelques questions à vous poser ce soir pour préparer votre entrevue de demain. Nous vous déposerons chez vous après l'interrogatoire. Dépéchez-vous, nous allons être en retard."

"Pouvez-vouz me donner juste deux minutes, s'il vous plait?"

"D'accord, mais pas plus!"

Amanoofwom opened his suitcase cautiously. But the soldiers suddenly brandished their guns in a "don't move" stance: "Ne bougez pas, monsieur!"

Amanoofwom put his hands up, and the crowd dispersed in terror. The young woman who was holding a bottle of water welded herself to Amanoofwom, crying with fear, instead of running away with the rabble. There were no shots, however. As a matter of fact, the soldiers had thought that the teacher was going to withdraw a Kalashnikov from his suitcase and shoot them up.

"Que vouliez-vouz prendre de votre sac?" one of them asked, while having his gun pointed at the teacher's temple.

"Je voulais prendre un stylo et du papier."

"Sûr?"

"Sûr."

"Que vouliez-vous faire avec ça?

"Je voulais laisser une note à un ami que je devais rencontrer ce soir."

"Votre ami n'est-t-il pas ici présent?"

"Non."

"Soyez sérieux, monsieur; vous arrivez à haranguer toute cette masse d'hommes qui ne peuvent même plus s'occuper de leur vie à cause de vos discours, et vous prétendez qu'un ami à vous a pu s'y absenter et qu'il vous a plutôt donné un rendez-vous pour le rencontrer ce soir!"

"Il n'est pas ici, malheureusement. Il veille sur son fils, qui a été opéré ce matin, et je devais l'y rejoindre après ce meeting."

"Est-ce vrai?"

"Vous pouvez vérifier, si vous voulez."

"D'accord, allez-y! Vite!"

Amanoofwom took a pen and a sheet of paper and wrote down something quickly. He folded the sheet and looked up, but the only person he saw next to him was the young woman, who offered him some water. The crowd was on the lookout, stepping back and forth according to the gestures of the soldiers. Amanoofwom turned to the young woman beside him and held her head, moving his face close to hers as if he was going to kiss her.

"Please, read this to the people once we have gone," he whispered, putting the sheet into her palm; and he was soon taken into the officers' van.

"Ne partez pas, s'il vous plaît," the young woman shouted while unfolding an A4 form. "J'ai à vous lire un message que le maître m'a glissé en partant. Ecoutez, s'il vous plaît!"

The mob flocked together around the young woman in massive bands, from all parts of the site. Here is what the young woman read to the people and to herself: "No one knows what may come out of this insidious invitation. But do not care about me. Care about yourselves. I have already told you that I will not always be with you. I will have to go. And what should matter is not what might happen to me but what you would do about the message that I brought. I have no future myself. My future is in your future. Yet your future depends on what you will do about the message I brought to you. I am certain that you already know what to do if I do not return. Do what you can do; I will be with you in spirit."

The young woman burst into violent sobs at the end of the dreadful reading. For sure she had lost the teacher, or whatever else she might have expected the genius young leader to be to her. She had definitely lost that man. The sentence 'I will be with you in spirit' was the finishing stroke that made it clear that the man himself knew that he would certainly not be back. It was about two o'clock when this happened on that Friday afternoon, some years ago.

CHAPTER 13

THE TRUE FACE OF TRIBALISM

Amanoofwom was taken to the office of Lieutenant Opianga, an army officer and cousin of the president. Opianga was in charge of presidential indictments. He was assisted by Colonel Marion, a French officer who was a member of the presidential guard. He was also said to be working for the French secret services. He had been sent either by the president or by the French secret services, or by both, to attend Amanoofwom's interview. The French wouldn't be left out of such an issue. Mr President's own palace was located within the French military base, commonly known as *Camp De Gaulle,* on *Carbonage Hills,* as the President was so loved and protected by the French political power, irrespective of his dictatorial cruelties over 30 years. No one knows the type of deal that the French had signed with that man to make them so blind over the blatant violation of the kind of democratic and human rights principles that they wouldn't dare violate in their own nation.

Lieutenant Opianga asked Amanoofwom to sit down on a chair placed in front of the desk while the Frenchman sat off to one side. Lieutenant Opianga then asked the four officers who had brought Amanoofwom in to leave the room, as he was going to begin a confidential interview with the culprit.

"Can I have your full name, sir?" requested Lieutenant Opianga, holding a golden fountain pen over a slim pad while a very sophisticated miniaturised tape recorder was lying near the inner left corner of the desk.

"I am Amanoofwom, Fridio Wúlyem."

"Date and place of birth?"

"I was born in Messanza on May Day at the end of World War II when I still was nearly 25 years old just before I saw light about a fifth score-year later."

"What does this mean?"

"That is what my mother told me. I have never tried to understand it myself. Perhaps you can help me understand it."

"Dear Amanoofwom, don't turn me on. I need your date of birth."

"Leave it like that, man. We have more important questions to ask," the Frenchman advised.

"OK, don't worry."

Anyway, Amanoofwom was still a mystery to many people. Nobody really knew where he had come from and when. He was a bit like God. Perhaps he too had no carnal begetter. Perhaps his mother too was a holy immaculata. And perhaps the man himself had not really been born the natural way on a real date and in a real place. Opianga had to turn to more important things, and thus he started: "Tell me, is it true that you are the Fanghish messenger who was sent by some kind of gods to overthrow our president and destroy our republican institutions?"

"That is what you have said; but I have never said anything like that."

"Listen, my dear, don't try to make a fool of me. Did you not say that you don't recognise the president as your president?"

"I have already said that I have nothing against the president, Lieutenant. You just don't want to listen to me. What I said is that the president is the president of his people. Yet the Fanghish people are not his people. The president is an Itéké. He is therefore, and in principle, the president of the Batéké, not that of the Fanghish. This is what I said."

"What the hell are you talking about?" Lieutenant Opianga ejaculated furiously, and he resumed, "My goodness! What is this rubbish of a president for the Batéké and a president for the Fanghish? Listen; if you have a problem with the president, then say so straight-away."

"No, dear Opianga. I have no problem with your president. I have already said to one of your men that I don't care about your president. The thing is simply that the Fanghish and the Batéké are not meant to be citizens of one common country. Things don't work like that."

"No, dear sir. You are the one who is trying to prevent things from working," the Frenchman interjected into the conversation.

"My colonel, you don't have any reason to say this, because things don't work like that in your Western world. Different peoples don't share common political institutions. The president of the Polish is not a Russian; that of the French is not an Italian; that of the Portuguese is not a Spaniard, etc., etc. Things do not work like that; and this is something you know. But why should you believe that anybody can rule over anybody in the case of Negroes?

"The fact – which we are trying hard to conceal in the case of Black Africa – is that there is no way in which we can expect different peoples of different cultural identities to share common political institutions. Because the concept of national – authentic – culture as practised in specific traditions and expressed in a predetermined language has such a power on human identification that it is consequential and fundamental to the constitution of nations and the erection of civilisations. This is why the peoples of the West that have thoroughly placed their languages in the centre of their development have built very successful nations by following the principle of the 'single language Tower of Babel'. For this, they have experienced such a perfect communication and mutual affection proceeding from the very fact of belonging to the same spirit. And they have worked together as brothers. And they have been rocketed so high to reach their God, or they are about to reach Him. And they have become powerful masters, making slaves the world over, due to the power of 'uni-culturalism' – 'uni-lingualism' – in the building of nations as revealed by 'the Word of wisdom'. But what strikes me dumb with disappointment is that these 'uni cultural' nations of the West have rather encouraged the niggers to erect their 'nations' on the basis of the failing 'multilanguage Tower of Babel' principle. And the resulting alienation and misunderstanding between the builders of such 'nations' is drawing them down into the abyss of backwardness and self-destruction. And the only excuse that we find is that 'the Negro is a fool'. But is there anybody who can avoid being foolish if assigned to build a tower with somebody who cannot communicate with him? If I ask for a hammer, you will bring me a wheelbarrow instead. Are we trying to say that God is a big liar?

"What the world – and even the African peoples themselves in their desperate campaigns for union and mutual acceptance between strangers – still fails to understand is that there is no way in which different peoples can share common political institutions. And they force niggers of different cultures together, and when people express their natural repulsion from instinct regarding those who are different from them, we call this 'tribal rebellion'. But this is absolutely wrong. The true fact of the matter is, rather, that different nations are simply at odds because political convergence doesn't work in a situation of cultural divergence. And such a virtuous *nationalistic* behaviour that nobody can blot out is being deemed *tribalistic* and regarded, in error, as a misdemeanour. The mistake in Black Africa is that we blindly regard colonially pre-empted pieces of land as countries and their funny names as nationalities, and fallaciously define Black African real cultural identities as tribes. But this is the cult of ridicule and belittlement that has been imposed onto the African peoples, because, truly, they are not tribes. They are nations.

"And this is not a poetic assumption to make things sound beautiful. The national dimension of Black African cultures is a sociopolitical reality that we are trying to ignore for the sake of foolish interests. But we are not aware that this is what causes every part of Africa to be likely to boil over and become blood-thirsty sooner or later. This is what my point is all about. There is no way in which we can expect different peoples to get on in one common political compound.

"All niggers are not the same, Colonel! The world's modern intellect has developed what you call 'African culture'. But this is wrong.

There exists nothing called 'African culture'. Africa is a continent on which we find many cultures different from each other. To me, an Itéké is not different from a Japanese; they are both strangers, except that one of them is the same skin colour as me. But I might then look at him as a Papua New Guinean inhabitant. We have nothing cultural in common, and we cannot build a common nation together. This is never going to work out. Therefore, cultural democracy is the only way out for the people of the subcontinent to build their countries as their cultures and languages go. That's when they will be peaceful, developed and civilised. This is my point."

"I understand your point, dear Amanoofwom, but what you fail to notice is that the struggle for cultural demarcation is completely anachronistic today in such a globalised era."

"No, Colonel. This is absolutely erroneous. What you do not know is that our Christian calendar is not very universal."

"What?"

"Let me explain, Colonel. There is a sentence that comes very frequently out of African people's mouths today. They often say, 'We are 300 years behind the Americans.' This sentence is very naïve. But it is very significant, for it makes it clear that we do not belong to the same historical era as the Americans. The implication of this remark in regard to your globalisation is that, if the Americans have already reached an era that allows them to promote globalisation, we, on our side, are not there yet. We are simply 300 years back in time. And this is true insofar as, if you look at the Americans 300 years back in time, you will find them still fighting against the Native Americans and the Mexicans over questions of cultural and political demarcation. Therefore, as we understand that we are 300 years back in respect of the Americans, it is completely erroneous for us to try and follow them in their globalisation policy when they are 300 years ahead of us. We will not succeed in jumping over steps by getting ahead of ourselves like that. We need to do what the Americans did 300 years ago to be in our real own era, and solve our own problems. Thus, cultural demarcation is not anachronistic to us, for that is still our era. This is the genuine reality: we are still in the era of cultural demarcation, and it does not help trying to run after those who are in a different era. Let them go! My goodness! We are not together! Moreover, if my claims are anachronistic, will you also concede this in respect of those of the Cornish who are fighting for the demarciation of Cornwall from England? Is their stance equally anachronistic?

"I don't really know what you want me to say. However, regardless of the Cornish claims vis-à-vis those from whom they look forward to getting their political independence, if you take a close look at the juncture at which our history finds itself today, you will probably find that your own claims, as well as those of the Cornish, are the very opposite of our contemporary political history."

"What do you mean?"

"What I mean is that, while the big blocs of the world are promoting union, and while the Africans are also thinking about the rise of the United States of Africa, you rather bring a separation project."

"Which are these big blocs?"

"Just look at Europe and see for yourself."

"I am very sorry, Colonel. But the European Union to which you are alluding is a very deceptive case. The EU is not a political alliance. It is very theatrical and dodgy. It is simply economic, commercial and atomic. It is a nuclear lobby. That is why you will never hear about anything called a 'central presidency' within the EU, because, as I have already said, the president of the Germans will never be an Italian. The president of the Russians cannot be a Welshman. And I don't see anybody – not even the initiators of the EU themselves – trying to debate this sociopolitical reality. Each European nation will contiune to fight for its national interests despite the existence of the EU, and Europe will always be divided and dangerously affected every time a serious problem involving national interest arises. That is why, in parallel, our idea of a United

States of Africa is a misconception. We talk about the United States of America as one country because the Americans are all Anglo-Saxons by the very fact that they have the same culture expressed in one single language: the Anglo-American language. So they can all communicate and work together as sons of one single national soul. But, if we created our United States of Africa, do we also have one single culture expressed in one single language to build one single nation?

"I tell you, dear Colonel, there is something magical that God Himself put in *language* that makes people stand as one. That is why, if a man does not speak the same language as yourself, there is no way in which you can build a nation together. I have already told you about the picture of *the Tower of Babel*. If I ask for a hammer, you will bring me a wheelbarrow instead. This is not a joke, Lieutenant. You can't build a 'nation' of several nations. That is where those who are promoting what they call 'globalisation' or 'one-worldism' are totally wrong, because life doesn't work the way they think it does. The concept of 'world citizenship' is not practicable in a multicultural universe in which every man is bound to defend his identity and integrity in his particular nation. Do not just let us think that, if a man goes to school to learn the English grammar, this means that he has become part of the English world. No. There is such a mysterious tie that binds a man to the cultural spirit of his mother tongue that nothing learned at school will ever be able to transcend it. Otherwise, how can we justify the fact that our great globalists and one-worldists still remain particularly attached to their nations? Why are they still Americans, English or French? Why do they not simply wipe out the boundaries between our countries so that men can move from place to place with no need for permission to enter such or such a country? Why do they not institute one central world presidency? How large and effective can a world government be? To what extent can they politically defend the whole world, which covers cultures and traditions of which they have no mastery? How can they speak on behalf of societies with which they cannot even communicate? Or else, are they capable of killing all the languages of our world leaving only one, which will be the world language? Can they create a world tradition? How sure are they about getting all people from all backgrounds fully adapted to their world culture? Is it possible for the Danish and the Zulu to share common *national* interests? Will the Mongolians understand and commit to the defence of the aboriginal patrimonies?

"I cannot formulate all the questions related to the impossibility of instituting a one-world system. I simply cannot understand the logic of those who create and promote concepts that they cannot fully defend. If the human mind is now experiencing philosophical recession, why not just shut up, instead of creating concepts that cannot be defended? Our world is not meant to be *one*. The oneness of this world fell short in the very beginning, once God Himself invented the cultural diversity that is the main feature of human identification; and this is not something that we can blot out by any artificial forcing.

"Consequently, each Black African nation needs to be considered in its cultural unity and be strictly demarcated from any other nations so that it can rise as a real country. That is what will give them the chance of laying the true foundations of their real countries, in order to grow in peace and expect to be developed through the improvement of their authentic values. We have to systematically revise the whole map of the subcontinent. We have to wipe out faulty borders and stop clumsy cohabitations in order to design 'the Map of Genuine Black Africa'. 'The Map of Genuine Black Africa' will give to the Hausa people, as a true nation, an authentic nationalistic impetus to develop their real Hausa country with a true patriotic devotion to the improvement of their cultural identity. It will give to the Igbo their real Igbo country; to the Douala their real Douala country; to the Myènè their real Myènè country; to the Yoruba their real Yoruba country; to the Wolof their real Wolof country; to the Bapunu their real Ipunu country; to the Zulu their real Zulu country; to the Umbundu their real Umbundu country;

to the Shona their real Shona country; to the Swahili their real Swahili country; to the Bakongo their real Bakongo country, to the Bamiléké their real Bamiléké country, to the Ubangui their real Ubangui country, to the Nguni their real Nguni country, to the Mina their real Mina country, etc., etc. This *uni-cultural* symbiosis is the only alternative that will nullify tribalism, that abysmal misconception. Because political convergence is not possible in a situation of cultural divergence. Am I wrong?"

"Je comprend pourquoi le chef d'Etat me disait un jour que, si vous avez affaire avec un fanghais, méfiez-vous d'abord un peu!" the colonel muttered rather desperately.

"Of course, you have to be a putrid, mediocre conman to mistrust very clever people," Amanoofwom said calmly, but in a very provocative tone.

"No, my friend! The thing is that you are not clever at all. You are poisonous. I have never met a human toxin like you. I presume that you are the second Hitler, who had to come," thundered the colonel.

"The name of Hitler does not terrify me, Colonel. Hitler was a normal and civilised human being who had his ambitions; and this is not my business."

"Did you say that Hitler was normal and civilised?"

"Yes, Colonel. Hitler was a perfect paragon of humanity and civilisation."

"What is this nonsense that you are talking!"

"Colonel, humanity and civilisation are about power. I have already said to my people that, if you are 'a man' because you belong to the genus homo by shape, you will not necessarily be 'a human being' if you do not belong to the *humanus* type by ability. The Romans themselves – the ones who invented both the notion of 'humanity' and that of 'civilisation' – were not referring to our natural 'manness' alone when they invented them. If you take dictionaries, you will find that the expression 'human being' is held from the Latin adjective *humanus*, which means 'cultivated', 'educated', 'organised'. That is why its derivative noun *humanitas* means 'culture', 'education', 'organisation', or 'civilisation'. And, if you try to look a bit further, you will find that the word *humanus* is directly linked to the word *cultus*, which means 'cultivation', 'education', 'organisation', 'refinement', 'decoration', 'sophistication'. Therefore, when the Romans used to say *ingenia cultiora* as referring to their own culture, they meant that they were the most sophisticated and refined culture compared to their neighbours, who – for them – were barbarous for being not very refined and well-organised. This is the reason why Roman annexations took impetus from the famous sentence 'homines a fera agrestique vita ad hunc humanum civilemque deducere', which means 'take men from their wild and savage life and drag them into our state of civilisation and political organisation'. In fact, the Romans felt as if they had a 'duty' to educate the primitive peoples around them to help them enter 'humanity' or 'the world of sophistication'. This is exactly what the *Oxford Dictionary of Advanced English* tells us too when it defines 'a sophisticated culture' as 'the one that has lost *natural simplicity* and learned *the ways of the world* with the *latest improvements and refinements*'. This simply implies that those who are not improved and refined are 'out of the world' and live 'on the fringes of humanity'. That is why they are very often regarded either as machines that can be exploited or animals that can be bullied and slaughtered when they become somehow embarrassing.

"Here, Colonel, you can clearly understand that humanity and civilisation are about those who are advanced and powerful and who feel free to exploit, bully and slaughter others for their own interests. I have already said that, in North America, the Anglo-Saxons bullied the Negroes and exploited them in slavery while they slaughtered the American Indians for being embarrassing to them; and that is exactly what Hitler did. He bullied the French because he found them inferior and perhaps exploitable, and slaughtered the Jews because they were embarrassing to him; and that is what all of you, humane and civilised nations of the West, have done and are still doing today. You bully and slaughter the non-human and non-civilised world around you. If, then, I say that Hitler was a normal and civilised human being who had his humane and civilised ambitions, am I wrong?"

"Is this what you also intend to do in your hunger for the achievement of a Fanghish civilisation?"

"Colonel, I have already said that we don't care very much about our neighbours. We don't need to exploit anybody, and we don't find anybody embarrassing enough to deserve extermination under our swords. This is not our ambition. Our ambition is to seek freedom and well-being for all peoples of the subcontinent in their nations as their cultures go. We don't need to catch slaves to develop our nation. We believe in our resources. We believe in our genius. We don't need the Batéké or anybody else to develop Síefangh! We don't need things like that. We do not need to behave the way you do: bully the world around you either just for secular imperialism or through your magnificent article number seven of the United-Strong-Nations constitution, through which you tell people that this is the 'best way to rid our world of the cruellest dictators in the image of Saddam Hussein'. But Saddam was not a cruel dictator. I know that such a statement may be truly shocking to you. But the reality is rather that Saddam was a Sunni, defending his Sunni stance against foreigners such as the Shia and the Kurds, who tended to stand against him and corrupt his Sunni identity. That is why he massacred them in horrendous conditions. And those among Saddam's own Sunni people who tried to fight him as they stood in support of foreigners were simply prosecuted for treason exactly the way the English would have prosecuted George Galloway for treason as he stood in support of foreigners against England. There is no human political apparatus that would not react in that manner.

"I know that some people would tell you that it is anti-political to just defend one's own tribe to the detriment of a greater interest of the country as a whole. But you cannot talk about a greater interest of the country if there is no country in the first place. Because, indeed, Iraq is not a country, to begin with. The Sunni, the Shia and the Kurds are not just tribes that should be tangled together in a faulty territory and fallaciously look at themselves as Iraqi people. There exists nothing called 'Iraqi people'. The concept of Iraqi people' is but a political misconception. And this is what created constitutional and judicial cruelty. The Sunni, the Shia and the Kurds are sovereign nations that need to be separated to give the chance to each of them to develop itself in peace where its sons will be able to work in national harmony to develop and defend it.

"Let the Sunni build their real Sunni country, the Shia their real Shia country, and the Kurds their real Kurdish country over the present geographical location of all their people. A Kurd is not meant to look at himself as a Syrian, or an Iranian or a Jordanian, or an Iraqi, or a Turk. These people will never feel liberated in these fake nationalities that set them apart ones from others.

"This is my claim, Colonel. It is not just a Negro African claim. It is universal, because the rule that stands behind it is universal. It is not by criticising other people's cruel nature or by making more colonies that we will solve the Balkanisation problem that causes ghastly atrocities in our beautiful world today. The Creator did not intend things to work like that.

"Thus, to come back to my own case, the only thing a Fanghishman like me needs today is to improve his own genius in his real Fanghish country that shall cover the present geographical location of his people; a country in which his mother tongue – the unshakeable symbol and instrument of his advancement in human history – rather than your French language, shall be the means for social communication, academic instruction, spiritual worship and political governance, just the way you do in France. This is my point, Colonel."

"Dear sir, your grudge against colonialism is historically irrelevant. Most nations, including those that you call 'the powerful nations of the West', have been colonised in the past. The

Spaniards, for example, were invaded and colonised by the Arabs; even the Greeks are reported to have fallen under the Egyptian influence;,and so on."

"Of course, Colonel, I understand this, and my deepest conviction in this matter is that colonisation is the most positive thing that may have come to us. The role of colonialism has always been to put more advanced cultures in a position to assist in cultivating less advanced ones. That is why I have no grudge against colonialism because it is something that has been highly instructive to us. It has successfully helped us into the groove of universal education. It has vastly trained our minds to the understanding of the most complex phenomena of existence. It has given us the ability to keep pace with the evolution of the world. I mean, it has simply illuminated us. Even those of us who were but primitives living roughly in the rain-forest in the open air have been made men thanks to colonisation. I find this extremely praiseworthy. But, to understand what should come next, you have to ask yourself the question as to whether or not the Spaniards are still using Arabic today as their official language. This is the touchstone of the true liberation of colonised peoples. We have to start consolidating our cultures in their entirety and get rid of our colonisers' expressions so that we can build our nations on the basis of the improvement of our own expressions. We have to be culturally sovereign to be politically independent.

"Our challenge today is that of exploring our cultures to build our nations through our spiritual inheritances. And this will not be confined to our folkloric cults and ritual dances. Each nation built upon its culture shall institute its own political system according to its intrinsic traditional and social realities and its spiritual convictions. And each nation shall institute its own academic system. Just as the Spaniards did after getting rid of the invading Arabic culture, we have to give to our children the chance of meeting scientific truths through their own expressions if we want them to be excellent in science. Your children of the West who are the authors of the great works that our children are consuming today are not particularly illuminated. They are just given the chance to do things the easiest way. They explore science in their mother tongues through their local mindsets. Science is a matter of vision and expression. Nobody can explore his visions and perfectly express them in a foreign language. If a man has a good vision while his language is not academically developed, he will be forced to express his precious vision in a foreign language, which will restrict the scope of his work. The result is that his work will simply be mediocre, not because his vision is mediocre, but because of his inability to express it. And we will think that he has no intelligence. Today, some people believe that a Negro cannot forge a good scientific invention or compose a good literary work. But what they fail to observe is that this is not due to the fact that the Negro is a Negro. The problem is that the Negro does not tackle science or write a book in his own language. How many English people can write a good book in Russian? The world wants the Negro to work twice as hard. The Negro African child is expected to be excellent in French grammar or English literature. But this is simply unfair. The Negro African child needs to build his life through the culture that his God gave him if we want him to be civilised. This is what my fight is all about."

"What you are saying may not be wrong. But the trouble resides in the diametrical opposition between Western history and your own ambition. We fought to build greater nations whereas you are fighting for a Fanghish country, a mere little portion of Gabon. Your fight is simply regressive. You'd better try the opposite if you want to build a great, powerful and civilised nation."

"Colonel, my nation is not a mere little portion of your Gabon. Siefangh is much bigger even than Gabon itself. This is why I am fighting."

"How?"

Amanoofwom leaned to the left to lift his right buttock off the chair, and put his hand into his right back trouser pocket. It came out with something like a little colour pad, which he then unfolded about six times to turn it into something nearly the size of an A3 form. He then spread it on Lieutenant Opianga's desk. He used to keep the sheet in his pocket in case he left his bag behind when moving out and about to discuss matters of his nation. It was like the Bible of an apostolic minister. Everything he stood for was clearly summed up on that sheet. It was like a teacher's mindmap. It was his mindmap. "Well, Colonel," he explained, "this is my nation. It covers all this space from Mbitom in the centre-east of Cameroon to Lambaréné in the centre-west of your Gabon, and from Nola and Ouesso in the Central African Republic of Congo to Mbini in Equatorial Guinea, but you chopped it into pieces with your malicious tomahawk."

Marion, unexpectedly, discovered a detailed map delineating the actual location of the Fanghish people and featuring a huge range of data related to Síefangh, and he seemed pretty intrigued by Amanoofwom's demonstration. But, all of a sudden, he shook his head and briskly turned round to say, pointing at a spot on the map, "No, my friend. I don't think this is true, because, I was here – just here – on a mission last year. The language that is spoken in this city is called Éwondo, yet you are talking about your Fanghish language. How can you then claim cultural sameness between the two?"

"I am sorry, Colonel. The Éwondo is but a Fanghish accent, just the way the Marseillean is to the French language; and we have several more Fanghish accents that cover the geographical space that you have on this genuine map of the Fanghish nation.

"The Éwondo speak Fanghish, but with an Éwondo accent;the Vute speak Fanghish, but with a Vute accent; the Etôn speak Fanghish, but with an Etôn accent; the Soh speak Fanghish, but with a Soh accent; the Beti speak Fanghish, but with a Beti accent; the Bulu speak Fanghish, but with a Bulu accent; the Nzim speak Fanghish, but with a Nzim accent.the Mvèñ speak Fanghish, but with a Mvèñ accent; the Ntumu speak Fanghish, but; with a Ntumu accent; the Okak speak Fanghish, but with an Okak accent; the Mekèh speak Fanghish, but with a Mekèh accent.; the Miwhô speak Fanghish, but with a Miwhô accent; the Ogowé speak Fanghish, but with an Ogowé accent; the Mbondomo speak Fanghish, but with a Mbondomo accent; the Boar speak Fanghish, but with a Boar accent; the Elin speak Fanghish, but with an Elin accent."

"Colonel, these are but regional Fanghish accents that your alien ears perceive as different languages, and those of us who are witless believe in your alien perceptions instead of looking at the reality of their own culture. Your alien ears perceive the Bulu and the Miwhô as different, exactly the way the alien ears of a Chinese will perceive the Marseillean and the Parisian as two different languages, for they really sound different to the ears of a stranger. And, yet, they are both but French accents. In England, for example, a native of Newcastle will give you the impression that he cannot hold a conversation with a native of Kent. And, yet, they all speak the same language.

"Regional variation within languages and cultures is a universal phenomenon, and the Negro cultures are not exempt from the universal. Some time ago, I had myself thought that the Mandingo, the Malinké, the Bambara, the Djula, the Djaka, and many other variations of them, were different languages. Because my alien Fanghish ears couldn't perceive the sameness of these Mandingué variations from the far west of Africa. Is this not enough to understand what is going on? And this is what is killing me. It is killing my people. It is killing my culture. It is killing my genius. And it is not only the Fanghish that are being killed. The whole subcontinent is going down. Our cultures are doomed to death. This is what kills me, Colonel."

"I am sorry, my dear Fridio, if you find your culture vulnerable enough to fall apart simply because a mere passport script calls you a different name; this is not to say that all African cultures are going to die like yours," Lieutenant Opianga remarked desperately.

"Dear Opianga, do you want to tell me that your culture won't die at all?"

"I don't even need to tell you anything. Just see for yourself how our culture is blooming. We have kept all our values alive, and we will continue to keep them alive."

"What are these values that you have kept alive, and will continue to keep alive?"

"My goodness! Where do you come from? Have you never heard of the Ndjobi? We even have a traditional king, whereas the Fanghish don't even have a damned leader."

"Who is your traditional king?"

"Listen to this ignoramus! Have you never heard of King Mokoko?"

"You see, Lieutenant. That is exactly what I am talking about. The royal palace of your King Mokoko is located in Congo, which means that King Mokoko is Congolese, whereas you have just told me that you are Gabonese. Tell me then, dear Lieutenant: where did you ever see a citizen having a different nationality from that of his king? Are you normal? I tell you, Lieutenant, the Mokoko controversy is but a trivial vagary out of hundreds of fallacies that clearly demonstrate our total disarray. That is why those who are trying to turn a blind eye and a deaf ear to such obvious aberrations are simply witless. Because, how consistent is it for you to regard yourself as a Gabonese in a 'country' that you are sharing with a Fanghish like me, but at the same time try to defend your Itéké identity through which you recognise that Mokoko is your king while Mokoko himself is a Congolese? Can you see how inconsistent your statement is?

"You first told me that you are Gabonese; but now you have come to tell me that you are an Itéké, and even that Mokoko is your king, whereas Mokoko himself is Congolese; in the meantime you have to learn the French language to have a rightful place in your society. Don't you ever stop stop and ask yourself some basic questions about who you really are? Are you Gabonese by your passport script, or are you French by your official language, or are you Itéké by your mother tongue, or are you Congolese by your king? What are you?

"I don't know if the African Negro pays much attention to the identity amalgam into which the world has put him to belittle, manipulate and bestialise him. While the French are French because their mother tongue is French, and because they go to school to meet scientific truths in French, and because, as Christians, they address their God in French, and because, on their papers, it is written that they are French; the Negro African, on the other hand, is torn between several identities. But how can we define a man who, for example, tells you that he is a Wolof because his mother tongue is Wolof, but who's got to speak French because this is the official language of his 'country', while he's got to pray in Arabic as a Muslim, and in the meantime, he tells you that he is Senegalese? Who can define such a man? Is he Wolof? Is he French? Is he Arab? Or is he Senegalese? What does he really think he is? How can we visualise the future of such a man? What is he going to be in 1,000 years? Obviously, the only future of such a man is Creolism. All Africans are meant to be Creoles; English-Creoles, French-Creoles, Spanish-Creoles, Portuguese-Creoles, Arabic-Creoles, etc., etc. African people will be just like the Jamaicans or the Haitians: kind of sub-English or sub-French, and so on. But this is not what will make the African Negro a dignified human being in 1,000 years.

"This is my point, Lieutenant. Creolism has no future in man's existence. It is the expression of indignity in human history. It is slavery. That is why, if you don't seek to reunite all the Batéké people in a real Itéké country in which Mokoko will be the legitimate sovereign of every single Itéké, just the way Elizabeth II is to the English, and in which your Itéké language will be the medium of social communication, academic instruction, spiritual worship and political governance, then you will never be able to make any claims about Mokoko, and Mokoko himself will have no values. Can you now understand me? Can you now see why our present borders are wrong? Can you now see why the map of Black Africa is shit, and why it needs to be revised into real cultural counties? Can you now see why you need to delineate your real Itéké country over the location of all Batéké people and elevate Mokoko as your real sovereign? I know that this may sound too hard a task to take up. But, if you are a normal human being, you won't run away from it."

Amanoofwom stopped. And nobody said a word after him. Nobody spoke any more. The three men just kept looking at one another in silence. The lieutenant and his assistant seemed to be dumbfounded, and the interrogation seemed to have reached a stumbling point. The objective was to find criminal charges in Amanoofwom's claims. But the interrogators were a bit like stuck. Opianga could not demonstrate that all Africans were the same; Marion could not contend that the Scottish National Party was an obstacle to British democracy; and it was hard to visualise different people speaking different languages building a tower together. What criminal charges could one make up now to convict Amanoofwom? Amanoofwom's contentions were heretical, of course; but it was *legitimate heresy*. The two servicemen kept looking at one another in total confusion.

After about fifteen seconds of silence, Colonel Marion made a facial sign to Lieutenant Opianga as to suggest the winding up the interview, while he said to Amanoofwom: "Do you have anything that you would like to say before we wind up the interview?"

"I don't really know if I need to say this here. I am a very worried man, Colonel. You know, ambitions are like a woman's breasts. A man who smiles at consolations at a time of failure is like a newborn baby that stops crying once administered with an artificial teat. Yet, you need to suck the real thing. There is no way in which a normal human being can work, fight and die for a fictitious nation. Our nations are very like Jim Carey's *Truman Show*. But they are most like reservation parks in which you just fling elephants and monkeys together for your own interests, though the elephants and the monkeys themselves have no future in such a territory. Our fictitious countries have no future in history, Colonel. This is what worries me. The chronic backwardness, civilisational inferiority and self-destruction of the African Negroes, for failing to explore their values in well-organised political units as their cultures go, is something that has made me very sick in this present existence. And my biggest worry is that my great-grandchildren are going to be like myself, or even worse: just slaves. This is what worries me, Colonel."

There reigned a short silence for a second time, after which Colonel Marion definitely resolved to wrap up the interview. "Well, I think that we will have to deliberate with General Idrissa (another cousin of the president) and see what to do next," he said to the lieutenant.

Opianga pressed on the 'stop/eject' button of the miniaturised tape recorder that was lying near the inner left corner of the desk. He then called upon the four officers who had been sent out earlier. They were still waiting for the end of the interview to receive the order to give Amanoofwom a lift back home. It was nearly three o'clock in the afternoon when the officers were called into the room and were, instead, asked to keep strict surveillance on Amanoofwom while Opianga and Marion deliberated with the general.

About two hours had passed when the officers received a radio message giving them a command that Amanoofwom could not decipher; and the teacher was soon taken into a tiny room in the basement of the same building, to stay in certainly overnight, at least. And, as the door was pulled shut and locked up, the man found himself in total isolation and desolation. From that instant, nobody can really tell what happened next. That was how Amanoofwom disappeared. He was then 25 years old, some years ago.

CHAPTER 14

THE ASCENSION

The news that Amanoofwom had been abducted spread all over Odzab and even beyond. But nobody knew where Amanoofwom had been taken. Some sympathisers even addressed alarmed letters of concern to Amnesty International. But no response was received. Ebongué, the closest friend, tried to lead a secret investigation into his friend's detention, but he found no traces of Amanoofwom in any prison, and nor could anybody tell him what had really happened. Family and friends were totally overwhelmed. To Mbeng, Atôm and Ongongora became more than a son and a husband. They became the deepest consolations of a devastated mother.

After several weeks, some people started thinking that Amanoofwom had surely died in prison. Others thought that he might have been assisted by a supernatural force and saved. Gatherings were organised in his memory. Talks were held in his name. But all this was very hush-hush, for the forces of public order would not allow any public gathering in the name of such an evil man.

Something incomprehensible then happened, however. Three years had passed when Okalghe, Ebongué's first-born, now thirteen, went on his way past the central post office to school one Friday morning. He had an assignment to hand in. In the PO Box he found a lot of letters, which he started tossing into the outer pocket of his rucksack one by one, reading the names shown on the back of the envelopes.

He went to school to hand in his assignment, and set out for home again. But he instantly thought that it would be helpful if he passed by his father's office to give him his letter. Indeed one of the letters was for his father. Okalghe got to his father's office and gave him the letter, and Ebongué put the letter on his desk to open it a few minutes later, after waving goodbye to his dear son.

As soon as he got back home, he slammed the whole pile of letters onto the table and started sorting the mail out, while sipping a cool glass of Coke.

"Whose letters are they?" asked his mother as she was passing by.

"There was one for daddy that I have already given to him."

"Oh! When?"

"I passed by his office on my way back."

"Ah, right! And the other letters?"

"Three for you, one for me, one for Engone, two for uncle Essuma, one for Obone..."

Messam suddenly turned to ask: "Who is Obone?" She did not recognise that name in the family.

"Obone is cousin Mekom's girlfriend; the girl who was wearing a crown-like silver hat at Aunt Oburu's birthday party."

"Oh! Is she Obone?"

"Yes."

"Ah, OK," Messam said casually, and Okalghe carried on reading the names shown on the envelopes to his mother.

Indeed, the post office of Messanza had never used the system of street addresses. People used PO Boxes, and the post office could not cope with providing as many boxes as needed by everyone. So only a few people, mainly high-ranking civil servants, could manage to have a PO Box. Then the whole family and friends of lower standing, friends of friends, friends of children, girlfriends and boyfriends of children, etc. used the same PO Box – with the strict permission of the owner, of course. But there was no way you could refuse, because, in doing so, you would cause somebody to miss an important opportunity for failing to have a mailbox. After sorting out the mail, the young Okalghe would then take his bike and act as a post office mail distributor, from door to door, as indicated by the names shown on the back of the envelopes.

Now, Okalghe had just finished the indoor distribution. He then took a few minutes to tidy his school stuff before getting on the bike for the outdoor distribution, when, suddenly, Ngule and Bifun came in through the front door asking where Ebongué was.

"He is at work. What is going on? Did he tell you that he was going to be here this morning?" Messam asked her husband's friends.

"No. In fact, he was at work, but he has just rung us saying that he had something very important to show us here. When he rang, he said that he was already on his way back home."

"Did he tell you what it is?"

"Yes. He said that he had just received a letter from Amanoofwom."

"Oh God! Amanoofwom is alive!" Messam shouted with emotion.

"Wow! It is must be the letter that I gave him this morning," Okalghe blurted out.

"Well, sit down. He will certainly be here in a minute. Do you want me to ring him and find out where he is now?"

"No. It is not necessary. He said that he was going to be home shortly."

In fact, once Ebongué opened the mail, what he saw was incredible: a letter from Amanoofwom. But what a letter! A light, thin and almost transparent sheet of paper bearing one single paragraph. Here is the content of the letter that Amanoofwom sent to his dear friend Ebongué, at the end of the third year after his disappearance:

I was told that faithfulness is one of the greatest virtues of our moralistic system, and I took it for granted until the day I discovered that even prisoners are faithful to their cubicles. One of my deepest convictions has been that all beings are meant to fly. Thus, any man who has had the chance to come into this world shall really live, or he will have to die. Therefore, my life's struggle has been to try and teach the ordinary man how to make wings and achieve a real ascendancy in history. But if each species ends up loving its nature in such a way that, while men praise God for having made them men, animals also praise Him for having made them animals, then happy be the camels! However, you shall not forget that the flip side of pudicity is to always leave you frustrated in the end: "why did I not dare!"

Ebongué recognised his friend's handwriting, style and signature, and he was deeply moved from inside. The contents of the letter did not seem to be of any importance right now. The greatest joy was first owed to the fact that Amanoofwom was alive. Ebongué put the letter into his pocket, struggling with emotion, and continued working. But he felt very disturbed about the letter and could not work at all. An hour later he made some excuses to his colleagues and went off.

Ebongué just had to indulge in some dancing and jumping with joy behind his steering wheel while driving back home. He gave a quick ring to his two nearest friends, Ngule and Bifun, requesting them to join him immediately in his house to share the historical event. It was miraculous to learn that Amanoofwom was still alive; and, best of all, that he was in a condition in which he could write to people.

Ebongué passed by Mbeng's house, where he shared the marvel with Amanoofwom's mother. But there was a problem. As Mbeng looked very carefully at the letter, trying to find her son's address so that she could reply immediately, she rather found instead that there was no sender's address. Ebongué consoled Mbeng, saying that perhaps Amanoofwom had just forgotten to put his address on the letter. This is something that happens to a lot of people. Ebongué reassured her that he would not forget next time. But that was not the only problem with the letter. Ebongué and Mbeng also noticed that there was no stamp on the envelope, so they could not even locate the place where the letter had been posted from.

Suppose that Amanoofwom had been released and was living somewhere around, completely free like a Messiah after completing his Messianic mission, and that the letter had indeed been put by him into Ebongué's PO Box; did he have a spare key for Ebongué's box? Anyway, Ebongué did not remember having given him a spare key at all.

Or else, suppose that Amanoofwom had been saved and deported to an unknown nation and that he would have had sent the letter to someone else living in Messanza; and that the person would then have taken the letter out and put it into a blank envelope, and then put it into Ebongué's box; who could that person be then? The only people who possessed a spare key were Okalghe and Messam, who by no means would play such a game with Amanoofwom. Who else could it be?

Nonetheless, Ebongué and friends celebrated the event in his house, where he found them already awaiting him and sharing the news with Messam and Okalghe. But once, in the middle of the party, Ngule said categorically to Ebongué: "We should write back now! Just right now!"

Ebongué instead frowned at him desperately, replying: "Ce ne sera pas possible!"

"Pourquoi?"

"J'ai vérifié la lettre avec sa mère, mais l'adresse de l'expéditeur n'y est pas du tout! J'ai juste oublié de vous le signaler en arrivant."

"Non! C'est vrai, ça?"

"Je vous vous le jure; cet enfoiré m'a écrit sans mettre son adresse!"

"Toi aussi, sois sérieux. Ce n'est pas possible, ça! Regarde bien."

The conversation between Ebongué and Ngule appealed to Bifun, who then turned to ask: "What is the matter?"

"No.it's just that…Aman did not put his address on the letter. So, we won't be able to reply."

Enraged, Bifun retorted: "You see! I told you that this guy is like a spirit. He always does things in a very bizarre fashion! Now what are we going to do? Maybe he will never even write again."

There came a silence clothed with an acid bitterness, and grumbling here and there. No one spoke to anyone. But everybody seemed to be indulging in painful and almost hysterical reflection to try to make sense out of it all as they registered their disappointment.

"Messam!" Ebongué called upon his wife, who was in the kitchen cooking some fresh fish in a palm nut sauce.

"Anh." That is the way women often respond when called by their husband.

"Can you please also serve us the rest of the 'Kuryebe' that I opened last night with Uncle Nguema."

"Owé!" That was to say "OK".

"No, Ebongué, I am not going to drink any more. I feel too bad to drink now." This seemed to be the reaction Ebongué received from both Ngule and Bifun.

"Sorry, Messam, forget about the drink; we don't really want any more."

The three friends took their leave of each other within the next few minutes. Ebongué did not give up on the matter, however. He felt like doing something about it. He wanted to break the news in the Fanghish public arena so as to rehabilitate Amanoofwom's status among them. But he had already been warned many times by the forces of public order. He had even been threatened with death should the authorities suspect him again in connection with anything concerning Amanoofwom. What he did, however, was to convene a secret assembly of a circle of acquaintances to share the contents of the letter and discuss it in order to grasp its profound meaning. But there are no reports about their interpretation of the letter's contents.

That was the last time anybody had heard from Amanoofwom. Today, however, despite the despair of those who sympathised with Amanoofwom on the one hand, and the opposition of the forces of public order, which cleared him away from the hoi polloi on the other hand, a lot of people still believe that Amanoofwom is a real living passion. They believe that he is not the kind of man who will give up on his fight. Some even believe that Amanoofwom will surely come again for the third time, and that he will certainly be a great leader to restore Odzab to that beautiful and prosperous Síefangh. For, as goes the old Fanghish saying, "ngue o akôme dzam enzing mboan mbeng, nal wha-mien bóghe dó"; this is to say, that "if you want something beautiful done, then do it yourself."

While the people are still awaiting their leader, Ebongué also has not lost hope. He is still looking forward to receiving a word from his friend. But, will Amanoofwom send any further letters, though? Will he really come back and do it himself?

Aba'a Memin [a'ba: 'məmin]
Aduma [aduma]
ákom ['akom]
Akoma [akoma]
Akoma-Mba [akom'a mba:]
Akure-Nzam [a'ku'rə nzam]
Alen Nkoma [a'len ŋkɔ'ma]
Aman [aman]
Amanoofwom [aman'u:fu:m]
Angône [aŋ'gonə]
Armah ['arma]
Atôm [a'tom]
Bakongo [ba'koŋgo]
Bambara [bamba'ra]
Bami [ba'mi]
Bamiliké [bamile'ke]
Bapunu [bapunu]
Batéké [bateke]
Bekale [bə'ka'lə]
Bekale-Be'Nguema [bə'ka'lə
'bə'ŋgə'ma]
Bekweñ [bə'kuɛŋ]
Beti [bəti]
Bibubua [bibubua]
Bibulu [bibu'lu]
Bifun [bifun]
Bikôndôm [bi'kon'dom]
Bingongom [biŋgoŋgom]
Biyeyem [bijəjəm]
Boar [boar]
Buiti [bui'ti]
Bulu ['bulu]
Djôb ['dzop]
Ebôna [ebona]
Ebongué [eboŋge]
Edwangane [eduaŋganə]
Ekot'e Beyem [ekot 'bəjəm]
Elám-Nzam [e'lam nzam]
Elíah [e'lia]

Elin [elin]
Elo'o-Nkwule [elo'o: ŋkulə]
Elolongh [eɓɓŋ]
Engone [enŋgonə]
Engông [enŋ'goŋ]
Enzamán [enza'man]
Essa-Bekang [esa 'bəkaŋ]
Esséna [esena]
Essône [e'so'nə]
Essône-Nkombot [e'so'nə ŋkombot]
Essuma [e'su'ma]
Etôn [e'ton]
Evoung-Mendang [evuŋ 'məngaŋ]
Eyang-Alouga [ejaŋ'aluga]
Eyano [e'jano]
Fangh [faŋ]
Fridio ['fridio]
Gabosep [gabo'sep]
Hausa [ha'usa]
Igbo ['igbo]
Ipunu [I'punu]
Itéké [i'teke]
kál ['kal] / ['ka:]
Kapla Bikuk-Ebuh ['kab'la bikugebu:]
Kenghle ['kəŋ'lə]
Kimbarranko [kimba'raŋko]
Kumameyong ['ku'ma'məjɔŋ]
Kuryebe [kur'jə'bə]
Lékoni [lekoni]
Maffo ['mafo]
Mba [mba:]
Mbeng [mbəŋ]
Mbini ['mbi'ni]
Mbitom [mbitom]
Mboga [mbɔ'ga]
Mbondomo [mbondomo]
Mebegue [məbəgə]
Mebegue-Me-Nkpaa [məbəge
'məŋ'kpa:]

Mebegue-Me-Nkpaa-*Ndzi* [məbəge 'məŋ'kpa:ndzi]

Mefan [məfan]

Mekèh [mək'ɛ:]

Mekie-Me-Kwule [məki: 'mə'ku'lə]

Mekom [məkom]

Melahn [məl'an]

Melen [mə'lən]

Menganga [məŋgaŋga]

Messam [məsam]

Messanza [mə'san'za]

Meyaba [meyaba]

Mfule [mfulə]

Mikolongo [mikoloŋgo]

Mimbará [mimba'ra]

Minko Mi'Obiang [miŋko 'miobiaŋ]

Minsisim [min's'sm]

Minzeng [min'zəŋ]

Miwhô [min'wo]

mohn-ñangh [mɔ'n ɲaŋ]

Morimó [mori'mo]

Mvé Mb'Essa [mve mb'esa]

Mvèñ ['vɛŋ]

Mvom-Eko [mvɔm ek ɔ:]

Myènè ['miene]

Nahn'Akom [n'aŋkom]

Ndjobi [nǯɔ'bi]

ndôm ['ndom]

Ndong [ndɔŋ]

Ndong-E'Nzam [ndoŋenzam]

ndzi [ndzi]

ndzihm'a éssa [ndz'ma 'esa]

ndzihm'a kál [ndz'ma 'kal]

ndzihm'a mohn-ñangh [ndz'ma mɔ'n ɲaŋ]

ndzihm'a ndôm [ndz'ma 'ndom]

Nguess [ŋgəs]

Nguíl, ['ŋgil]

Ngule [ŋgulə]

Ngwa Beyem ['ŋgua:'bəjəm]

Nhyemmam [njəmam]

ñia'e ngon [ɲi'eŋɔn]

Ñiengon ['ɲi:ŋɔn]

Ñiengon-Mebegue ['ɲi:ŋɔn məbəgə]

Nkole'e Engông [ŋko'leŋ'goŋ]

Nkom [ŋkom]

Nkombot-Evung [ŋkombor'evuŋ]

Nkorebot [ŋkorəbot]

Nkpaa [ŋ'kpa:]

Nnam'e Fangh [nnam'e faŋ]

Ntumu [n'tumu]

Nzam [nza'm]

Nzam-Elo'o [nza'melo:]

Nzam-Nkom [nza'm nkom]

Nzam-Ye-Mebegue [nza'm jəməbəgə]

Nzeng-Meyong [n'zəŋ'məjɔŋ]

Nzim [nzm]

Obone [obɔn]

Oburu [oburu]

Odzab [odzap]

Ogowé [ogowe]

Ohula-Nzam [owu'lanzam]

Okak [okak]

Okalghe [o'kalge]

Ondo Mebiam [ond ɔ]

Ongongor'-Evung [oŋgoŋg'evuŋ]

Ongongora [oŋgoŋgora]

Onohn [onɔ'n]

Onohn-Mebegue [onɔ'n 'məbəgə]

Opianga [opiaŋga]

Ouesso [wueso]

Oveng [ovəŋ]

Oyon [ojon]

Ozugle [o'zug'le]

Síefangh ['si:faʔ]

Sima Minko ['sma 'miŋko:]
Soh [s ɔ'ɔ:]
Taht'Ndong-Evung [t'at ndoŋ'evuŋ]
Tata Mba [ta'ta mba:]
Tsira-Ndong ['tsira ndoŋ]
Tsogo ['tsogo]
Ubangui [u'baŋ'gi]
Ugochukwo [u'gotʃuku:]
Umbundu [umbundu]
Vute [vutə]
Wessa [wesa]
Wúlyem ['wuljəm]
Yans ['jans]
Yans Milo Mi'Mbot ['jans milo 'mimbʔt]
Yésuh ['jesu:]
Yoruba [jɔ'ruba]
Yudi ['judi]